By Hand
& Eye

By Hand & Eye

George R. Walker & Jim Tolpin

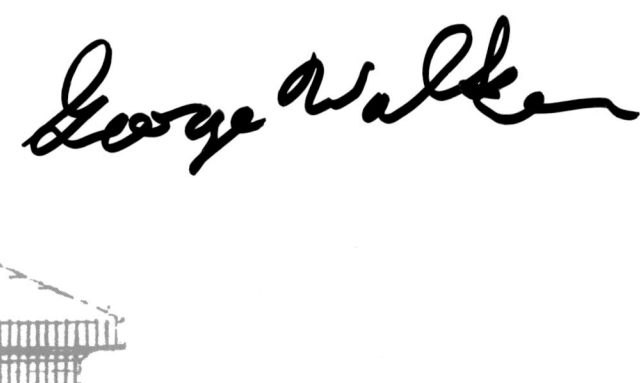

LOST ART PRESS : FORT MITCHELL

Published by Lost Art Press LLC in 2013
26 Greenbriar Ave., Fort Mitchell, KY 41017, USA
Web: http://lostartpress.com

Title: By Hand & Eye
Authors: George R. Walker & Jim Tolpin
Publisher: Christopher Schwarz
Editor: Megan Fitzpatrick
Acquisition Editor: John Hoffman
Design & Layout: Linda Watts

Copyright © 2013 by George R. Walker & Jim Tolpin

ISBN: 978-0-9850777-5-4

ALL RIGHTS RESERVED
No part of this book may be reproduced in any form or by any electronic or mechanical means including information storage and retrieval systems without permission in writing from the publisher, except by a reviewer, who may quote brief passages in a review.

This book was printed and bound in the United States of America.

Contents

Foreword...vii

Prefaces...viii

SECTION I: Making the Connections
Design at the Point of a Tool...3
Waking up Your Eye...19
Simple Shapes Combined into Forms...33

SECTION II: The Language of the Artisans
Understanding Proportions...43
Proportions Made Simple...59
Incorporating Curves...77
Classic Orders...87

SECTION III: Artisan Geometry
Traditional Tools...97
Basic Geometric Constructions...123
Generating Shapes...129
Generating Curves & Tapers...137
Developing Moulding Profiles...147

SECTION IV: Projects
About the Projects...153
Step Stool...156
Candy Box...158
Lap Desk...160
Tool Tote...162
Boot Bench...165
Coffee-for-two Tray...167
Cup Cabinet...168
Side Table...170
Vanity...172

Acknowledgements...175
Further Reading...176
Credits...178
Index...180

Dedications

To the memory of Professor Joseph Hartshorne, who got me started writing, and to my uncle Irving Pregozen, who got me started woodworking.

— *Jim Tolpin*

To the memory of Rudy Holloway, who saw things often missed by others, and to my father-in-law, Glenn Rafeld, whose presence is still felt in my woodshop.

— *George R. Walker*

Foreword

The material herein is a revelation in every sense of the word, for it not only reveals mysteries to us that were, according to the authors, common knowledge to furniture designers and makers in centuries and civilizations past ("artisans," to use the authors' term), but it teaches us how to approach our own design efforts in a wholly new (or ancient, really) way.

George R. Walker and Jim Tolpin introduce us to the language of pre-industrial artisans, and they discuss how period work is based on how we relate to our own bodies and the world around us in terms of proportion, ratio and scale. And they show us how to use that craft tradition and translate the tools and lessons of that prior age into useful strategies for design in our workshops.

In his section of "By Hand & Eye," George likens awakening the innate "designer's eye" to learning music: To build a song, one must first know and practice the simple notes of a scale. But once a composer internalizes those bedrock lessons and learns how notes combine harmoniously, the possible combinations are endless. The same applies to furniture: Internalize the shapes, forms, proportions and ratios that underlie a design and soon harmonious combinations will be easily recognizable.

Jim then introduces us to and teaches us how to use the simple instruments of "artisan geometry," with practical lessons on ratios and scale, and on drawing geometric forms. Then, he takes us to his bench to show us how he translates these lessons into everyday work, with nine projects developed using this pre-industrial artisan approach.

Together, George and Jim offer a harmonious combination of theory, tools and practice to help you unlock your innate design ability. That is, they teach you how to unleash and embrace your inner artisan.

Megan Fitzpatrick, editor

Preface
From Highboys to Flyboys

Hi, my name is Jim Tolpin, and I stink at design. Always have...and I thought I always would.

Which meant that most of my projects rarely strayed very far from measured drawings. I simply could not fathom how to come up with pleasing dimensions and proportions without endless trial and error. About four years ago, though, my attitude about design started to change as I began to notice a few things. Looking closely at some early American furniture pieces, I started to detect how the artisans might have organized the overall design. I was beginning to perceive some of the furniture's underlying geometry – the squares, rectangles and circles.

I didn't, however, fully realize the profound import of this unveiling until I attended George R. Walker's lecture at a Chicago furniture design conference. He confirmed that the underlying shapes were indeed geometric forms – and went on to fully open my eyes to the richness of the organization hiding right there in plain sight. He showed how pieces such as a Philadelphia highboy are composed of forms arranged in a harmonious symphony of symmetries, contrasts

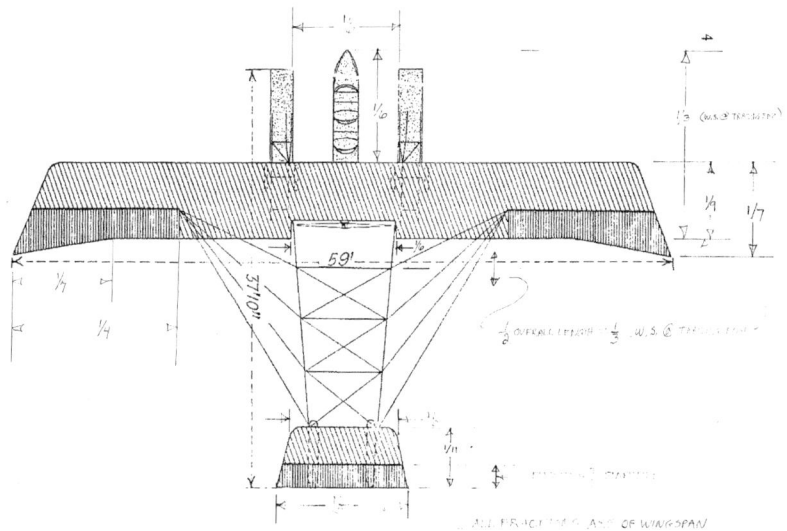

and punctuations, all executed through plane geometry. From the smallest detail to the general outline of the form, all the parts of the piece are related – not by arithmetic measurements, but by simple whole-number ratios. George's analysis was a revelation to me: The design of this highboy, considered by many to represent the epitome of Colonial furniture design, was the pragmatic outcome of an artisan executing plane geometry with a pair of dividers creating ratios in whole numbers – in exactly the same way a musician (from Amadeus to ZZ Top) employs the codified notes of the scale to either cover a song or to create an original.

I finally understood how the artisans (versus industrial-age engineers) came up with the designs for their furniture pieces.

Well that was pretty cool, but I long ago ceased to have much interest in recreating period furniture. These days I want to design and build all sorts of other things, from a hanging cabinet for my latte cups, to a bathroom vanity to satisfy the honey-do list, to an endless variety of vintage scale-model airplanes.

While in that last pursuit, a second revelation came to me that really dropped my jaw: I found proof that this ancient art of design was employed by artisan woodworkers to create far more than Colonial bling. Several months after George's lecture, I was looking at one of my books on very early aircraft and, while studying a plan view of a circa 1914 German navy seaplane, I suddenly found myself seeing inter-related geometric forms (see the drawing above). The moment I started to explore the plan further with a pair of dividers, a flock of ratios flew off the page, all relating in whole numbers to the wingspan. I shouldn't have been surprised. Like highboys, these early aircraft were being designed and built in woodworking shops under the hands and eyes of traditionally trained artisans – in both cases probably the best in the trade.

In an unbroken lineage from these early 20th-century artisans, back through the Colonial and Renaissance eras and deep into antiquity, these design strategies have remained intact as a tool of the trade. (Though as far as George and I can tell, this design tradition had gone extinct in the production furniture trade of the 1800s – as it was to also disappear in aircraft design soon after World War I).

For me, these revelations came just in time. While I had recently rediscovered the joy of working with hand tools in lieu of table saws, routers and sanders, I still hadn't cracked my fear of creating designs from scratch. Now, I was delighted to see that design was simply another skill that could not only be learned, but could also be thoroughly enjoyed in its execution – not unlike learning to wield a handplane.

Best of all, while I may have stunk at design in the past, the future is looking pretty bright – not to mention well proportioned! I hope and trust that you too will experience your own "aha" moments while reading this book and will feel the same way about your future adventures in furniture design.

Jim Tolpin
Port Townsend, Washington
May 22, 2012

Preface
Lifting the Veil

My journey into design began at my dining room table after toying with some drawings of the classic orders in an artisan guidebook from the pre-industrial era. The classic orders seemed a quaint relic of the past, but oddly, all the old books insisted they were the key to understanding design, and the masters spoke with one voice about the need to explore them. It started innocently enough. I cleared off the table and laid out a clean strip of poplar as a canvas. Using only a straightedge, pencil and dividers, I set out to draw a Doric classic order from the plates in Batty Langley's "The City and Country Builder's and Workman's Treasury of Designs..." (circa 1756).

After a few missteps, it slowly began to dawn on my eye how each part was linked together with simple proportions. That first attempt wasn't polished, but it did yield a sense of accomplishment – not to mention a nice drawing that felt good to me, knowing it came from my hand. But it also elicited a deeper sense that I'd brushed up against something profound. During the ensuing weeks I repeated the drawing, try-

This exercise upended my normal thought processes and revealed rooms in my head that I'd never before visited.

ing to be the diligent apprentice (but also because each time it was as if layers of smudge were cleared from my inner eye). I'm not sure of the exact moment, but somewhere between the third and fourth renditions, some gears broke free in the back of my brain and I began to think and see proportionally. I still wasn't sure how to pronounce all the things I was drawing, but I could see each part and sense how they knit together with the larger design. This powerful revelation lured me deeper into the literature of the pre-industrial artisan and inspired me to acquire a working knowledge of the craft element of design.

This gets to the heart of how Jim Tolpin and I had our eyes opened to the possibilities of this approach. Neither of us are trained designers, but rather experienced builders with a healthy curiosity. We both began experimenting with the practices and suggestions laid out in the period design guides. We set aside tape measures and began using dividers. We opted to use geometry to trace layouts, even when precision tools were easier and more convenient. Our goals were to learn to see, and to discover if the tradition might reveal relevant information for today's builder.

As a builder it's unlikely you'll ever incorporate a classic order directly into a furniture design. Yet the lessons those orders contain, and their ability to help you cultivate a good eye, remain relevant and exciting. These ancient design standards and the many geometric layouts that Jim so expertly shares are not mere historical curiosities from another era, but powerful tools to help you readily imagine spatial objects. And just as when learning to sharpen a plane iron or saw to a line, printed words can only act as a guide. The lessons have to sprout from your hands. So don't shortchange yourself by merely looking at the drawing exercises. Pick up those dividers and allow them to begin taking you on your own journey. This book is written for woodworkers who love building and who desire to take that next step in the craft. Once that threshold of design is crossed, a whole world of new horizons spreads before you.

George R. Walker
Canton, Ohio
May 28, 2012

Statue of Artemis

Hands cannot touch you where you move,
Swathed in dreams of deer in stride,
Apollos to answer you – all to prove
The age that shaped you never died…
for now along your marble ways
ancient line of light must ring
and flow at the touch of our musing eyes.
In Attic hush, the bright limbs sing.

— *Godfrey John*
(Late Canadian poet and essayist)

SECTION I

Making the Connections

1
Design at the Point of a Tool

2
Waking up Your Eye

3
Simple Shapes Combined into Forms

CHAPTER 1

FIG. 1.1.1. Dividers are much more than an icon of a faded past; they remain a portal into the artisan age.

Design at the Point of a Tool

Afternoon sunlight streamed across the wide pine flooring and up over a small Newport table. I turned my head and paused a moment, taking in the glow of the red mahogany top. With a pencil and a clean strip of pine to act as a story stick, I carefully nudged the small board against the table apron and began recording transition points, marking carefully where each element stopped and started.

This Newport table made by Al Breed is an exact reproduction of one of the true masterpieces of American craft. Originals sell in the seven-figure range, and this was as close as I might hope to get with a sharp set of dividers in my hands (museums tend to frown on that). My aim wasn't to record the table's dimensions to make detailed plans. Instead, I searched for a hidden song or harmony woven in the form, hidden in plain sight. I'd often read about the mindset of pre-industrial designers, how they loved to play with proportions and create frozen music in built objects, and I wondered if this table might contain a song. Sound far-fetched? Since antiquity, designers understood that a small handful

FIG. 1.1.2. Two Newport, R.I., cabinetmaking families, the Goddards and Townsends, built in a restrained style that reflected their Quaker beliefs and still exudes a vibrancy.

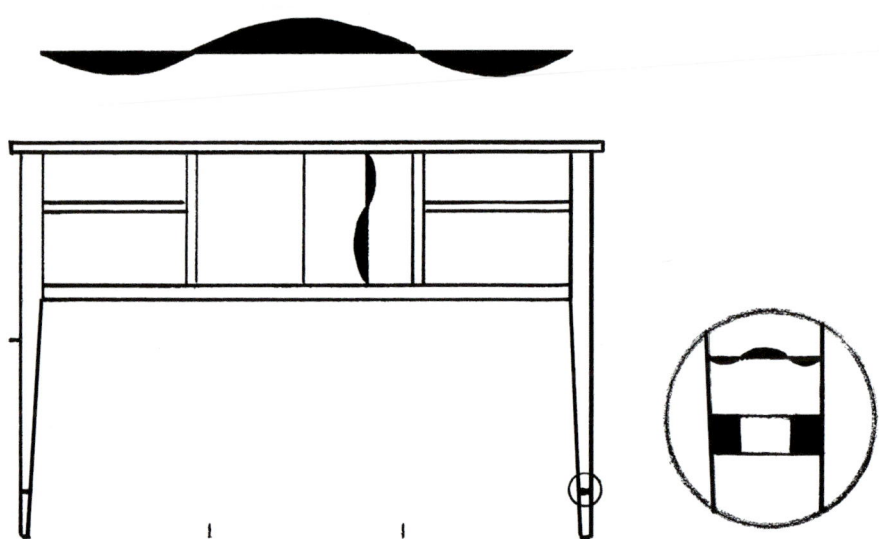

FIG. 1.1.3. Small cabinet shops used simple proportions to create pleasing designs. This sideboard uses the simple ratio of 2:3 to govern the form and organize the smaller details.

of simple ratios had a correlation with our musical scale. They spoke a design language built around simple whole-number proportions and applied them to a wide range of designs, from a tiny salt shaker to the entire layout of a city, and everything in between, including furniture.

With a square, each tick mark became a line on my story stick, transforming it into a map I could explore with dividers. My hands paced the divider points back and forth, adjusting the tool again and again, crisscrossing and retracing my steps. Then it happened. Like taking a pencil rubbing on the carved face of a weathered tombstone, a small series of overlapping notes appeared, running across the apron supporting the top: octave, fifth, fourth, fifth, octave.

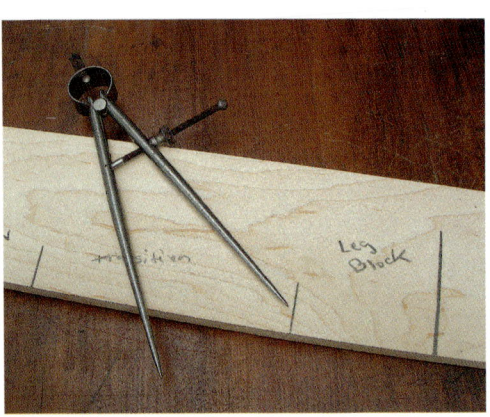

FIG. 1.1.4. Something simple hid just beneath the surface. After my dividers smoked it out, I marveled that I hadn't seen it earlier.

Not some grand symphony meant for a cathedral, just a subtle cello or flute piece with a few notes and a quiet rhythm. I'd been "looking" at that table for days but now I was "seeing" it. As I walked around it, the frozen music stood out clearly to my eyes. It was a moment of clarity, like when you spot a familiar landmark and the feeling of being lost vanishes. It also was a moment of connection, a rare glimpse into the artisan age. Connection, after all, is what design is all about: building things that connect and ring true. I want to be careful here and not romanticize this. It's not about going back in time and idealizing another age or being awestruck by period styles that were once the height of fashion. It's about drawing from our rich legacy of woodcraft to see what it offers the modern woodworker.

FIG. 1.1.5. Because the legs on a pair of dividers can be fixed, we can use trial and error to walk off a space into equal parts. Pace it off and make small adjustments so the divider point lands exactly on the boundary of the space.

That's the string that pulled Jim Tolpin and me together and got us so excited about what we call "artisan age design." Both of us marvel at the sheer simplicity of it, how it flows from hand and eye intuitively.

This is a gateway into a design language practiced in small cabinetmaking shops prior to the mid-19th century (though there are hints that it may have survived into the early 20th century). Lessons from that artisan age are still powerful and relevant because they are intuitive to our core. Do you remember when you first learned to sing as a child? Admit it, none of us can. It was so natural it sprang out of the mouth of babes. In the same way, this design language is a way of seeing and building that connects with how we are wired, tapping into roots deeply embedded in our makeup. It relies on proportions found in our own bodies as well as woven throughout the natural world around us. This powerful organic connection from nature is at the core of why these ideas hold sway (even if in the subconscious). We react differently to the song of a meadowlark than to the din from a nearby highway.

Let's be clear, though: Traditional design is not a list of "Thou shalls" and "Thou shalt nots" etched in a pair of bookmatched mahogany slabs. Instead, it's a collection of observations about how we relate to our environment. Because it's based on more than 2,600 years of human experience, some inescapable patterns emerge. We tend to connect to visual compositions that convey a sense of harmony and movement. We also react intuitively to designs that can be easily read by our eye and

> "Tradition is tending the flame, it's not worshiping the ashes."
> — Gustav Mahler

tell a story. Our eyes avoid, or react with apathy, to designs that give a sense of aimlessness or lack a spark of life.

The tool set and skill set from the craft tradition sprouted from this design approach. Jim and I share a solid conviction that traditional tools and skills, when asked to speak their native design language, become a sum greater than their parts. Almost like sliding them back in their original groove. Which begs some questions: Did the tools give birth to this language of design or was it the other way around? Did we invent dividers because we saw patterns and proportions in nature and felt compelled to explore them? Or, did we discover nature and its proportions after we attached two sticks at a fulcrum? We'll never know the answers, but it sure is fun to think about. What we do know is that we have inherited a tool set capable of translating images in our minds directly onto the work itself. This powerful and profound ability relies on simple shapes that we can imprint into our internal blackboard, creating pictures that we can manipulate, experiment with and change.

So for me, standing there "seeing" that Newport table was truly a liberating moment. This wasn't magic, just a handful of simple proportions. This was something I could get my arms around and begin filling in the gaps in my head that held me back from making confident design choices. I sensed my craft journey had turned down a new path, and my woodworking would never be the same.

Now Jim and I both stumbled onto this by different paths. We have different backgrounds, likes and dislikes. Jim is drawn to contemporary work with an eye shaped by a fondness for the sweet but utilitarian lines of wooden boats and airplanes. I'm drawn far more to traditional work inspired by simple furniture that cabinetmakers built in country shops than that from polished urban centers. Yet we're both energized by this approach that springs naturally from hand to eye. As each discovery unfolded, we learned to set aside our assumptions and began listening to what the craft tradition had to say.

The Artisan Age

If we could somehow walk into a pre-industrial cabinetshop, we might find much that's familiar. Wood hasn't changed its working characteristics, and it's still a valuable and expensive commodity. We'd recognize the joinery, no doubt marveling at the speed a journeyman could bang out a dovetailed drawer or chop a mortise. Where differ-

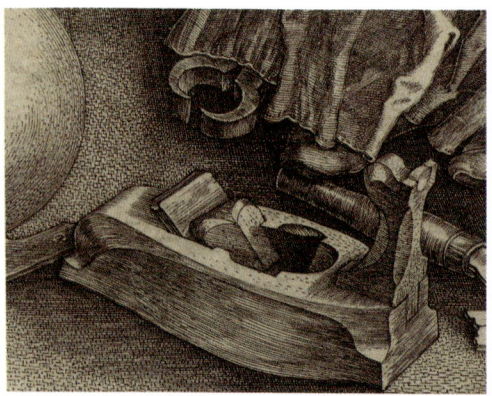
FIG. 1.1.6. Knowledge not shared is knowledge lost.

ences become glaring in that pre-industrial shop is in the artisan's approach to design. This was, after all, the golden age of the artisan – a time when builder and designer were one and the same. Designers were not a separate class of specialists working out of a fourth-floor office (or a separate country, as often happens today). The same artisan who crafted the furniture also designed it right at the bench. It's no accident that the ancient word for designer was "architect," derived from the Greek word *architekton* – a combination of the root words *archi* (chief) and *tekton* (builder). In other words, master craftsman.

FIG. 1.1.7. Geometry was the doorway to knowledge, and simple geometry was practiced in all the building arts.

The idea that a designer and an artisan should be separate specialists is a new concept brought on by the demands of industrialization and mass production.

Apprentices in a cabinetshop learned a wide range of skills on their paths to become full-fledged journeymen. They mastered sharpening, joinery and use of materials alongside basic trade math and reading. Design skills came into play also, and they consisted of two elements: craft and art, which were considered inseparable. The craft part of design centered on learning simple geometry for layout as well as the mastery of the laws of nature. These laws are defined not only as the knowledge of the various properties of wood itself but also as a profound understanding of the proportions, harmony and symmetry of structures that could be built with it.

Such mastery of design imbues a work with individuality, character and personality. The craft element forms a foundation that ignites the art element. This book's aim is to

FIG. 1.1.8. Dividers united the design world of architecture with all other arts.

help you build that craft foundation. That craft is not separate from art (as it's often portrayed in the modern way of thinking) but rather integral. It's like a musician practicing the scales or a painter mastering the color wheel. We never leave the base behind to progress to a higher level. We can't be expected to design without the craft base any more than we can run without balance or play music without notes.

Divide & Conquer

Emblazoned on guild crests and banners (not to mention Lost Art Press hats), dividers were iconic. But it's easy to fall into the mistake of thinking icons were always mere symbols, and not reality itself. Dividers, were, however, quite real and ubiquitous. They have been found everywhere throughout history, showing up in tool chests and tool inventories across every building craft. They range from simple hinged points to specialty dividers fitted with cutters, knives, inkers and gouges. They were fashioned from wood, bone, ivory, steel, hand-forged iron, brass and precious metals. Some were made small enough to slip in a shirt pocket and others large enough to step off the huge gears of water-powered mills. Beyond

FIG. 1.1.9. One pair of dividers with a fanciful flair made on a blacksmith's anvil, and another crafted by a maker of scientific instruments.

the building crafts, dividers were in common use by surveyors, navigators, scientists, doctors and artists. It's safe to say that dividers were, in fact, the most ubiquitous tool of the artisan age. But the question remains: Why is that?

Dividers jump between two worlds: the imaginary and the practical. Or to be more clear: the worlds of the eye and the hand. First, dividers are tools of the eye or, more accurately, the inner eye, whose role is to help us step off spatial shapes and proportions. But there's far more to it. Because we use our hands – a critical portal to our mind – dividers are a direct link into our imagination. That linkage with our hands and inner eye is key, enabling us to see and to lay out designs spatially in that blackboard tucked away inside us. Just as a guitar allows us to experiment, to play with sound and to ultimately create music, dividers are our instrument for experimenting and playing with space, helping us draw pictures in our mind's eye.

This understanding of how we use dividers is key to making the lessons of this book a working part of your craft experience. These pages are filled with scores of lessons that explore space with dividers and pencil. Think of it like exploring music by playing a guitar. The physical act of playing will transport you far beyond where intellect alone can take you. In the third section of the book, the "practicum" written by Jim, you'll learn (or, for many of you, relearn) how to use a compass and straightedge to perform a number of practical geometry constructions. In the last section, you'll explore a number of recent designs by Jim as he shares insight into this "design at the point of a tool."

Dividers were used by artisans to understand the world around them and to transfer that knowledge to built objects. Artisans found that dividers could unlock proportions occurring in nature to give their designs life and believability. The building arts shared a common knowledge of proportions, which Renaissance designers used to unpack the works of antiquity. It allowed cabinetmakers in Colonial America to understand and interpret designs coming out of England and the Continent. That timeless access is still available to the modern artisan, linking the entire craft with a continuous thread. It could be argued that dividers are a greater invention than the wheel. While a wheel and axle form a simple machine that carries a load, a set of dividers carries ideas. They reveal things hidden in plain sight. They show us things that we've never seen before.

Dividers are also the tool of the practical, the go-to tool to step off distances, transfer offsets and scribe layout lines at the bench. Thus they are also the tools of the hands. The same tool that enables us to step off imaginary space in our minds allows us to design at the point of a tool. Once we become fluent in the language of proportions, the flow of ideas back and forth from mind to hand becomes intuitive. This is a powerful concept impossible to overstate. When that threshold is crossed, it's a profound moment – the point where you begin to truly design by hand and by eye. For both Jim and me it was a watershed moment.

From Making to Manufacturing

So why did dividers fall from grace? Why have we let them slide back to being simply iconic, to losing their connection to the very heart of artisan craft? The answer may be found in the Industrial Revolution, which put an end to the artisan age. By the mid-19th century, industrialization, mass production and the acceleration in invention of modern building materials pushed the design process away from the workbench. Automation discouraged the artisan way, and it required a whole new mindset. Workers needed to learn the language of machines, not of proportions. Instead of tools serving as an extension of the artisan's hands, the worker became an extension of the machine. None of our traditional hand tools required numbers to be transferred to make them perform. Handsaws didn't come equipped with dials, scales or verniers. Chisels could be wielded freehand or made to follow a simple layout line struck from the point of a tool. It was only as cutting tools were bolted to machine fixtures rather than guided by hands that we began needing numbers to feed machines.

It came to pass that craftsmen's labor was focused on production and no longer on design. That close connection that an artisan felt between hand, eye and work was lost. Machine power and automation put noise, fast-moving cutters and layers of steel between hand and eye. Dividers couldn't speak the language of machines and mass production; they spoke the language of the artisan age, and that voice was nearly extinguished.

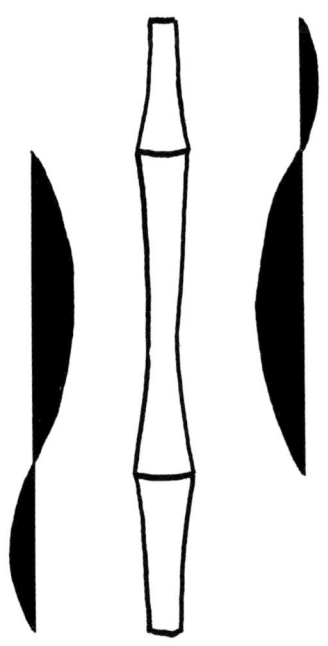

FIG. 1.1.10. Lesson #1: Measuring tools such as this ruler occupied a different role in the tool hierarchy.

FIG. 1.1.11. *(right)* Without thinking, an artisan could size up major and minor elements, diameter to height and the proportion from narrowest to thickest in section.

When Rulers Didn't Rule

What, exactly, is the language of the artisan age? To put it simply: It is a design approach that speaks to proportions scaled to whole-number ratios. Measurements as we know them in a modern sense were largely unknown and unnecessary to the artisan workers. Today we think of dimensions, tolerances and measuring accurately with precise rulers, micrometers or digital readouts. The pre-industrial measuring tools of the artisans were "Fred Flintstone-like" by today's standards. Rulers frequently went no finer than ¼", and were often hand-stamped and crude. If we were to use those crude rulers as our primary tools to design and build, we would no doubt struggle. Reason being, the approach was with an entirely different mindset. Instead of asking, "How high is this base dimension in inches?" pre-industrial artisans would have asked, "How tall is this base in proportion to the case above it? How wide is this leg in proportion to its height? How much does this leg taper in proportion to its width at the widest part?" A seemingly small difference that's much more than a quirky relic from another age, it's a difference that placed them in another universe far away from the industrial thought process. It was the design language of the artisan age.

From 3-D to 2-D – The Built vs. the Graphic

What I have been discussing here is not, I assure you, conjecture. Historical design books support and illuminate this language, and there's ample evidence that many established cabinetmakers read and studied these books. Most of these guides were architecture-based, which informed the use of proportions to organize a design. Don't worry, though. We aren't going to take a painful detour that requires we learn to design buildings before we tackle furniture. We look to these books because they focus on the art of the built object, on how these things occupy three dimensions. This is in distinct contrast with furniture design trends following the Industrial Revolution that shifted toward the thinking and approach of graphic design. Much of today's design literature leans heavily on graphic arts that focus on the visual object (as opposed to the built object). You may be surprised to learn that terms such as "positive and negative space," "line weight" and "visual tension" are the language of contemporary graphic arts, not of architecture or furniture design.

This architecture-based design language draws on an a tradition going far back into antiquity. It emphasized proportions inherent to the human form and to those found throughout nature. Apprentices were encouraged to study something called the classic orders, an ancient architectural form that was the culmination of thousands of minds working for literally thousands of years. These classic orders are thought to embody the highest level of proportional composition and we believe they served as a wellspring of inspiration to the artisans of antiquity. The orders contained the DNA, that is, the genetic sequence, of their proportional

When 12 Trumped 10

The language of the artisans was all about finding, generating and laying out whole-number ratios with a compass and straightedge. They were not using rulers to work to arithmetic derivations of a numbered measurement. So while using a scale based on one to 10 works fine to resolve numerical formulas, you do often end up with decimal fractions of a whole number. That would require an artisan to lay out to a numbered ruler – not to mention having to deal with decimal places. Another downside in using base-10 is that 10 doesn't readily break down in whole-number fractions: You are limited to 1/5 and 1/2. A one-to-12 scale, on the other hand, gives you 1/6, 1/4, 1/3 and 1/2 – the ratios of which can be easily counted out on one hand (thank you ancient Babylonians) as shown in the drawing below. Note that you use your thumb as the counting cursor.

Divisions of 12 also came into play for easily laying out right angles – especially so when dealing with large constructions. Thanks to the work of the ancients (Thales and later Pythagoras), artisans knew that when you broke 12 down into three, four and five divisions, you could easily create a right angle. Step out three divisions on one leg (which could be a marked stick or knots on a rope), four on another and five on a third – and when you set the ends together they form a right angle. As you'll see later in Section Three, Artisan Geometry, working with proportions and executing constructions (such as generating rectangles from squares to a variety of ratios) through the use of fractions of 12 makes the process intuitive and quick.

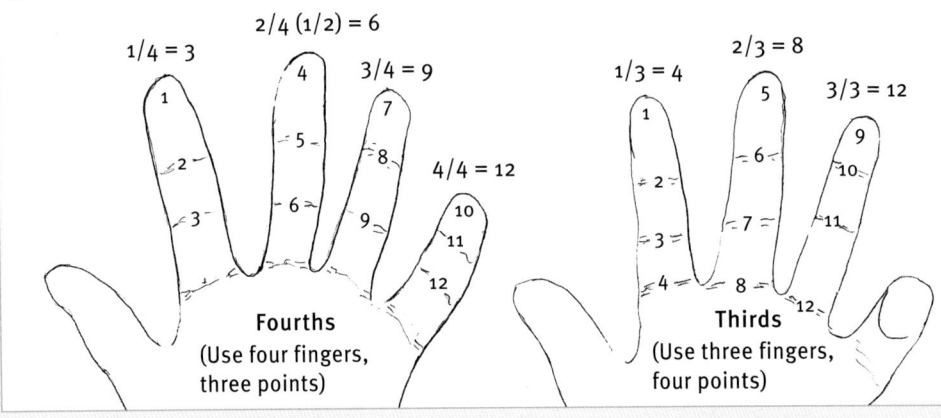

FIG. 1.1.12. Divide 12 on one hand into thirds and fourths (using fingertips and knuckles).

systems. Artisans became intimately familiar with them through the oral transmission of masters coupled with long, careful study. In a very real and practical sense the orders gave artisan designers a common vocabulary to communicate and share ideas. Even today, for the modern woodworker, drawing the classic orders can reshape our ability to imagine and visualize proportional relationships.

The Classic Orders – A Drawn-out Process

I'll be the first to admit that period design books can be a slog. Seventeenth and 18th-century authors slathered on the verbiage, taking an entire page to say, "That dog is fat." Rest assured, you need not become fluent in King James English to learn their contents; you just need a willingness to practice some design-focused exercises. All pre-industrial design literature contained some common threads: Proportions were paramount, as was a seemingly odd obsession with the classic orders. Almost all the books began with a series of plates detailing the orders and stressed the need to study them. Batty Langley, a popular author of guidebooks for the artisan classes, suggested drawing each order six times. As I mentioned earlier, the classic orders were thought to embody a standard of perfection that could not be improved upon, and their mastery was considered equivalent to an artist (painter) learning to mix colors or to a musician learning the scales.

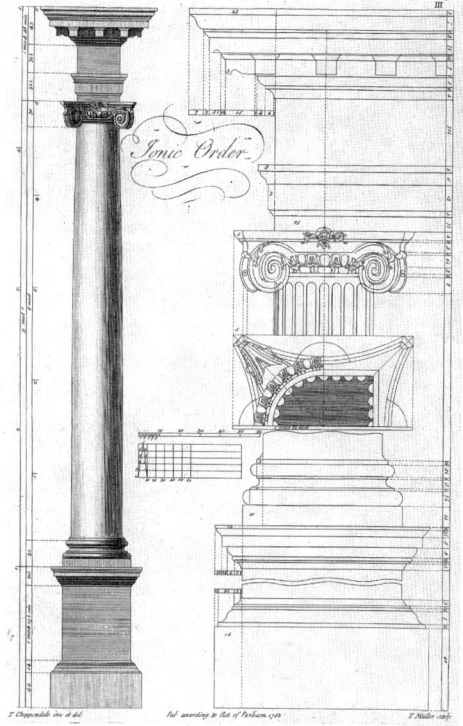

FIG. 1.1.13. If you were an apprentice in the artisan age, you learned this Ionic classic order by heart.

"I can feel the heart-throbs of the ancient Greeks in their marble gods and goddesses."

— Helen Keller

Historicist to Modernist

Before going further, it might help to understand the traditional mindset concerning inspiration and design. I'd like to credit Steven Semes for the concepts presented on this subject from his book, "The Future of the Past."

There's a wide spectrum of thought on how to approach design, with extremes at both ends. At one end is the approach we'll call "historicist." This is a view that looks to the past for inspiration and desires to preserve the tradition – some might say embalm it. This view tends to consider masterful work in a glass case, to be studied and copied. In the furniture world, this is the reproduction camp. This isn't confined just to period furniture builders (of which I'm proud to be a part), but it also applies to Arts & Crafts furniture or Sam Maloof rockers. This approach has real value and springs from the craft itself. Artisans have always looked to masterful work to inspire and elevate their own. With some great masterworks, one could spend a lifetime of study and not hit bottom. In modern circles, the historicist is often looked down on and misunderstood, but this is actually at odds with much of our cultural tradition. Somehow it's not creative to attempt to capture the fire and life in a Federal-era Virginia sideboard, but it's another thing for an orchestra to revel in the attempt to recapture the beauty of Beethoven's Symphony No. 5. Beyond that, attempting to reproduce masterful work has always been a pathway to learn. Painters often copied the works of masters to discover the depths of technique.

FIG. 1.1.14. Many accomplished builders who enjoy reproductions view the process much like a musician attempting to perform a great musical composition.

FIG. 1.1.15. Many think that Rembrandt funneled a lifetime of tragedy in this painting of a lost son reuniting with his father. Entire books have been written exploring this one masterwork.

The limitation with the historicist is that the masters who originally created these great works were never historicist themselves. They didn't set out to create masterpieces by copying in excruciating detail. Because the focus is often on the physical objects themselves, a historicist can miss some of the real treasure. It's possible to craft an exact reproduction of a Philadelphia highboy by candlelight with period-correct hand tools, yet still miss the underlying proportions that filled the design with life and power.

The other end of spectrum is bookended by the modernist. This view gazes to the future for inspiration, often disdaining the past. Modernists are driven to constantly explore new ground and new ideas. The craft tradition is thought of as stifling and as a barrier to creativity. The aim is to create something outside or beyond the craft tradition. A modernist is free to look anywhere for inspiration but the goal is always something new. Standards are seen as a potential limitation, and often intentionally avoided (except occasionally in the context of flouting them). Yet modernists legitimately spring from the tradition in that pushing the boundaries has always been a hallmark of the creative process.

FIG. 1.1.16. Modernism pushes the boundaries of furniture making, often turning to new materials to achieve the vision.

This preoccupation with the new comes with limitations, however. Because woodcraft has been explored for more than 3,000 years, the potential for creating something totally new is a colossal challenge, unless you extend beyond wood as the primary medium. Modernism came into its own only as man-made artificial materials (plastics, foam, composites etc.) made it feasible. Modernism intentionally confronts a long tradition of highly evolved design knowledge (including the craft element of design covered in this book) which, we believe, carries great risk. We respond to design cues on a much deeper level than mere fashion. Design is not to be trifled with lightly. It is for this reason that much pure modernist work is polarizing.

Somewhere between these two extremes is the traditionalist, or the craft tradition.

FIG. 1.1.17. This design gives a nod to the past but has a timelessness about it – a quality often found in traditionalist work.

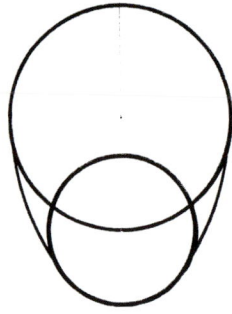

FIG. 1.1.18. Drilling down to the bedrock of inspiration, this simple egg shape is pregnant with possibility.

FIG. 1.1.19. Is it just an egg? Or is it a human face?

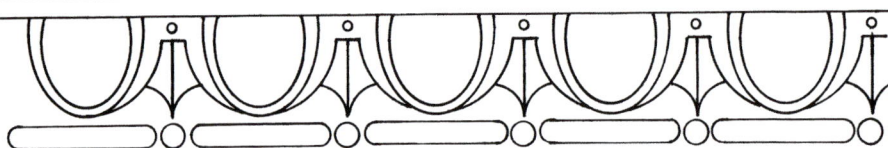

FIG. 1.1.20. Is this just whimsical carving or is that an egg hiding in there?

FIG. 1.1.21. Is it just an egg, or a vase?

FIG. 1.1.22. Or is it part of the turning in this chair leg?

Here, the aim is to enrich by respectfully extending the craft, always looking forward to find fresh inspiration, but with one eye mindful of the past. The traditionalist is concerned with the underlying principles that bolster a masterpiece and seeks to interpret that knowledge in fresh ways. It's more focused on the craft than on any style or fashion, and draws inspiration from nature, built work, architecture, furniture and fine art. A traditionalist recognizes there are standards to both provide structure to build on, and underlying principles to inspire. A traditionalist looks at a source of inspiration differently than either the historicist or the modernist. Ideas are not frozen in the past or dismissed because they are not original. Instead, the question becomes, "What is the creative potential in this?" or, "What possibilities does it contain that I can build on?"

This traditionalist approach is not about slavishly worshipping the past or ignoring our craft tradition. Instead, it's about extending the artisan age by building relevant work in the context of our time. To achieve that goal requires us to gain a solid foundation in the craft element of design. We must reunite the design language, the tools and the skill set. This journey begins by learning to see, awakening the "by eye" part of this amazing design language.

It's hard to get more basic than an egg, right? It's just a major and a minor circle connected by some curved lines. How much creative potential does this shape contain? Look at the photos at left and consider this.

Conclusion

At first, the use of very simple visual building blocks (i.e. simple shapes and proportions) seems to be rote and mechanical. Delving deeper, it soon becomes apparent to me that it's the opposite. This turns out to be a highly evolved design language that uses proportions just the way a writer learns to use words to create a unique story, or the way a composer learns the language of music to create a song. The language of the artisans was not a compendium of rules; instead, it was a compendium of tools.

CHAPTER 2

FIG. 1.2.1. It takes a sharp pair of eyes to get a clean look at this feathered acrobat.

Waking up Your Eye

On the southern shore of Lake Erie lies a narrow strip of cottonwood bramble called Magee Marsh. It's the last bit of shelter for migrating songbirds before they take flight across the open water. Stiff headwinds can cause a massive pileup with thousands of birds hunkered down, and hundreds of bird watchers converging to witness the spectacle. It's called a fallout. To a birder, a fallout is an event on par with a solar eclipse.

The first time my wife, Barb, and I stumbled into one, I wasn't prepared for it. The air bristled with brightly colored warblers as we stepped under the shelter of the tree canopy. I felt a puff of air on my cheek as a blur of yellow feathers darted close to my ear. Veteran birders around me ooh-ed and aah-ed, "There's a black-throated blue, and just above it, 5' back at 2 o'clock is a redstart!"

But my eyes weren't quick enough and I didn't know how to look, or what I was looking at. Over and over I just missed something wonderful and rare. A 9-year-old boy wearing a T-shirt proclaiming "Birding is not for Sissies" tried in vain to help me, but after a few minutes, politely slipped away. That first morning I wondered to myself if I'd ever

> "For all men, not just architects, are capable of appreciating quality; but there is a difference between laymen and architects (designer/builders) in that the former cannot know what a building will be like unless he has seen it completed; while the architect knows perfectly well what it will be like...from the instant he conceives it in his mind, and before he begins it."
>
> —Vitruvius, 1st century B.C.

get this. I didn't seem to have the eye for it. In spite of early doubts, gradually my eyes and brain started to mesh. As the day wore on, I began to see clearly those winged jewels I'd only read about in books.

This book is the equivalent of a "fallout" to awaken your designer's eye. Despite any doubts you might have, you already possess the inherent ability to see with your inner eye. It is, in fact, simply waiting for you to awaken it. You'll see what once seemed impossible and quickly gain the confidence to spread your creative wings. With some practice, the ability to see and unpack a design will become as natural as breathing.

Looking for Clues in all the Right Places

We live in a media-saturated world filled with images bombarding us every waking moment. Yet, as Vitruvius observed, we're still plagued with a common dilemma: A layman looks while a designer sees. My own craft background, molded by modern industrial practice, left me dependent on measured drawings. The ability to visualize seemed beyond my grasp in spite of a lifetime of building things with my hands. Granted, I had strong opinions about furniture, art, cars and guns, and I knew immediately what I liked or considered ugly. But truth be told, I could only detect the glaringly obvious. Even then, I struggled to pin down what caught my eye. I could admire a masterpiece, but could not explain what tipped the scales in its favor. I'd look at a chair and think, "It's off; there's something awkward or clumsy about it," but rarely could I voice with certainty what looked awry. This is a little embarrassing to admit, but even if I started a project with clear pictures and plans, the image I formed in my head never seemed to match the actual parts

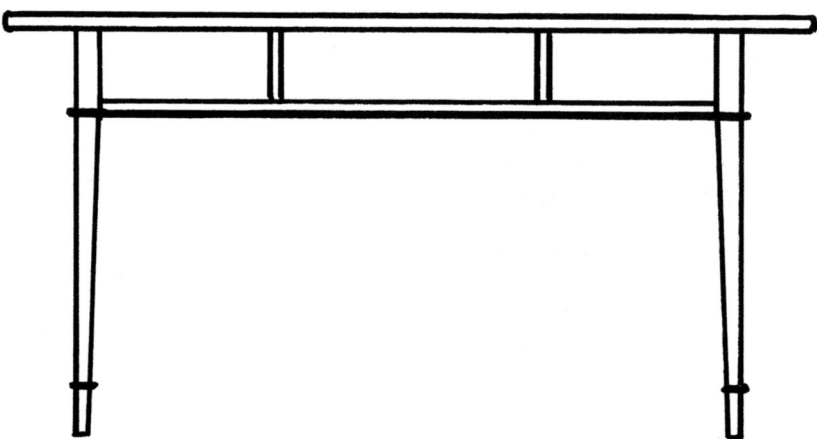

FIG. 1.2.2. Is this just a small writing desk or something more? My untrained eye would have said, "Nice work, nice lines," with little more meaningful comment to add.

as they came together. This reinforced the feeling that I couldn't trust my eye. Not that I couldn't "make to print"; I couldn't "see to print."

Our modern industrial approach doesn't awaken the eye. It's just the opposite; the aim is duplication, and that's achieved by removing the human element. I started my professional life in the trades as a machinist. Blueprints were my world and point of reference; drawings, measurements and tolerances were my comfort zone. Mistakenly I assumed that's what artisans had always relied on, just with a more primitive set of tools. I had no idea that the artisan age used drawings in a completely different way than anything I'd been taught.

In spite of my misconceptions, my own background in the trades gave me subtle clues that something had been broken. My apprenticeship as a machinist began in the 1970s, right at the sunset of the hand-drafting era. Apprentices got a taste of drafting in the engineering shop, a massive open room with row upon row of tilted drafting tables. Just a few years passed and those big drafting boards disappeared as computer-aided design (CAD) technology emerged. Down in the factory, those dog-eared paper drawings were stored away in a vault and replaced by crisp, freshly printed computer drawings with immaculate graphics. A few years later, machines came equipped with a monitor, eliminating the need for a paper drawing. The next step allowed machines to download the drawing directly into the machine controller and eventually, no image of the actual part was required, just data. Oddly enough we still called them "drawings" even though they con-

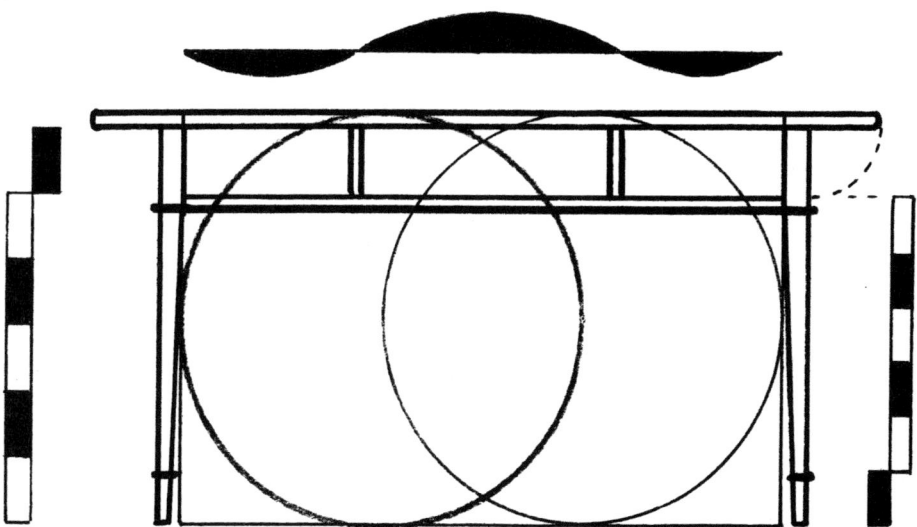

FIG. 1.2.3. You can learn to see what lies beneath the surface. This is what we are talking about!

tained no pictures, just code. Industrial drawings reached a new pinnacle; they could speak directly to machines in their own native tongue. What a success. It took nearly 200 years from the dawn of the Industrial Revolution for technology to finally and entirely remove the human worker from the equation.

Now don't get me wrong; this isn't a rant against technology. The ability to mass-produce and duplicate things with precision is crucial to our modern society. From safe baby food jars to fail-proof landing gear on an airplane, our world today is unimaginable without it. But at its core, measured drawings and the way we use them in our modern industrial approach focuses on duplication. It removes human error but at the expense of creativity by limiting choices and dictating rigid commands. Worst of all, by emphasizing measurements and ignoring proportions, it masks relationships between parts and how they relate to the whole. We look at a historic drawing and conclude the details shown to build it are sketchy. Conversely, an artisan-age craftsman might conclude that our modern drawings contain everything but the kitchen sink, yet they obscure the essence of the design. The creative spark requires a different set of conditions to ignite. It feeds on choices, options and the ability to see. In short, it needs the human element restored so that a dance can emerge between the play of hands, eye and the wood itself.

Looking for Clues in all the Wrong Places

I recognized some common threads just beneath the surface in pre-industrial craft that struck a chord. It possesses a connectedness, not just by including the trappings of nature, but also something deeper by interweaving the rhythms of nature and our relationship to it. The emphasis on proportion, harmony and contrast are timeless connecting points. Now, I don't like everything produced in the past. Some styles, such as Gothic Chippendale that drips with gee-gaws, I think of as Frankenfurniture. It's best left behind to a narrow band of history along with olive-green refrigerators and vinyl tops on cars. But I found myself drawn to some of the simple, hon-

FIG. 1.2.4. The artisan age sometimes gives us a wink and quietly lets us know there is more beneath the surface.

FIG. 1.2.5. Drawings can take many forms and serve many masters. Which ones best feed the designer's eye?

est work that displayed not just a high level of technical skill but an underlying knowledge about design. I'd look at a carving detail that seemed to sprout from the end of a chair arm and know there was more to this I needed to understand.

Given my background, my first thought was to look for answers in the shop drawings from the pre-industrial era. It was here that I found my first surprise; drawings were almost non-existent. At first I reasoned it was a fluke due to the scarcity of paper or its ephemeral nature. Looking closer, I had to admit that reams of day books, indenture records and estate inventories managed to survive, so why not drawings? Of the small handful that somehow did survive, none would even qualify as a true drawing in the modern sense; they are often similar to a crude sketch scratched out on a napkin over lunch. I could not imagine how thousands of workshops during long periods of time produced such a vast collection of incredible work. How could shops separated by long distances, even oceans, replicate styles and disseminate and experiment with regional interpretations without the assistance of drawings?

Drawings are a means of communication. Some speak the language of machines (duplication) and some foster creativity and speak to our inner eye. Woodworkers have a wide range of drawing options to assist in the process of designing and building furniture. CAD programs are now widely available and allow projects to be viewed in virtual 3-D. Yet in some important aspects they may still fail to make the inner connection with our designer's eye. One is the pure physical aspect that makes visualization possible. I'm reminded of Beethoven who late in his career suffered the tragedy of deafness. Somehow he continued to compose by sawing the legs off a piano so that as he played, he could feel the notes through the vibrations in the floor. The great master still needed the physical connection to visualize and compose. The physical act of drawing manually with pencil and dividers taps into a portal in our mind via our fingertips in a fashion that differs from our hands pushing a mouse. Many forms of drawing, and even full-sized mock-ups, don't automatically guarantee we see the design from a proportional standpoint. Seeing a width dimension on a table leg does not mean you will be able to visualize the relationship between width and height, and between the space that adjoins it. Walking off those spatial relationships with dividers helps the mind to think and see proportionally.

Drawing on the Bright Side of the Brain

Traditional proportional drawing drafted by hand ignores dimensions. It instead relies on simple geometry and dividers to compose an image that conveys the proportional scheme. It employs a vocabulary of proportional notes that we can visualize internally. Because this type of drawing relies on proportions rather than specifications, it moves another step closer to a pure image in the mind. Pro-

FIG. 1.2.6. This period drawing contains no dimensions, just a proportional key at the bottom. Artisanage cabinetmakers were so immersed and adept in proportions that they could quickly grasp and build the design with little more than this key.

Concept Sketching

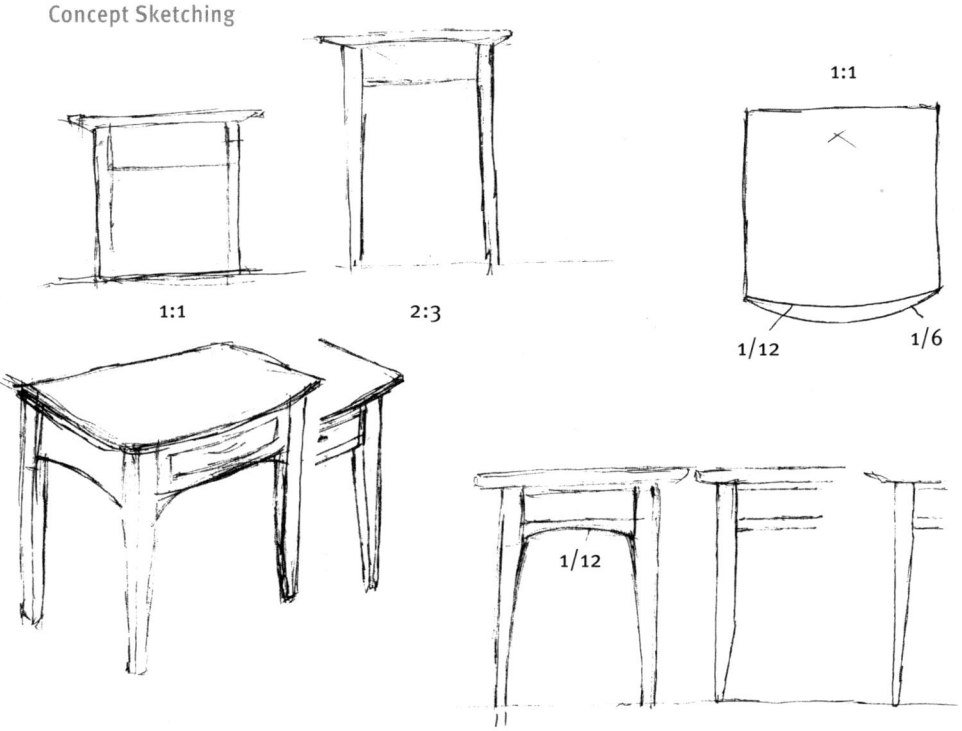

FIG. 1.2.7. Freehand sketching is a fluid exploration of line and form intended primarily to connect internal ideas with a physical image. For those familiar with the language of proportions, these drawings can provide a powerful link through our senses into the drafting board in our minds. Like the proportional drawing, though they contain no dimensions, they may provide enough information to execute the design.

portional drawings can provide enough information to execute a build with simple tools; the drawings are organized in a way that meshes with traditional bench techniques. Even if you are adept with digital or industrial drawing, this type of drawing is not a step backward. Instead, it's a concrete method to begin making that connection with your inner eye.

Our goal ultimately is the drawing that takes place in your head. This is speaking the language of design from the artisan age in its purest sense. It's what Vitruvius wrote about when he said an architect could see clearly from the instant he conceives it in his mind. It uses a simple language of visual notes to create spatial music to help you acquire the ability to conceptualize internally. This is at the opposite end of the spectrum from the industrial approach – using that ability to spur creativity and provide a practical means of expression. You may still choose

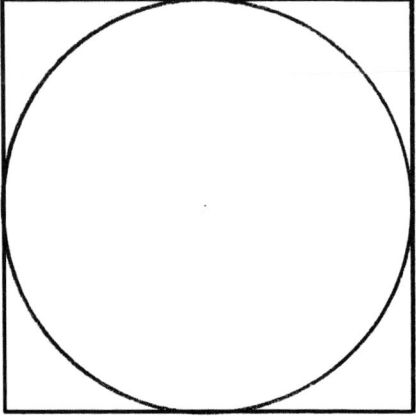

FIG. 1.2.8. Our task begins by learning to visualize a small set of simple visual notes.

to employ modern drawing techniques and (egads) SketchUp, but the goal is to always encourage the flow of clear images from the drafting board in your head.

Make Your Designs Sing

This concept of clearly seeing a design in the mind's eye is a learned skill. Let's do a little experiment. Take a moment, close your eyes and sing the "Happy Birthday" song silently to yourself. You weren't singing out loud were you? (If you did, start again and sing it just in your head.) Could you hear it? Think about this for a moment. No audible sound, but you

FIG. 1.2.9. The single square (left) is at one end of the scale and the double square (right) is at the other.

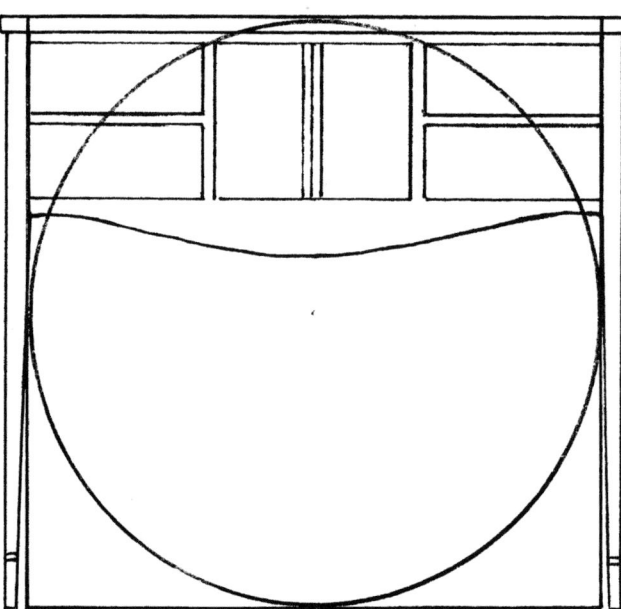

FIG. 1.2.10. Relax. We won't try to convince you there are squares and circles under every bush (you'll find that out for yourself after a while).

could clearly hear it in your mind. Try this: Sing it silently to yourself again but at a slower tempo. Can you still hear it, only slower? Can you imagine it sung in another voice? How about a deep, clear Nat King Cole version? How about a sultry Marilyn Monroe singing to John F. Kennedy? Can you hear the song played on an instrument? A piano? Try a trumpet. How about bagpipes? Stop! Cruelty alert: Step away from the bagpipes. The point is, you have the amazing ability to visualize already.

You not only could hear the song, but you could manipulate it, express it with different voices and instruments. I'd venture a guess that if you thought about it, you have hundreds of songs tucked away in that stereo in your head. Chances are, few of you have ever formally studied music. In fact, most of us could not write down the musical score for the song. It's not about notes you can write on paper, but notes you can hear in your mind.

Music at its simplest is made up of a handful of simple building blocks we call notes. Musical styles and genres can span a huge range from Bach to John Lee Hooker to ZZ Top. Underneath it all is the same handful of simple notes. Accomplished musicians, including the likes of Yo Yo Ma, practice the musical scales daily. The scales are nothing more than a note sequence arranged to keep a sparkling clear image freshly imprinted in the mind. Do you doubt that a musician develops a heightened ability to imagine music? The reason we struggle to see spatially is that we never learned a set of visual notes.

Close your eyes again and visualize a square. Can you see it clearly? If not, take a moment and draw a square with pencil then try again. Now close your eyes and imagine two squares side by side, one next to the other. Now imagine two squares arranged one on top of the other. Can you see the squares clearly? It doesn't matter how big the squares are, or whether they float in space. They can be solid or simple line drawings. The important part is that you can see them. Now do the same visual exercises again, only this time imagine a circle. Then visualize two circles, a pair side by side, and a pair one on top of the other. Consider the circle and square to be interchangeable. There's lots more to say about the circle later, but for now all you need to realize is that they are both easy to visualize. Congratulations. You have just taken baby steps in learning to see. You have just imagined the visual notes that bookend the range of our visual scale. The single square or circle begins the sequence, and the double square or circle completes it. In between are a handful of intermediate notes. The circle and square are the basic building blocks, and though it might seem like a small step to you now, in reality you've taken a giant leap toward unlocking your inner vision, and toward making your designs sing.

A DRAWING EXERCISE

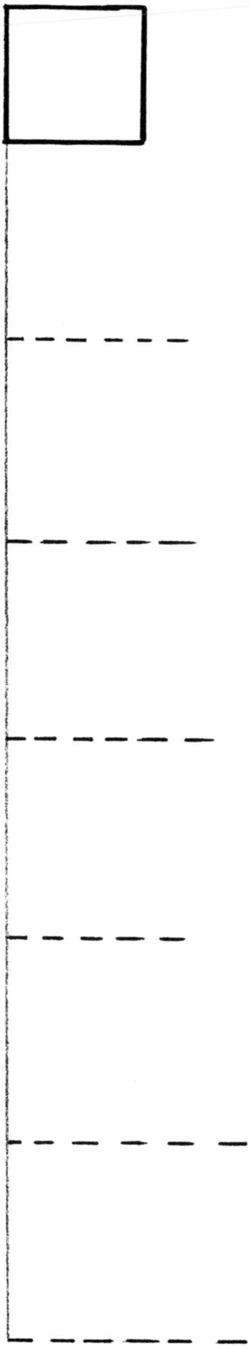

FIG. 1.2.11.

Creating a Visual Scale

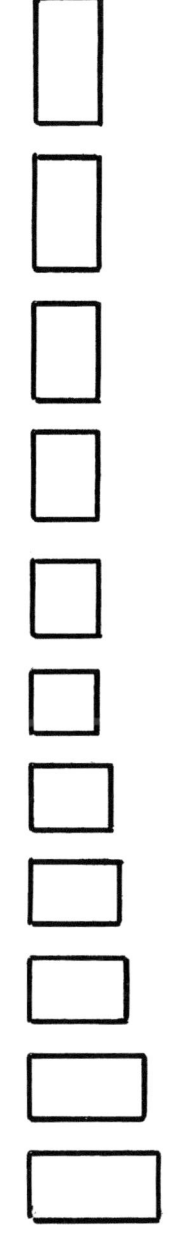

You just imagined the two notes that bookend the scale; let's draw the entire sequence. Adjust your compass to draw a circle that will just fit inside the square at the top of the previous page. Leave your compass at the same setting and on the line at the bottom of the page draw two circles side by side but just touching. Encompass them both with a rectangle.

You have just drawn the visual notes at the bottom and top of our visual scale. Pre-industrial artisans had a fancy name for these. They were called a square and a double square. Take a moment again to close your eyes. Can you see the shapes clearly?

Now that you know how to draw a double square, can you think through how you might draw two circles that overlap to create a square and one half square? Draw that and encompass it with a rectangle. If this is confusing you can turn to page 30 for an example drawing (1.2.13), but it's important that you think through this and draw it out.

Using the same logic of overlapping circles, can you draw a square and 1/4 square, a square and 1/3 square, a square and 2/3 square, and, finally, a square and 3/4 square? Encompass each with a simple rectangle.

You have just drawn the basic rectangular building blocks needed to construct forms in your head and at your workbench. You may or may not have drawn them in a sequence that goes from small to large. If not, draw them again in sequence starting at the top right side of the page.

IMPORTANT POINT: We created a set of visual notes that extend horizontally. You can also arrange these so they extend vertically.

You have just tapped into something profound on three levels:

FIG. 1.2.12. The same notes can cover a range of space either horizontally or vertically, with the single square in the center.

(CONTINUED ON NEXT PAGE)

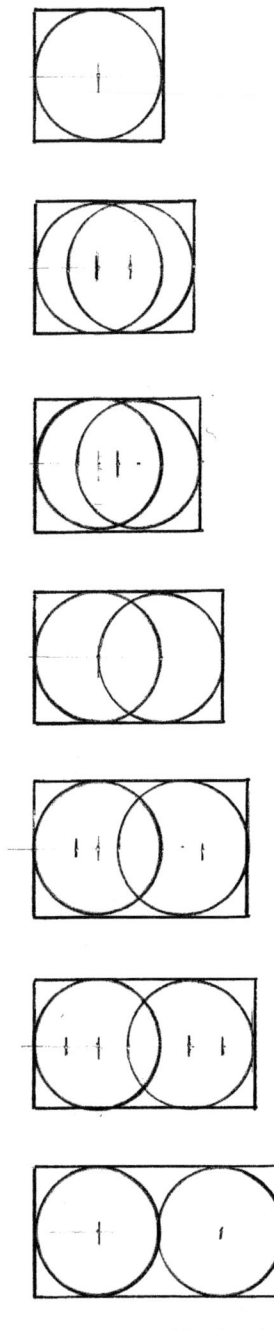

1. This is a series of visual notes that can be visualized with clarity. The single and double square are intuitive; those notes in between can, with only a small amount of practice, also become clear.

2. These simple shapes are easy to apply in practice with just a straightedge and compass. Thus, they dovetail perfectly with actual shop layouts at the workbench.

FIG. 1.2.13. In this visual note sequence, the center rectangle is a square and one-half.

FIG. 1.2.14. Anything look familiar? Gibbs describes these as square, square and one-half, double square, etc.

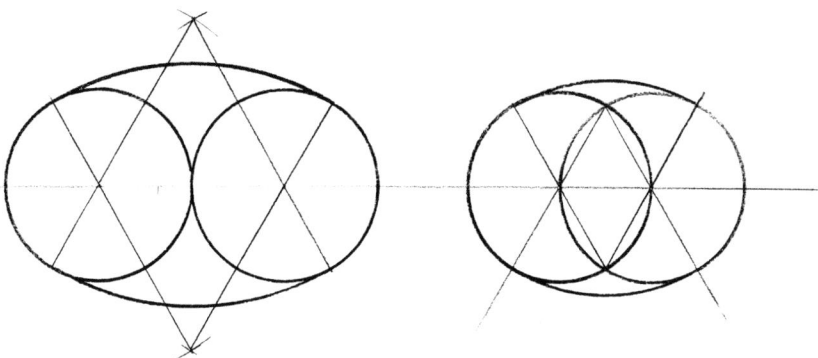

FIG. 1.2.15. Can you plainly see the connection – how these ovoid shapes use the same simple notes as the rectangles? Can you visualize them in your mind also?

3. These notes have deeper connections (more to come on that later). For now it's powerful enough just to know that they are easy to imagine and practical at the workbench.

Perhaps it's so simple we look beyond them for something more complicated.

At left is an engraving from James Gibbs's "Rules for Drawing" (circa 1732) on different window configurations. Throughout historical design books these series of simple visual notes show up in examples of ideal room sizes, fireplace openings and furniture.

We use circles to generate these simple rectilinear shapes. By extension, the same can be applied to ovoid shapes.

Conclusion

Now you have a simple scale to practice and become familiar with. You can begin to combine these just like a songwriter arranges notes in a song. Yet music is more than just notes on a scale or tossed about at random; music employs melody, harmony and rhythm. In the next chapter, we'll take a closer look at how to begin arranging these visual notes to create fresh, lifelike compositions. It begins with understanding forms and the ability to look at the underlying bones in a design.

CHAPTER 3

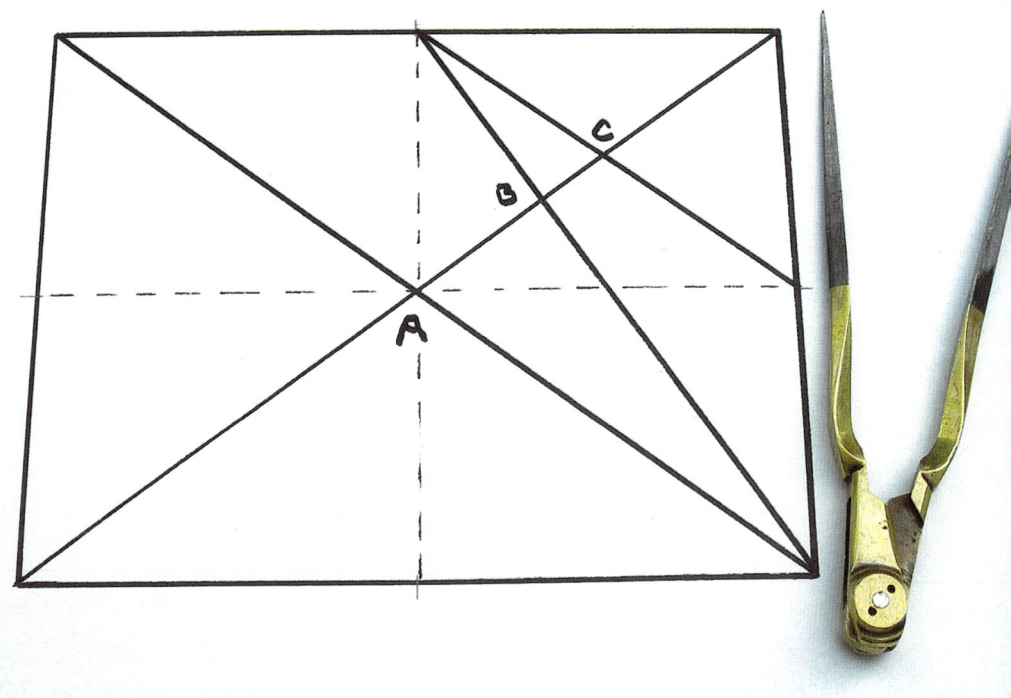

FIG. 1.3.1. Using simple geometry to locate these points divides this rectangle into halves (A), thirds (B) or quarters (C).

Simple Shapes Combined into Forms

My first taste of geometry was in the seventh grade. Mrs. Knox taught by the fear method, wielding a long wooden paddle that she kept tucked away under her desk but within easy reach. She distilled the learning of geometry to its simplest form: Memorize theorems or be beaten. The thought never occurred to me that geometry might be useful, let alone a beckoning doorway into a hidden world. Art and beauty conspired to keep their secrets hidden, and they anointed Mrs. Knox to ensure it.

Admit it. You may not have had the bejeebers scared out of you in geometry, but chances are you were force-fed an endless pile of theorems. Both Jim and I want to assure you we are not headed there. This isn't about formulas and theorems, but about a simple, pure form of geometry that's illuminated with a string, a straightedge and a pair of dividers. It underpinned all the artisan trades much the same way Latin and Greek lie at the root of Western languages.

In the artisan age, apprentices learned a working man's practical geometry. So this is about learning a pure, simple geometry that will help you visualize shapes in your head as well as quickly execute layouts at the workbench. Today we often think of geometry more in a mathematical setting, as a method to find a numerical answer that involves the resolution of angles and lines drawn on a page. Pre-industrial artisans thought less about numbers and more about visualizing space and proportions, and how those spaces related to our human form. Geometry was a straightforward, practical language of design to understand and clearly see proportional relationships.

It's far too easy from our vantage to discount this ancient approach. It seems to sprout from nowhere as Western civilization stepped onto the stage of history. For much of that history, it was not just the language of design but also the language of science. Architects used it to design cities and buildings, and astronomers tried to explain the cosmos using simple proportions. Scholars finally broke away from this track in the 16th century, favoring the scientific method. Yet the artisan class still clung to it, carrying it on through oral traditions into the 20th century (as we saw in Jim's analysis of the designs of the earliest "aeroplanes" in his preface). Although we discovered new ways to advance science mathematically, proportions still found an accepted role when a design required beauty. Christopher Wren, one of the giants of British architecture in the 17th and early 18th centuries, was also an accomplished scientist in the fields of astronomy and medicine. As an influential member of Britain's fledgling scientific society he embraced the new mathematics of the Age of Reason. Yet he left perhaps the largest body of design work from his era, all based on the older language of simple geometry – simple shapes and whole-number proportions. Ultimately it wasn't science, but the relentless pressure to mass-produce driven by the Industrial Revolution, that caused the language to fade from use as small artisan shops disappeared from the landscape.

The bond between this design language and the tools and techniques of the craft tradition cannot be overstated. This practical geometry is expressed and visualized with lines, points and simple shapes. In theory a point has no size, no height and no width. It only possesses a location. We use dividers to step off proportions and generate shapes that create reference points on our work at the bench. In reality that pinprick left by the divider leg has a physical size, but it's just large enough to register a location for a marking knife to strike

FIG. 1.3.2. Christopher Wren, better known for designing St. Paul's Cathedral in London, built this monument to the great fire of London, which also acted as an instrument to conduct astronomical experiments. Here was an overlap of the new science of reason with the older legacy of proportions and beauty.

a line. In theory a line has no height or width (just length). Our line struck with a knife has a physical size, but it's just enough to register a chisel for a precise joinery cut or leave a mark to guide a handplane. From a simple geometry standpoint, we employ the most accurate baseline possible using dividers, a straightedge and knife. We might add a miter square for speed and convenience, but we take care not to add a layer of remove between our minds and hands. These methods place design in our fingertips, right down to the point of a tool.

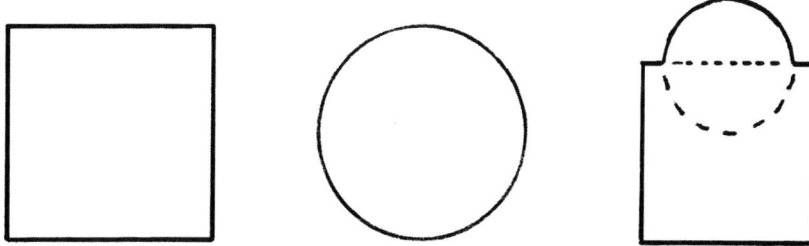

FIG. 1.3.3. A "shape" is a simple figure, either rectilinear or curved, that cannot be broken down any further (e.g. square, rectangle, triangle, circle). A shape can be either in two dimensions or three (e.g. cube, cuboid, cone, cylinder, pyramid). A "form" is a combination of simple shapes to create a composition. This clock-dial form (above right) combines a square and a circle.

FIG. 1.3.4. A form can be used in a macro sense, to define an entire composition and all the major shapes that define it.

FIG. 1.3.5. A form can also be used in a micro sense. This brass key cover is made up of two circles overlapping a 2:1 rectangle. It's a small form that complements the overall furniture piece.

Simple Shapes/Complex Forms

A form is a simple shape, or a combination of simple shapes, that defines the overall visual boundaries of a volume. This is often loosely referred to as the lines of a piece. It's a good exercise to train the eye to look beneath the surface and see the underlying bones that make up a form. It's easiest to look for these in a façade and deduce the simple shapes in two dimensions. As you get more comfortable you will begin to see these shapes as solids (i.e. cubes, spheres etc).

Forms can be internal, made up of the actual walls of a building or the sides of a cabinet. But, it's also helpful to understand that some designs are governed by a simple shape that governs the form externally. A circle or square can define the extremities of irregular-shaped

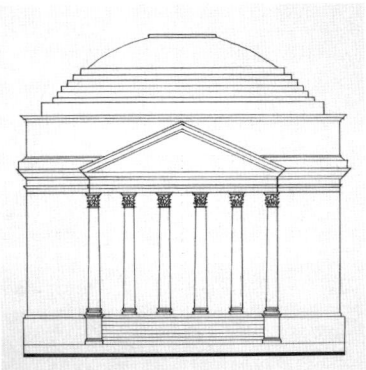

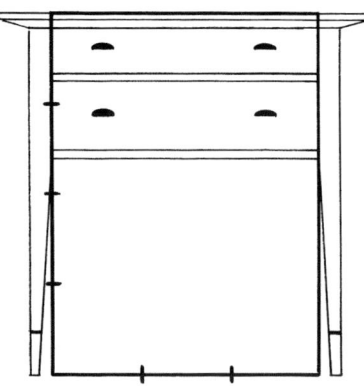

FIG. 1.3.6. This form is a circle that drops straight down to the ground from the equator. Or you could imagine it as a sphere with a cylindrical drum rising from the ground to the equator.

FIG. 1.3.7. Although much of the mass of this piece is air, it's governed by a 3:4 rectangle that defines the top, sides and floor.

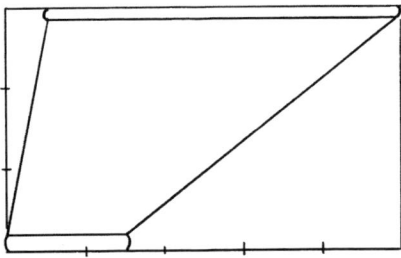

FIG. 1.3.8. This form is a circle enclosing just the tips of the starfish's arms. Contained within that circle is a series of overlapping triangles.

FIG. 1.3.9. In this case, a rectangle governs the height and width, even though the foot is cut away on one end. A simple shape can define a form even if much of it is just air.

designs. The ability to visualize this simple shape makes the complex simple, and it becomes much easier for your inner eye to comprehend. You'll take a large step in understanding this design language when you develop the ability to see simple forms in these more complex designs.

From Macro to Micro

A thread running all through this traditional design language is that most lessons apply on the macro level and then echo on a smaller scale. In this case with forms we see simple shapes governing the big picture as well as the smaller details. One of the ways that we relate to an object is how the form is composed as it relates to its scale. The overall governing shape, that big rectangle or circle, is the impression we see from a distance. It might be a building across a city square or a bookcase at the end of the hallway. That overall form is what our mind takes in at first glance. From a distance we focus on how the design fits in with its overall surroundings.

As you move closer and interact visually with the object itself, the proportions of sub-elements come into play. Because our field of vision is limited, the overall form may become impossible to take in. Traditional design usually includes smaller elements to keep our interest as we draw closer. This is where figured grain and the smaller simple shapes cause our eye to flow over the design. It's important to note that just as the overall form is related to its setting, the smaller sub-elements, even down to the details of carving, are related proportionally to

FIG. 1.3.10. This sketch of a period mirror and table includes some hints of the room setting. If you look past the ornament, notice how the mirror frame aligns with the adjoining woodwork. It's scaled to harmonize with other elements in the same space.

FIG. 1.3.11. Details meant for close-up view are not visible from a distance. We expect to look someone in the eye when at speaking distance; from farther away, eye color is invisible. Each view, macro to micro, has a different story to tell and a different means to achieve it. Exaggerating a detail meant for a close-up view so that it's seen from a distance may result in a disturbing effect.

A DRAWING EXERCISE

Capturing a Form

Here's a drawing exercise to help you unpack the simple shapes in a form and help you begin to see proportional relationships. You'll need a piece of paper, straightedge, pencil and dividers. Pick out a small object you can place on a table such as a child's chair, or sketch a larger object from a distance. During this exercise you need to remain in the same spot while you draw the entire object.

Hold your straightedge out at arm's length in your non-drawing hand. Use the end of the straightedge and your thumb to pick off the overall width of the largest rectangle that governs the form. Use this measurement to draw the bottom side of a rectangle. Using the same method, capture the height of your subject and with that you can complete a rectangle that's proportionally accurate. Congratulations. You've just defined the simple shape that governs the form.

Now look at your subject and determine the next-smallest shape that's internal to your larger rectangle. Use the same method as you work from large to small to fill in the

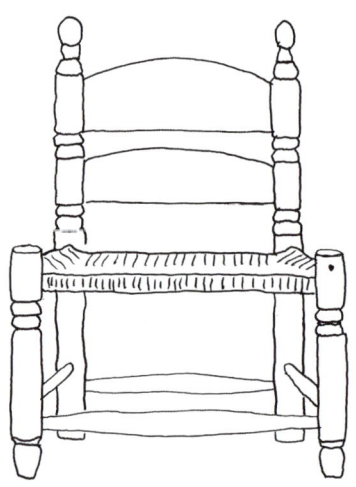

FIG. 1.3.12. This exercise will help you pick out the major shapes in a form as well as the smaller shapes that are internal to it.

the larger form. Traditional designers strived to make all the parts in a composition relate proportionally to each other as well as to the whole.

Finally, we have the close-up view. Except in small objects, it's now too close to take in the overall form; carving, inlay and texture give the viewer a reason to delight in the maker's composition.

It's impossible to overstate the role that visualization plays in the ability to design. Happily, it's a learned skill that you can improve by applying some effort. In the next section, we'll share some ways to integrate that knowledge into your practices at the workbench.

details of the form. Dividers are handy for visually plucking smaller elements and guiding your detail drawing. I would encourage you to use a sketchbook and practice this on a variety of objects. Challenge yourself to draw and unpack irregular objects. Once you begin to see them as a collection of simple shapes, a whole new world will open up to you.

FIG. 1.3.13. Make sure your arm is outstretched as you pluck every part. We are not after a numerical measurement, but instead gathering how each part relates proportionally.

FIG. 1.3.14. Use each measurement to draw in the simple shape on your form.

SECTION

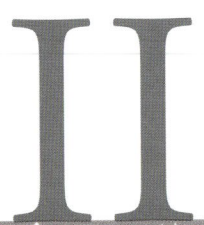

The Language Of the Artisans

1
Understanding Proportions

2
Proportions Made Simple

3
Incorporating Curves

4
Classic Orders

CHAPTER 1

FIG. 2.1.1. The star cluster known as the Pleiades is found in the myths of all the world's peoples. It is a common "language" that binds us together across oceans and eras.

Understanding Proportions

The Big Dipper lives up to its name: a large constellation of bright stars emblazoned across the night sky. The Pleiades, on the other hand, is a small cluster of stars tucked away and hardly noticeable. The cluster is said to contain upward of a hundred stars, but you can hide them behind your outstretched thumb. Under city lights the Pleiades is barely visible as a faint silver glow, while out in the country under dark skies you can make out six or seven pinpricks of light bound together in a tight knot. Yet mysteriously our eyes are drawn to this tiny gem. I've witnessed it often with first-time star gazers.

After we trace out the big, bright constellations, a finger points skyward to Pleiades, and a curious 12-year-old scout asks, "Mr. Walker, what's that little clump of stars all alone by themselves?"

What follows is always fun. I ask them how many individual stars they can make out. Most can spot six, some with sharp eyes can spy eight or nine. Then I share how that little group of stars shows up in the lore of every culture. The writer of the Book of Job penned nearly 4,000 years ago, "Canst thou bind the cluster of the Pleiades?" Called the Seven Sisters by the Greeks, the Lost Boys by the Blackfeet tribe in North America, Subaru by the Japanese (look closely at the nameplate of the car maker), the Pleiades played a major role in the mythology of ancient cultures all over the world. I like to think they bind us together. When I look up and see that glow against the black winter sky, I'm reminded that our ancestors shared the same sense of wonder and awe.

> "An understanding of the orders and their proportions is an entry into an ancestral code appreciated by everyone but never fully understood by anyone."
>
> —Robert Adam

The skeptic in me can say without blinking that the methods and techniques we are exploring in this book can stand on their own without the help of mystique or myth. Using circles and simple shapes as a spatial language conforms to our brain's ability to process information much like a binary code enables a computer. Yet there is a part of me that wants to live in a world where there's still room for wonder. Why does birdsong in springtime sound delicious? Why the universal search for beauty that spans all cultures and all eras? We don't pretend to answer these questions but, for the sake of stoking your passion for design, it's fun to learn how this language came down to us on the wings of science, myth and wonder.

Jim and I have a little running joke based on the ancient's fascination with the circle, and how in their eyes it's woven into our DNA and the DNA of the universe. Each time we see another example – and we've run across a slew while researching this book – it's like a wink from the ancients. We smile and say to each other, "It all circles back to the circle!" (For those of you who enjoy digging into some of these ideas and concepts, Jim and I will be writing more about this in the weeks and months to come on the "Rabbit Holes" page at georgewalkerdesign.com.)

The idea of a design language built around a circle seems at first blush too simplistic. How could something so basic, easy to draw, easy to imagine and found abundantly in nature, be so central? Actually it's precisely because of all those reasons. The circle allowed builders to see and unpack the world around them, to make sense of the natural world. And the circle allowed them to use the simplest of tools to etch out their own designs in wood, clay and stone.

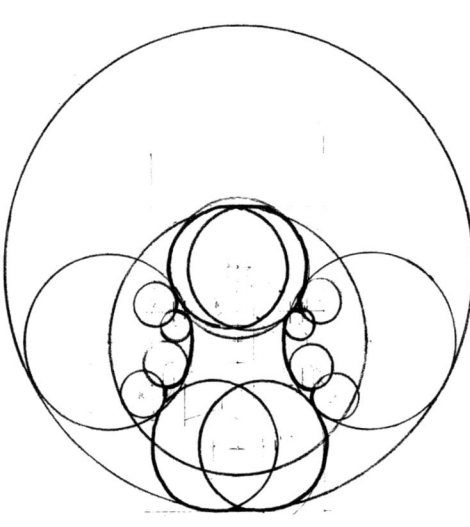

FIG. 2.1.2. Hidden in this assembly of circles is the outline of a violin body. Can you see it? This is a reconstruction of the archetype violin form that Stradivarius used.

It's possible to use a compass and a few circles to create some amazing designs. Yet this goes far beyond using circles like a set of building blocks. It's about a circle of knowledge that links together a chain of ideas about nature, the human form, the classic orders, simple proportions and music. I first met Jim at a Woodworking in America conference on design in Chicago. He attended my presentation on traditional design and the next day I slipped into the back row of one of his sessions on designing furniture using our own bodies as the template. Jim shared his design approach for building a step stool using his handspan to lay out the proportions. It was simple and elegant, and I immediately recognized his approach was a close relative to what I was exploring. It may seem a bit odd in our numbers-focused world to use a handspan to lay out a design, yet the reality is that all our furniture forms are built around the human anatomy. Sideboards are 40" tall and table and chair heights are all standardized in inches or centimeters, but they all are based on a height that meshes with our human frames. Later, in Section Four: Projects, Jim details this approach on a number of different projects. If you can put aside prejudices that favor a tape measure, you'll find this a liberating and fun approach. To my way of thinking, we were both entering the same chain of knowledge – just from two different spots on that circle.

FIG. 2.1.3. Nature, the human form, classic orders, music and proportions: all these are intertwined and connected to form a circle of knowledge about design.

This is a collection of observations of many thousands of minds during more than 3,000 years. Its roots extend into pre-history with the Greeks having a prominent role (they wrote about it, so they get much of the credit). Basically, it's wisdom about how we perceive and react to the world we live in. Our surroundings today might seem a world away from that of our ancestors, but though we live in a modern environment, we cannot erase our basic human makeup. We still respond to fear, pain and pleasure, and all things critical to life and survival. We respond so naturally at our core that much of our reaction is not apparent unless we pay close attention. There is a natural temptation to look at what the ancients said or accomplished and either romanticize them and make them more than reality warrants, or look at them with a modern prejudice and undervalue the true significance. The value for the modern woodworker is somewhere between these extremes.

Our ancestral code has a way of showing up no matter how modern, chic or ridiculous our pose. We've reduced miniature dogs (or dog-like things) into fashion accessories – canines bred to be carried in a handbag. This latest bizarre twist in dog-man relations is tempting to pass off as just another fad. Yet behind it all we've been sitting by dogs in the firelight for millennia, sharing danger, food and warmth. Perhaps there's something more to it that prompts a woman to keep a dog close by her side? Or why do we insist on installing a fireplace in our

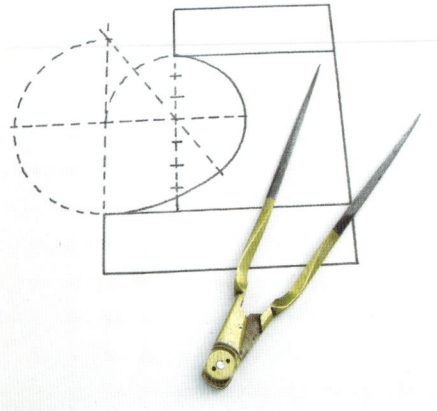

FIG. 2.1.4. Circles can be combined to create harmonious forms with seamless transitions.

modern, centrally heated home or high-rise apartment? We even use technology so our hearth isn't real fire, just an electronic image of logs burning happily. Is it fashion, style or something deeper in our bones?

A large office complex with an ocean of cubicles sandwiched beneath a low ceiling has a distinct vibe. The soulless, pancake-like arrangement in these human warehouses grates away at us. Stand near the exit door and watch as people step outside after working in a cramped cubicle. The most common reaction – often without a thought – is a quiet sigh of relief. Traditional architects, however, paid close attention to how a room's interior space felt. They clearly understood that the key to making a room feel comfortable and inviting was to make its height harmonize with its overall footprint. They knew that a large room with a low ceiling feels stifling, and that a small space with a high ceiling feels cavernous and evokes a feeling of insecurity in most people.

The front of a large cathedral is focused around a massive entry door. Does that mean that the designer expected very large parishioners? Obviously the large door is scaled to the large facade, which was, in turn, scaled to the idea that this was the house of God – not that of puny man. A smaller door would not only be inappropriate, it would look out of place – like a small mouse hole chewed into the base of a wall.

Where Proportions Come From

Again, this might sound far too simple, but it really does start with a circle. Let's begin by exploring this form as a simple shape. Geometrically, it has some unique properties: It's a curved line with no beginning and no ending. That idea of no beginning or ending gave it a connection with eternity and with the wonders of the heavens that appeared to us to stretch out forever. Thus the circle symbolizes the cosmos. The fact that any point on the circumference is the exact same distance from its center also meant that a circle is a self-contained manifestation of symmetry. The focus or center point of a circle is the equivalent of zero, in that it has no dimension and occupies no space. Yet that focus point has a fixed place in space; weird – almost like a black hole.

Later we'll dive deeper into symmetry, but for now consider this: "Symmetry is the deepest thing we know about nature." This statement, made by Steven

Weinberg (a Nobel laureate in physics), was not referring specifically to the visual symmetry of forms, but to the underlying symmetrical balance of all the forces that occur throughout the known universe. These include the relationship between electricity and magnetism, the balance of "dark" and visible matter and energy, and the equivalency of the forces due to expansion and to gravitational attraction. We don't understand why this great cosmic balancing act happens (and we perhaps never will), but we do know that if it didn't, our universe would cease to exist.

FIG. 2.1.5. A circle is the most fundamental of forms.

Nature is filled with examples of circles that inform our senses from the earliest moment. A newborn's limited vision at birth extends just a few inches – just far enough to make out its mother's eyes. It's one of the first images we store in our memory. Some are mistakenly under the impression that circles are a rarity in the natural world, and I've been challenged on "circles occurring naturally" several times while speaking in front of groups. I've always answered by asking the whole group to start naming some

FIG. 2.1.6. Children, as they learn to draw, always begin by using the circle as a symbol to depict people and animals. Is this coincidence or something more?

examples. After a slow start, a torrent of circles pour in (cross-section of a tree trunk, an elephant tusk, ripples created by a stone tossed in still water). Always the same response after we quickly fill up a blackboard: "Enough already! We got it! You made your point! Dang!" Maybe it does all circle back? Perhaps we might learn something if we sit by the ancients and listen to what they had to say.

Circles can be visualized with clarity. It's so solidly imprinted in our minds that we can use it as a mental building block. Think back to Section I, Chapter 2, and our silent singing exercise. You were able to visualize a song and then visualize a circle (and its counterpart, the square).

Connection with our Human Form

While the circle on one level embodies the cosmos, it also forms a link with the human form. The iconic drawing below by Leonardo da Vinci is actually an ancient drawing exercise practiced by artists to understand the ideal human form. Outstretched limbs can be encompassed by a square and circle with the navel at the center. This depiction of the idealized human form came from the writings of Vitruvius, a first-century B.C. architect who committed into writing a long tradition of design knowledge from antiquity. The circle connecting with our human form is the next big link in this chain of ideas. The ancients, both pagan and Christian, thought of the human form as encompassing perfection and the embodiment of beauty. They saw man as God's highest creation. They took note that our bodies contained symmetry. Our form is encompassed by a circle, the embodiment of symmetry, and also exhibits a mirror image in the left and right sides. They also to understood that the human form could be unpacked and expressed using simple proportions. For example, our eyes are positioned halfway between the top of the skull and chin, our bodies are eight times the height our heads. Obviously, individuals have small differences from these ideal proportions, but as a general guide, they provide profound insight into our form.

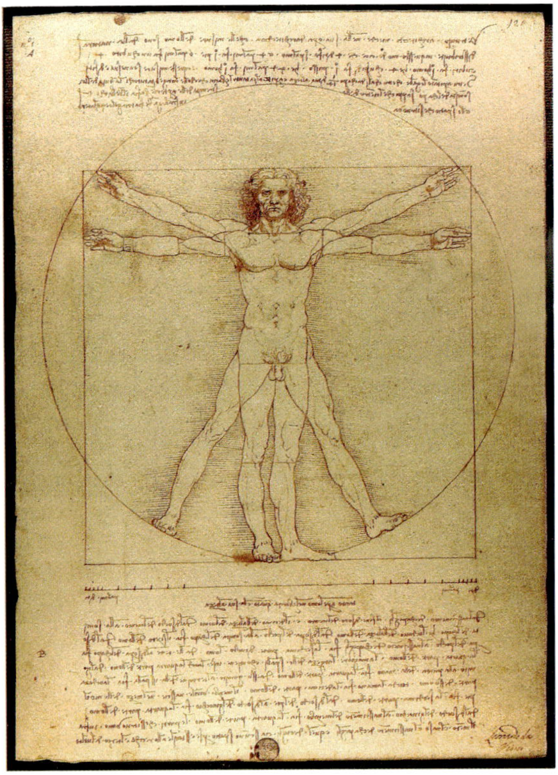

FIG. 2.1.7. A circle can define the boundaries of a form in a subtle fashion by capturing the inherent symmetry – in this case, the human body.

FIG. 2.1.8. Leonardo da Vinci illustrated how we perceive the proportions in the human form by exaggerating just one or two proportions to create a "grotesque."

The idea of proportion or "ratio" comes from the root word "reason." Proportion at its simplest is how one part relates to another as well as to the whole. Animals and plants abound in endless variety, but all produce offspring that conform to a type. Although a huge variety of types exist, individuals all conform to a scheme of proportions. Body parts all have a consistent ratio with other body parts. We may be taller (and fatter) than previous generations but overall our proportions remain the same.

Polycleitus, a Greek sculptor who lived circa 400 B.C., studied and wrote about the proportions woven into the human form in his book "The Cannon." His work as a sculptor catapulted Greece into the Golden Age. Before him, human depictions were static, mere symbols of human forms. His in-depth knowledge of the proportions knit into the human form imparted life. His figures looked as though they might step off the pedestal and throw a spear. No originals survived, but even Roman copies bristle with vitality. This deep knowledge of proportions gave artisans of the ancient world a key to explore the human form, which they regarded as the embodiment of beauty. Those same proportions found in the human form also found expression in the built world through architecture.

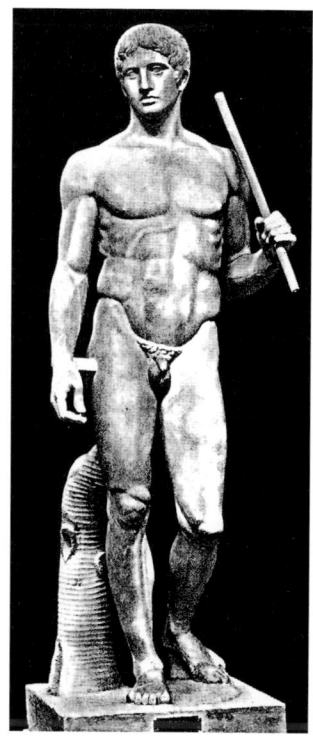

FIG. 2.1.9. The study of the human form reached a peak in the golden age of Greek sculpture circa 400 B.C.

A DRAWING EXERCISE

Proportional Linkages

Draw a rectangle with a simple ratio between height and width of 3:5. Now, randomly adjust your divider points with a few turns on the adjustment screw and draw a second 3:5 rectangle. Because these two are governed by the same ratio, they are said to be in proportion. Now draw a third 3:5 rectangle, but this time go back to your original and step off half the width. Use that to draw the final rectangle that's one-half the original. All three of these are in proportion, but the first and third are additionally linked because one is connected proportionally to the other (1:2).

This idea of the human form encompassing beauty is woven into the architecture from antiquity. It was the key for the built world and all related arts. In the ancient world, architecture was the mother of all art. Understanding proportions was fundamental to the architect, sculptor, painter and artisans in wood, stone and metal. This connection between the ideal human form and the built world is the next link in this chain: circle, to human form, to proportions, to the built world (hang in there, we are getting closer to furniture). Designers strove to impart the beauty of nature into built works. Frequently they anthropomorphized the human form into the bones of their designs.

Connecting with Architecture

The term "classic order" is a modern name for an ancient architectural form used in the construction of temples. At its simplest, it's a column supporting a beam or lintel. But it's much more than that. These columns became highly stylized and refined, and reflected strong links with the natural world and the ideal human form. The columns reflected a link with nature in several ways. The stylized stone shafts mimic old-growth timbers used in the construction of the earliest prehistoric temple structures. The taper of the shaft and the mouldings at the base reflect an origin found in the old-growth forests (which you must remember, were at the time not far away from the great cities of ancient civilizations). King Solomon contracted with the king of Lebanon to harvest great timbers of cedar for his temple and palaces.

Over the centuries, five orders, or types, evolved, each containing within its fabric shadows of the human form. The different orders reflected gender, with Tuscan and Doric depicting a masculine athlete or warrior, while the Ionic, Corinthian and Composite reflected a feminine figure or virgin.

The orders also were built around distinctly human-derived attributes. Although we have a mirror image of our left and right sides, vertically our bodies have a distinct beginning, middle and ending: feet, torso and head. The classic orders are likewise organized around this arrangement of beginning, middle and ending, each with pedestal, column and entablature. Smaller sub-elements within the order also repeat this theme. The column is made up of a base, shaft and capital. This vertical organization is carried into many other forms beside the classic order. Not surprisingly, this simple sequence finds itself repeated in the structure of good storytelling and music, with both benefiting from a solid beginning, middle and ending.

The orders also share a strong proportional link. Just as all our body parts are connected proportionally into a unity, every element down to the smallest detail is connected proportionally with the whole. Thus the orders were thought to possess a perfection of their own.

From a craft perspective, the importance of the classic orders to the pre-industrial artisan can not be understated. The majority of all historic design literature

UNDERSTANDING PROPORTIONS

FIG. 2.1.10. These iconic architectural forms are known as the classic orders. They are one of the most highly evolved and intensely studied forms in human history.

FIG. 2.1.11. The mouldings on this column are stylized depictions of forms from the natural world.

(including furniture guides) prominently feature the classic orders. It's almost as though the authors realized they wouldn't have any credibility if they didn't pay homage to the classic orders. In my own case, I read the glowing prose and wondered if it would be foolish to dismiss so many respected voices. I first approached the classic orders thinking they might reveal some proportional formulas that might help unlock the design secrets from the artisan tradition. After diving in, it began to dawn on me that there was something much deeper at work. I suspect I could spend years plumbing their depth and not touch bottom. But here's my take on what they meant for the pre-industrial artisan, and hopefully what they can mean for you, the modern woodworker: The classic orders schooled the artisan designer on three levels.

First, in an age when design and building were carried out under the classical tradition, knowledge of the orders introduced the apprentice to the language. The orders are a doorway into the world of plinths, architraves and the seemingly endless ways that mouldings and ornament might be employed in a classical setting. Especially in America, few artisans had the luxury of specializing, and there is ample evidence that cabinetmakers frequently produced architectural interior work such as fireplace mantels and bookcases. The ability to design furniture and architectural work that would complement a classical room setting was an important skill set.

Second, the classic orders are a something of a primer in the application of basic proportions. They are chock-full of simple proportional sequences that an artisan might rework and apply to a wide variety of design problems. Almost like a small series of guitar chords, proportional sequences from the orders equip the artisan with an arsenal of proportional tools. A familiarity with the orders greatly increases the comfort level in using and manipulating proportions.

Last, and most important for the modern woodworker, the classic orders are a proportional standard that can impart a sense of perfect proportional pitch. Truth be told, the orders themselves rarely show up explicitly in furniture design. That's not surprising because they evolved to suit the needs of stone temple construction. Yet the most profound lesson they offer is that they provide a foundation for making informed design judgments. Working through the classic orders enables the artisan to clearly see proportional relationships and establish an intuitive "North Star" to make course corrections.

For all these reasons (and especially the last one) we are following the path of the craft tradition to explore the classic orders. I hope that as you work through some of the exercises preceding them, you too will be inspired to walk through this ancient doorway.

FIG. 2.1.12. The idea of a beginning, middle and ending is found throughout classical design and finds its origins deeply rooted in the classic orders and the human form.

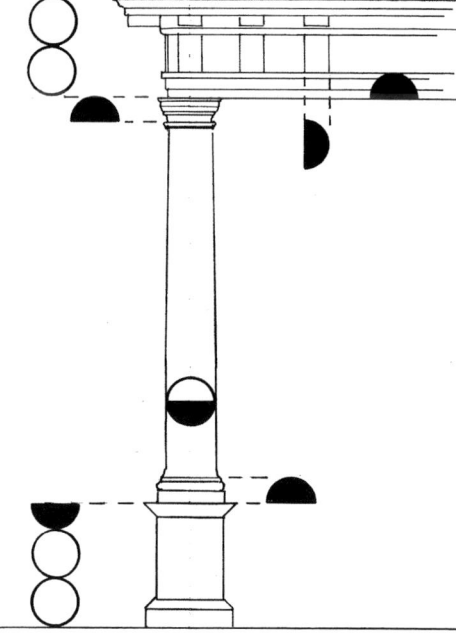

FIG. 2.1.13. On this classic order, the diameter of the lower shaft is the module that's echoed throughout the composition. A module can tie together dissimilar elements that may not be in close proximity.

Proportional Linkages

Also connecting the human form and the classic orders is the idea that all parts are connected by simple proportions. The human form in all its complexity could be unpacked by exploring the simple proportions of one part to another. This was the basis of the Greek achievements in sculpture, and it became the foundation for classical painting. Proportions, or what was termed "measurement," was considered the craft element of the art, necessary to empower an artist to launch his (or her) creative potential.

Any work conceived using simple proportions will contain a module, an internal proportional unit that's either multiplied or divided to define other elements in a design. This is an internal key that acts as a unit to create proportional linkages for other parts in a composition. Proportions are unique to each design and a given module is arbitrary. When you step off a 3:5 rectangle, those divisions are actually modules. Yet there is a little more to it than just randomly picking any element and calling it a module. A small element such as a moulding might be related proportionally to the whole design but must be multiplied many times to step off the larger parts of a form. Using dividers to step off a height that's 54 modules high is unwieldy. Using a large element from the form doesn't work well either, because you are forced to reduce it into awkward fractions to scale smaller parts. Sculptors used the height of the head to proportion a human figure, our height being eight modules high. Designers from the Renaissance used the diameter of the shaft at the base of a column to proportion every other element in a classic order from big to small.

They then divided the column into 60 minutes, so even the smallest moulding could be expressed in relation to the column diameter. Design guides from the 18th century such as the popular works by Batty Langley took it a step further and moved away from a strict use of modules. They simplified proportional layouts and avoided using fractions of any kind. Yet there is an attractive thing about using modules. They seem to repeat themselves in other elements of a composition. The diameter and half-diameter on a Doric classic order defines

> "As [the art of measurement] is the foundation of all painting, I have set myself to the matter of teaching the essentials to young people eager for instruction in their art, and giving them reasons for taking up measurement with ruler and compass, so that they can recognize the truth when they see it. In that way they will not only be eager to know their art but will also acquire a surer and profounder judgment."
> — Albrecht Dürer
> Dedication to
> *The Art of Measurement,* 1525

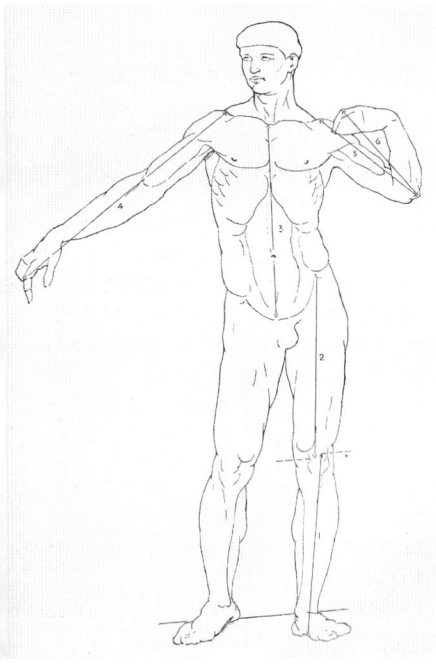

FIG. 2.1.14. Artists used the human head as a module to proportion major elements in the human frame.

the height of the base and capital, the decorative triglyphs and the projection of the cornice. Think of it like a musical chord that ties a melody together. Once you begin working up designs with proportions, a module will intuitively step to the forefront that you will reach for instinctively. Using a module to size other elements in a design is a way to bring a unity. I don't get worked up trying to discover a module in an old design or designating one in a new design. They seem to rise to the surface on their own. Jim offers his own practical advice on the use of proportional modules in Section III. This isn't something forced; it's intuitive and organic.

Connecting with Music

Pythagoras, a 6th-century B.C. Greek scholar renowned for his discoveries in mathematics, is also credited with unlocking the framework that underpins Western tonal music. He accidentally stumbled on a connection between simple whole-number proportions and musical tones. The story goes that while walking by a blacksmith's shop he paused to listen to the sound of two smiths pounding away at their anvils. Each blacksmith produced a unique sound as he struck his anvil. By chance they both struck at the same time and produced a unique third tone or harmony. This got Pythagoras' attention. He quickly realized the anvils were different sizes, and this led him to a series of experiments about the relation between proportions and musical tones. Building a crude stringed instrument, he discovered that two strings of different lengths could produce a harmonic tone when plucked together. These tones corresponded with simple ratios: 1:2/octave, 2:3/fourth and 3:4/fifth. To the ancients, this became yet another confirmation that these simple ratios were a connection with something greater. Thus a handful of simple ratios became the proportions of choice for the

"The proportions of the voices are harmonies for the ears; those of the measurements are harmonies for the eyes. Such harmonies please very much, without anyone knowing why... ."

— Francesco Giorgi

built world. They can be employed to size one part in relation to another, or used to govern simple shapes and bring a harmony between height and width in rectangles or ovals.

Circle Back

At its simplest, there are three ways proportions are used. Think about the ways you might divide a small stick that is the length of your forearm. Separating it into two equal pieces creates symmetry. It leads the eye by using a mirror image or a ratio of 1:1. Break the stick into major and minor parts and you create contrast. Contrast gives life to a design by introducing harmony. It often uses simple whole-number ratios such as 1:2, 2:3 etc. Finally, break off just a small piece from one end of the stick. This creates something called punctuation. It visually emphasizes the beginning or ending of the larger part and often signals a transition to another part.

Let's put some legs to this knowledge about proportion and see how it's possible to infuse a design with life using symmetry, contrast and punctuation.

A DRAWING EXERCISE

Locked Ratios

Go back to the series of visual notes you created in Section I, Chapter 2. Take your dividers and step off the simple ratios for each of those rectangles. Remember that the square is a ratio of 1:1 and the double square is 2:1. You should find the following ratios locked in those rectangles: 1:1, 1:2, 2:3, 3:4, 3:5, 4:5 and 4:7. Note that these rectangles are simple to visualize and also coincide with Pythagoras' harmonic ratios.

FIG. 2.1.15. This knowledge comes to life as we learn to translate it to the work at the point of a tool.

CHAPTER 2

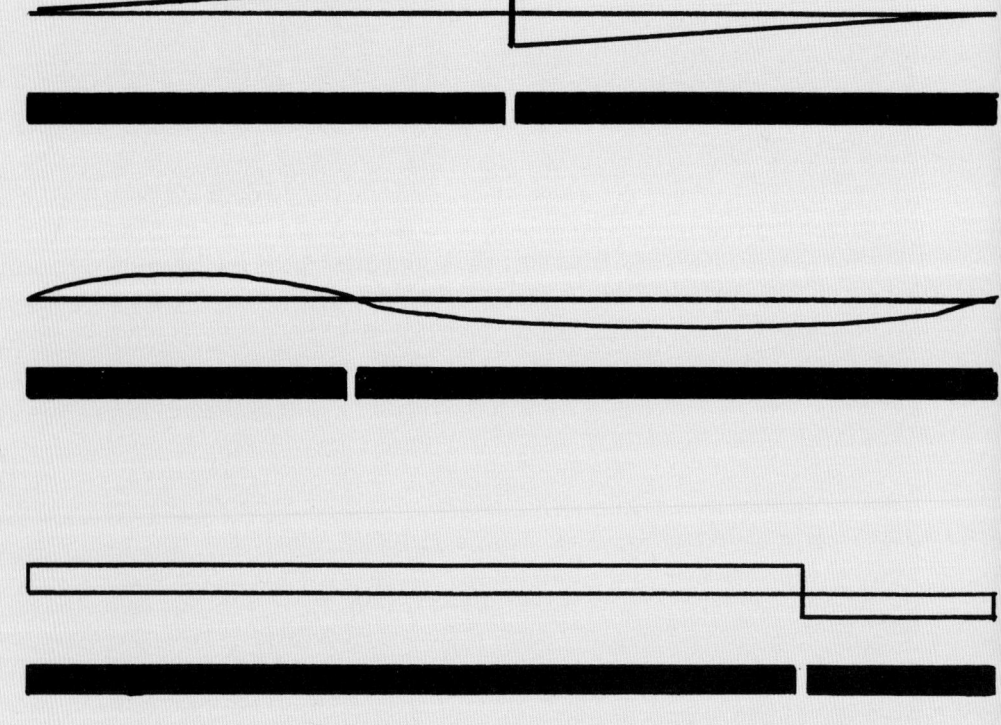

FIG. 2.2.1. In simplest terms, there are three ways proportions are used: symmetry, contrast and punctuation.

Proportions Made Simple

Gaining a solid footing in how proportions work provides a framework to inform your judgment. Furniture design often boils down to making something both really simple and really good. Simple doesn't mean "easy" and good is elusive – like that perfect sunset. That's a razor-thin line to balance on. On either side it's easy to stray off course. Simplify it, pare it back, scrape it down to bedrock and run the risk of a design becoming stark and cold. Try the opposite tack: Inject some life and a sense of motion, force it a wee bit too much, and it takes off like a circus wagon pulled by wild ponies.

Here's the good news. Proportions are at their essence simplicity itself. Although they can be combined in an infinite number of combinations, at their core they do just three things: create symmetry, contrast and punctuation. That's the key to designing something really simple and really good.

My wife and I have a different definition for the word "lost." Her idea of lost is being momentarily unsure of the route to a new store at the shopping mall. She might say to me, "I'm late because I got lost trying to find the new shoe outlet." My concept of lost is wandering for days without food, unable to identify a landmark. I might say to her, "I'm late because we missed the canoe take-out and got swept over a waterfall." According to Barb's definition I've been lost countless times;

> "Even in literature and art, no man who bothers about originality will ever be original: whereas if you simply try to tell the truth (without caring twopence how often it has been told before) you will, nine times out of 10, become original without ever having noticed it."
>
> — C.S. Lewis

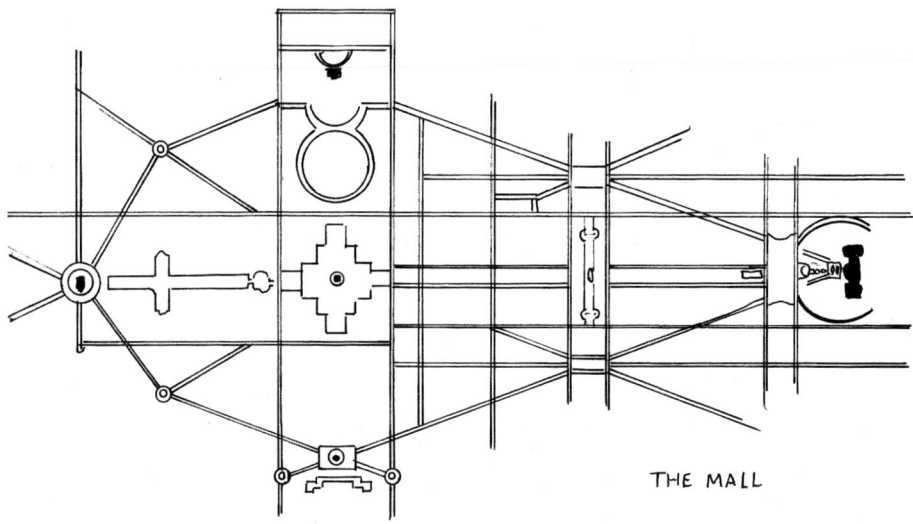

FIG. 2.2.2. The Mall in Washington, D.C., employs symmetry and sight lines with grand results.

she's quick to point out that I can't find the Target store at the mall. Views differ, but everyone agrees that getting lost is not desirable. For our ancestors it was a matter of survival. It meant the difference between safety and real danger. We have powerful built-in reflexes that continually read our environment to seek out clues that signal warmth and safety, and to avoid danger and chaos. Is it any wonder that designers would explore methods to play off these reflexes?

Originality

Before we dive into symmetry in a practical way, we first need to address a common misconception about the issue of "originality." Because this artisan design approach relies on simple geometry and a limited number of whole-number proportions, some see a danger that this can confine and restrict a designer's options. In truth, any design approach has the possibility of being prescriptive. Even modernists can find themselves handcuffed by the need to always invent something new. But as we've discussed earlier, the concepts that underlie this artisan design language are fundamentally meant to inform rather than to constrain. In this chapter, we'll see that symmetry is an especially good example of a design tool that leads to the freedom of innovation. While symmetry is commonly used to create axis lines that lead the eye, it does not always have to be used that way. We have already touched on the idea that the circle is a symmetrical shape with all points on the circumference equally distant from the center. A circle can be used to define the outer edges of a form, or used as a series of smaller building blocks to assemble a larger form. Thus, even an asymmetrical design containing a number of elements based on circles also contains symmetry. In addition, plenty of traditional designs do, in fact, employ the opposite – asymmetry – so perhaps we should be asking not whether to employ it, but rather a more basic question: "Do I understand what I'm after, and is symmetry a good option to achieve it?"

Symmetry & Axis Lines

Symmetry can be employed on a large scale to create axis or sight lines with dramatic results. One of the hallmarks of traditional design is to use axis lines (also referred to as lines of sight) to lead our eye to a destination. On a macro level this can be seen in the layout of cities. The Mall in Washington, D.C., is an iconic, grand-scale example with its view of the reflecting pool leading the eye from the steps of the Lincoln Memorial to the Washington Monument, and then to the Capitol beyond. Interspersed between these primary points are a series of secondary axis lines that carry the eye out to the White House and to other monuments. While a pronounced, primary axis line can stand on its own as a visual path to guide our eye forward, this effect is made stronger by having a symmetrical layout flanking it on both sides. Conversely, when we see an element such as a door or drawer on one side, we immediately look for a corresponding element on the other.

Symmetry & Mirror Image

Symmetry is a tool we use to create a mirror image, or a simple ratio of 1:1. While an axis line can be a physical feature to lead the eye to a destination, we can also use symmetry to create an axis visually by positioning mirror images on either side (left and right). Even though

FIG. 2.2.3. Even though there is no physical axis line, the symmetrical layout of drawers creates the effect of one, pulling our eye to the carvings.

FIG. 2.2.4. Bilateral symmetry shows up in countless forms in the plant and animal kingdom.

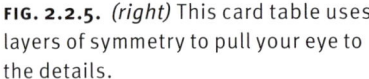

FIG. 2.2.5. *(right)* This card table uses layers of symmetry to pull your eye to the details.

there may not be any physical line such as an aisle way, our brain creates a sight line running between the opposing twin elements. Note that this works only on bilateral mirror images: east vs. west or left vs. right. We might recognize the division between two images north and south, but they do not create a sight line that carries the eye forward.

Symmetry shows up abundantly in nature. It's most prevalent in the animal kingdom where it seems odd to find the rare example such as a halibut with both eyes on one side of its head. Botanists have concluded that flowers use symmetry to attract insects, much like a landing pad for a helicopter, leading a honeybee straight to the source of pollen. In furniture it could be a panel of burled maple or a carving. This use of symmetry can cascade down in scale even to small details such as hardware. Period brasses were often symmetrical, pulling the eye to a tiny detail.

Introduction to Contrast

One of my favorite places is Brumbaugh Woods, a few acres of old-growth hardwood forest. The short hike to it gradually builds with anticipation. The first

FIG. 2.2.6. Symmetry works no matter what the scale, from the layout of a city to this escutcheon.

half-mile cuts through a woodlot, clear-cut 30 years ago and left to re-grow. Maples and hickories provide a monotonous view of middling-sized trees, choked by dense underbrush and poison ivy. Then the trail spills into a power line slash cut and finally descends into another world, the old timber. Wow…It's open and airy as though entering a great concert hall, yet with a deep stillness my wife describes as the "holy of holies." Giant columns of black oak and American beech support a towering ceiling 80' above the forest floor. In spring, it's carpeted with millions of flowers – bloodroot, trout lilies and spring beauties, while high above a pair of wood ducks search for tree cavities in which to make a nest. A beam of sunlight trickles down and then vanishes. Though the eye is first struck by the old giants, this isn't just a collection of old trees; this is much more. Spaced apart in a secret rhythm, trees of every size play a part, making it a living forest. In spite of the fact that it's a public space, the local kids haven't yet gouged their names in the smooth bark of the beech trees.

FIG. 2.2.7. Trees of every size offer constant visual delight during a stroll in Brumbaugh Woods.

We know all about monotony; we're surrounded by it. We build efficient and monotonous warehouses to store cars, people and books, organizing our world into skin-deep and visually dead grids that lack contrast and lend the eye no foothold or reference point. One way we, as designers, can break up this ubiquitous monotony is to use contrast. This design strategy invites the eye to explore, to take a closer look, and, it is hoped, to achieve some measure of visual harmony.

Harmony in the musical sense is the combining of two different voices that together create a third voice. In music it involves two notes far enough apart that they are clearly distinct, yet close enough so that the frequencies combine to create a harmonic tone. We touched earlier how Pythagoras discovered that harmonic tones had a connection with simple whole-number ratios, 1:2 being an octave, 3:4 a fifth and so on. This grew into a tradition in the classical world that music and geometry were one and the same. Thus music is geometry expressed as sound, and those same proportions creating audible harmony in music lead to visual harmony in built objects.

Up through the 18th century, this musical connection was thought to confirm something artisans had been using for centuries long before Pythagoras. Certain combinations of simple ratios lend a pleasing effect to a spatial composition. Indeed, we do seem to inherently connect with compositions arranged in a hierarchy where major and minor elements complement rather than compete.

FIG. 2.2.8. Major and minor paired together makes for a more interesting composition.

Don't be misled by the terms hierarchy or major vs. minor, as though its a competition of one part lording over another. Just the opposite is true: When major and minor combine they create something unique, each part bringing out the best in the other.

Nature is filled with examples of major and minor paired in complementary roles, and we know that humans have taken note of this for millennia. Describing the sun and the moon, the author of Genesis wrote, "A greater light to rule the day, and a lesser light to rule the night."

Using Contrast to Define a Form

Contrast is often used by designers to define an overall form. We learned earlier that a form is a combination of simple shapes. Often the design is governed by a circle or square, which embodies symmetry, or we can introduce contrast by expanding the square into a simple rectangle. How does employing a rectangle bring the possibility of harmony to a form? It's simple: Because the sides are unequal, it follows that the height is in contrast with the width.

One of the earliest detailed descriptions for a piece of furniture is of the Ark of the Covenant, a wooden chest that existed in a Hebrew tabernacle of 1,300 B.C. The front view of the chest is described as being $1\frac{1}{2}$ cubits high by $2\frac{1}{2}$ cubits wide. We can simplify this ratio to 3:5 – and because the ancient cubit was approximately 18", we know that the chest measured 27" high by 45" wide. ("And Bezalel made the ark of acacia wood: two cubits and a half was the length of it, and a cubit and a half the breadth of it, and a cubit and a half the height of it" Exodus 37:1.)

A DRAWING EXERCISE

Minor & Major

Go back to those simple visual notes you drew from a square in Section I, Chapter 2 (the sequence of rectangles from a square to a double square). Use your dividers and determine how the minor side is proportioned to the major. Hint: The minor side on the double square is half of the major, or 1:2. Each of these simple rectangles has a ratio that corresponds with Pythagoras' harmonic tones. The major and minor sides are linked in a harmonic ratio.

So you see, these are more than just simple combinations of circles that are easy to visualize. They are also shaped by simple whole-number ratios: 1:2, 3:5 etc.

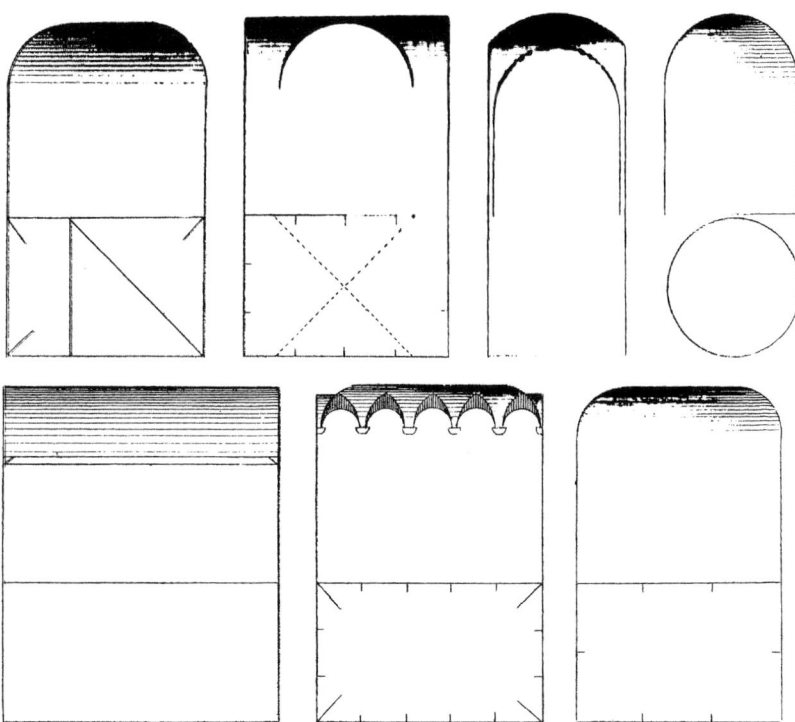

FIG. 2.2.9. Palladio illustrated footprints for rooms and the vaulted ceilings above. Note that he shows a square, a circle and then some simple ratios: 3:4, 1:2, 3:5, 2:3.

From the dawn of the written record, forms using just a small handful of simple rectangles defined the shape of furniture. Most likely the artisans learned this design strategy from the long oral tradition of their trade, but historical design books also give some clues to how they put it into practice. Oft repeated are room layouts that show an ideal footprint for a room. They don't list dimensions but instead proportions – 1:1, 1:2, 2:3, 3:4, 3:5, 4:7, 4:5…. Do these sound familiar? Builders employed these simple rectangles to size rooms that were thought most inviting.

To establish a form we begin by thinking about the primary way the piece will be viewed. For case pieces, our focus begins on the shape that defines the façade; for tables and other pieces viewed mostly from above, we begin with the shape that defines the top. In both cases the starting point is often one of the simple rectangles from our visual scale. At a later point we may choose to adjust it or add curvature, but for now this gives us a starting point to build upon.

Once the major shape is established we can begin dividing up the internal spaces in the design much like an architect might define room spaces in a building. Artisan-age designers placed emphasis on how a room interior might feel, so they focused on proportioning the room space bounded by the interior walls, not the outside of the exterior walls. Similarly, in the furniture of this era, we often see spaces sized to simple whole-number ratios that fall just inside the legs or to the inside of cases – but for a different reason. All the important joinery coincides with the inside of the case or marries into the insides of the legs. All drawers and doors are made to fit to the inside of case openings. It's natural, then, that if the artisan was using dividers to lay out proportions and joinery details, the two would be built around the same reference points. Quickly dividing up proportional sequences is simplified if you don't have to account for the thickness of the case components. All the artisan needs to do is simply divide up the void.

FIG. 2.2.10. Any element in a room that's part of the interior composition often employed simple rectangles. Here a fireplace opening is five parts high by six parts wide.

The Magic of Three

The Greeks thought that the number three was the first real number because it contains a beginning, middle and end. Much of the foregoing discussion has been about pairing major and minor to create harmony. Whenever three spaces or elements are set close together, they all tend to vie for our attention at the same time – sort of like a room full of 8-year-olds all squealing, "Pick me! Pick me!" A solution using contrast is to set up a hierarchy in which you make one part of the three the major element. Often it's as simple as using a sequence like 2:3:2 or 3:5:3. Just think of the same simple ratios except now with three elements. This tack combines symmetry with contrast and is often used on the horizontal arrangements of small drawers.

The idea of using contrast to complement is not confined to proportions. Carving can have a more profound impact if contrasted with a smooth surface. We can contrast textures, colors and straight lines versus

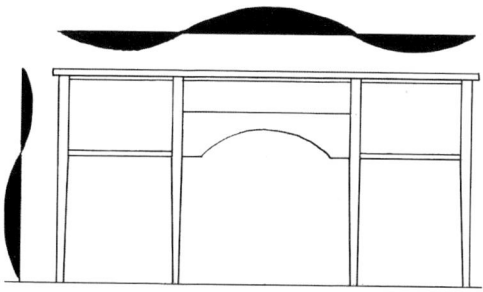

FIG. 2.2.11. This overall form is governed by a large 2:1 rectangle. The smaller rectangles that make up the interior spaces are all bounded by drawer openings or the space between legs.

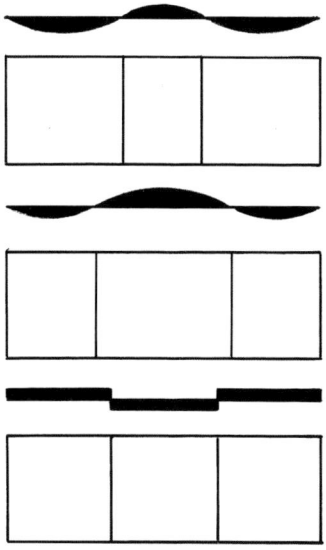

FIG. 2.2.12. Which layout does your eye find more interesting?

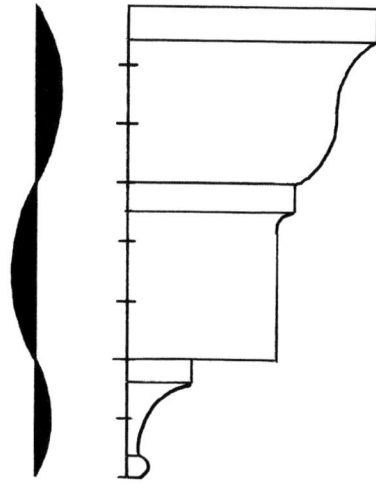

FIG. 2.2.13. Even though the two upper sections are the same height, they appear to contrast because they employ such different shapes.

FIG. 2.2.14. Note that in this piece, the designer made the center section just slightly wider than the side bays. The fact that the outer bays are horizontal drawers while the middle bay uses vertical doors, also adds to a sense of contrast.

curves. Often the proportional contrast lies hidden beneath these more obvious visual elements.

We have explored proportions that mirror (symmetry) and contrast. Now let's take a closer look at using proportions to create borders and transitions.

Introduction to Punctuation

I wince at the sound of an electronic voice on the telephone that apologizes and without waiting for my response, puts me on hold. Early electronic versions of artificial voices on answering machines were even worse. The robot voice, a talking bullfrog speaking through a whirling fan blade made such a hash of simple numbers: "ZEERoh…SEVen…." Beyond just butchering each word, it also strung phone numbers together like a child learning to read out loud. My mind locks up when a soulless machine grunts out a monotone phone number: "NINe…NINe…SEVen…SIXX…FOUR…FOUR…ZEERoh…." We've yet to teach a robot to say, "Nine, ninety-seven, sixty-four, forty." In genuine speech, words flow together naturally with pauses and bridges, like a series of stepping stones across a stream.

Punctuation is employed to create pauses and transitions to organize a design into something our eye can take in and comprehend. It's used on the macro level to establish a beginning, middle and ending of the overall form, and can be woven into the smaller details within a form to visually string elements together.

Use Punctuation to Organize a Form

Punctuation can be used to organize a design by creating a distinct beginning, middle and end. This is one of the defining features of traditional design. So much so that it's woven into the way we tell a story, sing a song or design a building. Our own bodies illustrate this tripartite arrangement with feet, torso and head. Because the human form lies at the very core of this traditional approach,

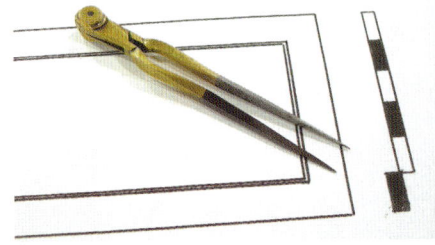

FIG. 2.2.15. Punctuating a form creates a distinct beginning, middle and end.

designs are primarily organized vertically, with the beginning at the bottom and ending at the top. Without thinking, when we take in a design we note how it's anchored to the floor and how it terminates at its highest point. In nature we find abundant examples of organic transitions. Trees don't just jut up from the earth like a utility pole planted by the phone company. Though largely hidden from sight, the roots flow into the tree trunk just above the soil, bulging out in response to

FIG. 2.2.16. This small inlay plays an important visual role. It tells the eye that one part is ending and something different is about to occur.

the mass above. Pre-industrial artisans wove this theme into their designs, sometimes boldly creating a beginning with a ball-and-claw foot. Or they took a subtle tack and established a beginning with a small bead, inlay or slight change of taper. Brash or subdued, they help the design tell a story.

Also note that most of our traditional moulding profiles have a correlation with the transitions or borders we encounter in nature. The series of torus mouldings swelling at the bottom of a column shadow the swelling of a tree trunk at the roots. The gentle arch of a cove moulding mimics the transitions found in tree branches as they spread to form the canopy.

The classic orders are a textbook of this beginning, middle and ending, with punctuation woven into the form from the major parts down to minor details. From a proportional standpoint they offer several practical examples of how to achieve punctuation, a reminder that it's about the principle and not about any specific proportions. Probably one of the most profound lessons they offer is the way they help us see the internal relationship between the larger element and smaller. Punctuation is achieved by dividing up a space into five or more equal parts

FIG. 2.2.17. Traditional moulding profiles often took their cue from nature.

and having the part at one end act as the beginning or ending. The physical act of stepping off the space with dividers helps us see more clearly the proportional dynamic. When I first began making design judgments, I often had a hunch something wasn't working. I might sense the feet on a chest were too large. But it wasn't obvious to my eye that I was uncomfortable with the relationship between the height of the feet and height of the case above it. Walking through the different examples of punctuation in the classic orders drove the lesson home. Now, without thinking, I size up border elements with the spaces they punctuate. Often a border might be too narrow and look weak or, conversely, be too wide and look clumsy because the border element competes rather than complements. As you make the connection between the space and its punctuating border, it becomes easier to see how parts relate.

The classic orders are filled with examples of punctuation woven into the overall form as well as the smaller details. The overall form on all the orders are organized vertically by dividing the entire height into five equal parts and making the bottom part the beginning. The bottom part, or pedestal, punctuates the space above it. On a Doric order, divide the remaining height above the pedestal by five again to establish the ending at the top. This top space is called the entablature and punctuates the space below it. The Ionic and Corinthian orders use a slightly different punctuation sequence, dividing the upper portion by six parts to create a more slender feel.

FIG. 2.2.18. Two simple punctuations at top and bottom create the major parts of this order. The bottom (beginning) portion is called the pedestal, which supports the column (middle), which in turn ends with the entablature.

FIG. 2.2.19. Does your eye sense anything amiss with the relation between the top and the structure below? Knowing the top punctuates the space below it helps to visualize where this feeling arises.

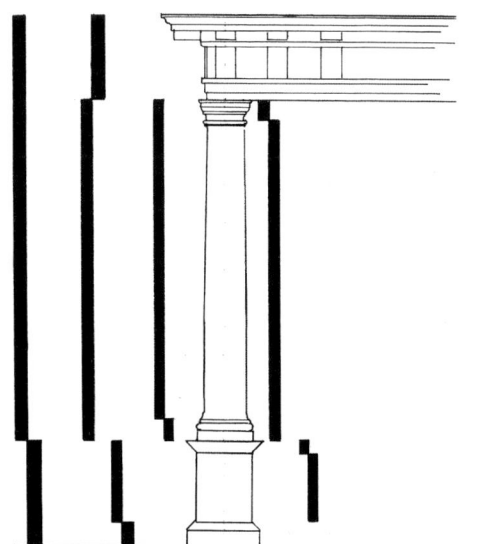

FIG. 2.2.20. This idea of punctuation repeats itself. Note that the proportions vary (they are not all one-fifth) but still convey the idea of beginning, middle and end, echoing throughout the entire order.

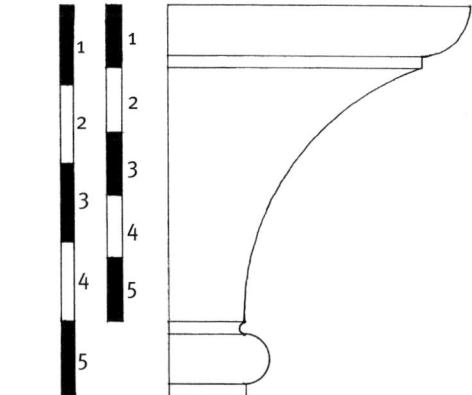

FIG. 2.2.21. A moulding or inlay detail can incorporate punctuation, in effect weaving this idea of beginning, middle and end down to smallest details.

There's ample evidence from historic design books that artisans became familiar with a small handful of proportional sequences and the visual effect they lent to a composition. I like to think of them as an array of spices. It's more important to begin by getting a sense for the flavor they impart, rather than for the actual proportions themselves. You can begin to gain a working vocabulary of these proportional relationships by drawing Doric classic orders in the exercise in Section II, Chapter 4.

Punctuation to Establish a Border

Punctuation acts like a visual warning track in a baseball outfield. As the outfielder races to catch a fly ball, the warning track signals that the field is about to end and the home-run fence is fast approaching. Punctuation tells the eye that one part is ending and another is beginning. Our eye doesn't like to suddenly hit a wall or slip over a cliff. That's why printers format a text with margins to make words easier to read. Borders help us locate transitions and play an important role. A door frame is a good example. It plays no functional role yet plays a vital visual role of highlighting the opening. Note that on a tall vertical space such as a window or door frame, we don't use the height to establish our punctuation. That could result in a heavy band if wrapped all the way around. Tall vertical shapes (doors) are punctuated across the width (east and west), while long horizontal shapes (drawer fronts) are

The Human Form Hidden in Plain Sight

Critics point out that modern builders and architects can fall into a malady called the Greek Temple disease: slapping together classical elements from antiquity to somehow capture a sense of power and integrity. Of course, they do so without a clue about where these qualities came from, and how they came to be imbued in buildings from antiquity. It's an easy conclusion to make if we focus on the surface without considering there might be something deeper. It's true that many of our revered civic buildings often were modeled after temples from antiquity. Historical design literature emphasized the perfection found in the Greek and Roman classic orders.

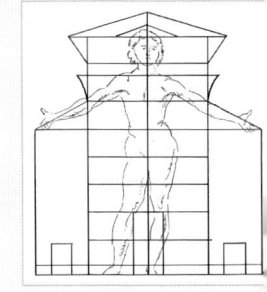

FIG. 2.2.22. The human form resides just beneath the surface.

Yet the tradition reveals something deeper than a fascination with carved stone columns. To the Greeks, the classic order was the embodiment of the human form, but also of the building itself. Sweep them away and the roof collapses. The Romans extended the idea that the orders embodied the human form, yet applied new materials: concrete and brick. The result was that walls could support a building without requiring the orders for structural integrity. Yet they still used the classic orders to organize the façade, even though columns often had little or no structural role. They began to shadow the orders using shallow representations, sinking pilasters and half-columns into a wall to suggest the order. Later, designers completely eliminated columns or pilasters but continued to weave the proportional sequences to organize a façade. An exterior or interior wall could be divided into beginning, middle and ending using mouldings and paneling to echo an invisible classic order. Not just walls, but just as the order has internal elements that repeat the beginning, middle and ending, other elements in an interior – windows, fireplaces, furniture, candle stands, lamps – all could shadow the classic orders. Because the orders embody the human form, designers were in essence filling their homes with a host of human figures large and small.

FIG. 2.2.23. Because classic orders are anthropomorphized forms, it was even thought that an interior with multiple layers of objects based on the orders was filled with human forms.

punctuated along the height (north and south).

This brings up another practical issue. A series of drawers, doors or spaces in the same composition with multiple sizes would call for different-sized banding or border elements for each space. Yet that's seldom the case in built work. Select one door or drawer front from the mid-range and use it for all. It's more important for all the composition to display a unity through similar borders. Graduated drawers that get larger toward the bottom of a case are a good example. If you choose to incorporate a punctuation with banding or inlay, work up a border for several of the smaller drawers and trust your eye to select which border will complement all.

Tweaking a Design Using Punctuating Ratios

It used to frustrate me to hear someone with a creative bent opine about making the smallest tweak to hit some mythical sweet spot. Somehow they seemed to magically know that adding ¼" to the width of a door frame would spell Nirvana. I might agree that the door frame did seem to look better, but it all seemed like magical guesswork or voodoo. Part of clearing through the fog is to gain some understanding of how elements harmonize or punctuate. Using these principles, we can unpack examples to help develop that inner sense. Secondly, we need a practical approach to make small

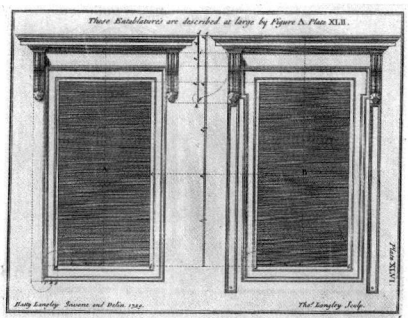

FIG. 2.2.24. Palladio suggested a rule of thumb for establishing the casing around a window opening. Divide the space into five or six equal parts, and use one-fifth or one-sixth as the casing.

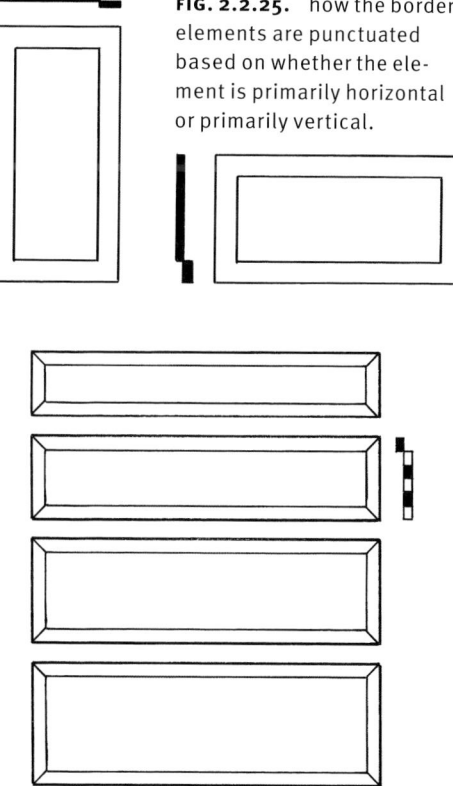

FIG. 2.2.25. how the border elements are punctuated based on whether the element is primarily horizontal or primarily vertical.

FIG. 2.2.26. We selected the border for one of the smaller drawers to punctuate all. That border ties all the others together in a unity.

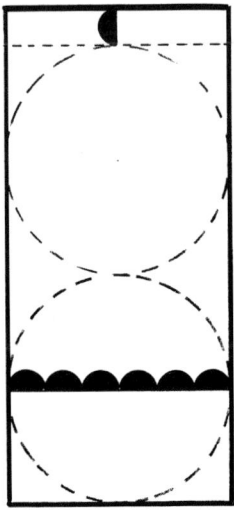

FIG. 2.2.27. Adding 1/6 to the height or width of a door opening is a way to tweak it to your eye. This double square was tweaked taller by adding 1/6 the width to the height. Period guide books described this as "two squares and a sixth."

adjustments to an element or shape. We already established that a small series of simple ratios (1:2, 3:5, etc.) can cover a range of simple shapes to define a form. Classical designers often used punctuating ratios to make a small tweak. These are large enough to make a visual difference without looking forced. The top diameter of a column shaft is one-sixth smaller than the shaft diameter at the base. If we want to bump a square just a bit wider without making too dramatic a shift, we bump it just a little wider by one-sixth. A long 2:1 rectangle can be tweaked just a bit longer using a sixth of the width.

Conclusion

All this time we have been building this design language using simple proportions and intuitive geometry. Until now, we've stuck to rectilinear shapes with plane surfaces, all rooted in nature and the ideal human form. Yet nature and the human figure abound with curvature. It's no surprise, then, that the craft tradition celebrated curved surfaces – often to extremes. In the next section we'll turn off the efficient interstate of straight lines and onto a scenic byway filled with curves. We'll learn how to visualize them, unpack them and combine curves into lively and honest compositions.

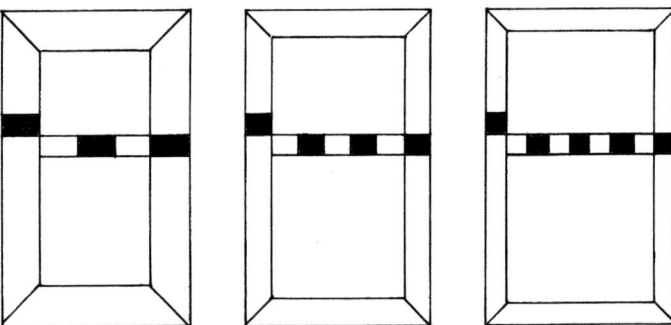

FIG. 2.2.28. This principle applies to tweaking border elements. If 1:5 seems too bold, try 1:6, 1:7 or 1:8. We are always concerned that the border element has a relationship with element it's linked with.

Designing with Ornament

Traditionally, ornament and mouldings were employed to punctuate and emphasize a form. Even though they've been overdone, it doesn't mean they don't have a valid place. Our woodworking design tradition has seen wide swings in taste concerning ornament, embellishment and mouldings. Some periods drip with overcooked gingerbread, some scrape clean down to the bone. A few contemporary designers even abhor figured wood, and some modernist designers dictated that ornament should be allowed only if it looked machine made – no hints of man's hand. It's difficult today, with the pendulum swung away from traditional ornament, to see how it was originally viewed, especially when bursts of excess litter our furniture history. It might be helpful to understand the original craft intent and not simply write off traditional ornament and mouldings as a relic of another era. Ornament must complete a design – similar to the effect of leaves on a tree or feathers on a bird. It's not an add-on, it's not a strategy to rescue an inferior design. Abraham Swan (circa 1757) wrote, "If the original design be bad, superadded ornaments will make the whole appear like a clown in a laced waistcoat."

The bones underneath must be good or ornament will only make the whole design worse. That's the reason so much mass-produced 20th-century Colonial-style furniture fails so pointedly.

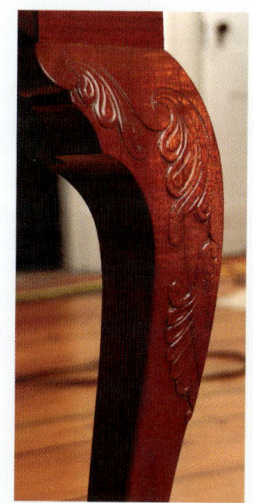

FIG. 2.2.29. The subtle carving on this table leg accomplishes several things at once. It highlights the form, provides interest for a close view and emphasizes this object's place of importance in the life of a home.

Ornament and mouldings must have a function. While we think today of function as primarily a structural element (a way to meet a physical requirement), the craft idea of function was much broader, because the definition of function included visual appearance. Mouldings or other ornaments were used to emphasize a form, create a visual border, transition one part to the next or to create layers of interest on different scales (such as a close view). Another function of ornament is to set something apart. As reflected in Swan's quotation above, this human need to embellish what we value is the reason that even our ancestors of modest means felt compelled to use ornament to decorate a powder horn, dowry chest or quilt. The question to ask is not whether the ornament or moulding adds to the design, but whether the design lacks something without it.

> "[Architectural ornamentation] liberates us from the tyranny of the useful and satisfies our need for harmony."
> — Roger Scruton

CHAPTER 3

FIG. 2.3.1. Nature creates curves out of once-rectilinear granite blocks.

Incorporating Curves

In Maine's Acadia National Park, there's a spot called Monument Cove. Huge blocks of pink granite tumble down a sheer cliff into the pounding surf below. Massive stones that just recently broke free (in the last 1,000 years) echo their crystalline structure, forming stone obelisks and rectilinear blocks the size of a locomotive. Up at the farthest reaches of high tide, the ever-pressing forces of nature slowly grind the square blocks into cloud-like shapes, while down in the heart of the relentless surf, those rough granite clouds are transformed further into shiny smooth cobblestones. It hardly seems possible that these gentle curved shapes were once the rectangular blocks just a few yards beyond the crashing waves. When the surf is especially rough, you can just make out the clanking ring of stone tumbling against stone, nature making one thing from another (not unlike the artisan at the bench) – gentle curves from jagged stone.

It seems obvious that a design language rooted in the natural world would celebrate curves. On the simplest level, organic growth abounds with curvature. Nature uses gentle curves where a branch joins a tree trunk, and it's this organic transition that inspired artisans to create mouldings to join one furniture part to another. This differs from a machine-made object such as a power-line pole, where the cross braces jut out abruptly. The efficient cross brace might function perfectly, but the visual effect is the immediate recognition that it's the product of industry. Curved transitions

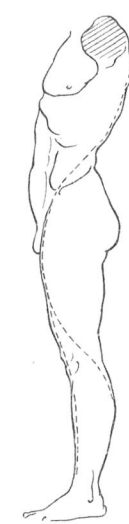

FIG. 2.3.2. The human form may lie at the root of our fascination with curvature.

play several roles. Yes, they have a load-bearing capacity, but they also play a visual role. Curves lend an object believability. The artisan substitutes the cutting action of a spokeshave or moulding plane for the forces of nature, but the visual results share a connection.

Light & Shadow

A flat surface reflects light in a single, monotone pattern. It's always a function of our eye in relation to the light source, but the reflection from a flat plane is one-dimensional, static and can appear cold. Curved surfaces respond to light in a dynamic pattern: the reflection appears three-dimensional, fluid and warm. A convex surface reflects light outward with an area of maximum reflection at the apex, gradually fading into shadow on either side. Concave surfaces deflect light inward, resulting in zones of shadow that gradually fade back into areas of light. Depending on the relation of our eye to the light source, these areas of maximum light and shadow shift as we move about a room. We often think of reflection as something shiny, chrome-plated – but it can be subtle differences such as shimmering green reflecting off the contours of a patch of moss. Variable reflectivity imparts depth and evokes a sense that the form is alive.

FIG. 2.3.3. We tend to think of light and shadow as a function of how shiny or reflective an object is. Actually, it depends more on the dynamics of curvature.

Tactile

Curved surfaces also have a tactile quality. We respond not just to visual cues but also to messages from our hands and bodies. Imagine a hammer with a handle that's triangular in cross section. In fact you don't have to stretch the imagination that far. The bane of most mass-produced hand tools is misshapen handles that grate and chafe our hands. Even if the shape is OK, our hands are such sensitive receptors that we tend to balk at the feel of plastic or metal grips. We not only prefer handles that conform to our hands, but the best totes and

FIG. 2.3.4. This doesn't mean plain surfaces don't employ light and shadow, but it does belie the fact that reflected light is far more appealing if it's contrasted against shadow. That's all a dentil moulding is – a facia broken up to introduce shadow and texture.

handles have some sophisticated curvature that marries with our human form. We prefer chairs that reflect and conform to the curvature of our bodies. A ladder-back chair is an example of a functional yet uncomfortable chair. Adding a few slight curves makes a dramatic transformation. The form becomes friendly and warm, not just to the body, but to the eye. Almost anything on a piece of furniture that we touch with our hands is enlivened by the addition of curvature.

Visualizing Curves

Design is more about seeing than about designing. At first blush, curvature seems difficult to imagine with clarity. Curved lines are fluid and don't have the same distinct anchor points as rectangular forms. They often lack clear borders between one curve and another. While straight lines intersect abruptly, curves flow into other curves and straight lines seamlessly. Curves can be regular, based on a circle. Curves can be irregular, based on a parabola. Curves can be fast, slow, concave, convex or combined in ways that include all of the above. A seemingly infinite range of possibilities can make turning off the straight line interstate highway a scary proposition. I know many woodworkers who stay clear of projects involving

> "I sometimes wonder if the hand is not more sensitive to the beauties of sculpture than the eye. I should think the wonderful rhythmical flow of lines and curves could be more subtly felt than seen. Be this as it may, I know that I can feel the heart-throbs of the ancient Greeks in their marble gods and goddesses."
>
> — Helen Keller

FIG. 2.3.5. Curves also invite us to reach out and touch.

FIG. 2.3.6. Chairs, more than any other piece of furniture, are pieces we connect with. How many times have you heard someone refer to "my favorite chair?" Often a part of that connection is some tactile curve that embraces our touch.

curved work. At one time I thought it was the limitations based on the machine setup in the average woodshop. That's a factor, but I now believe that what looms larger is our inability to visualize curvature.

Curvature is one area of artisan-age design where modern woodworkers are onlookers – mere knuckle-dragging Neanderthals compared with our forebears who spoke and sang the language of curvature at a level we can barely fathom.

Curves in the Craft Tradition

We might associate straight lines with modern designs, but pre-industrial artisans swung between the straight and curved. Furniture from the Queen Anne period (circa 1730-1760) avoided any trace of straight lines. Not surprisingly, American Federal-style furniture was a reaction to the flamboyant curves of Chippendale and Queen Anne. Clean, straight lines replaced the cabriole legs with ball-and-claw feet. Yet those Federal pieces created something profound by contrasting straight geometric shapes with gentle curves. Subtle serpentine curves worked into the fronts of sideboards and tables, and garlands of inlaid vines and ribbons, hinted at life and warmth.

FIG. 2.3.7. Period chairs are a study in curvature.

FIG. 2.3.8. Federal work shifted away from the bold sculptural carving of earlier work, yet still relied on gentle curves to impart life to the designs.

INCORPORATING CURVES

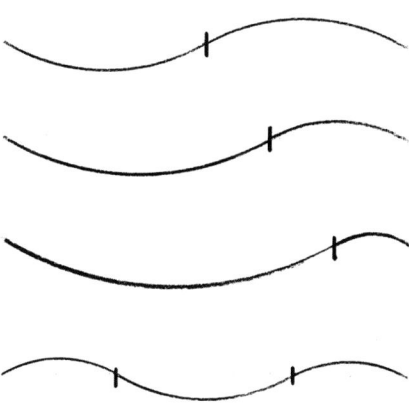

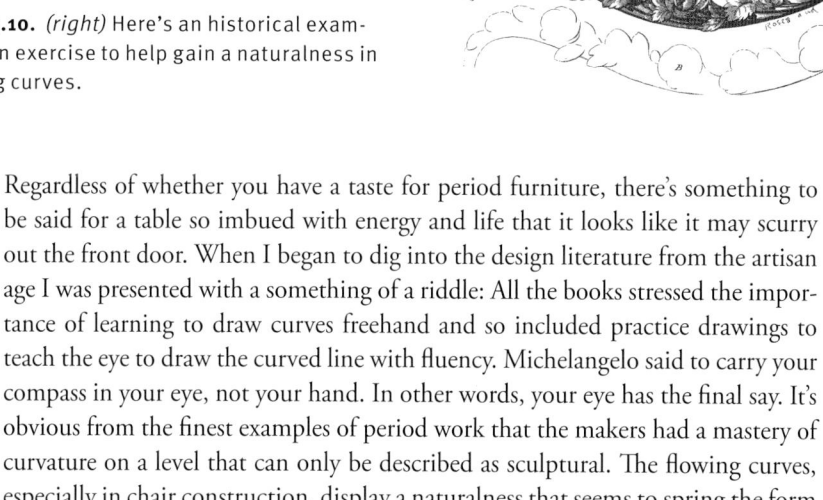

FIG. 2.3.9. Symmetry, contrast and punctuation can be applied to curves.

FIG. 2.3.10. *(right)* Here's an historical example of an exercise to help gain a naturalness in drawing curves.

Regardless of whether you have a taste for period furniture, there's something to be said for a table so imbued with energy and life that it looks like it may scurry out the front door. When I began to dig into the design literature from the artisan age I was presented with a something of a riddle: All the books stressed the importance of learning to draw curves freehand and so included practice drawings to teach the eye to draw the curved line with fluency. Michelangelo said to carry your compass in your eye, not your hand. In other words, your eye has the final say. It's obvious from the finest examples of period work that the makers had a mastery of curvature on a level that can only be described as sculptural. The flowing curves, especially in chair construction, display a naturalness that seems to spring the form into motion; it's a celebration of curves far beyond that which could be created through arcs generated with a compass.

Yet a closer look at the engravings in those old design books reveal some simple methods to visualize a curve and build that connection between hand and eye. Actually, two categories of curved elements show up. Yes, there are plenty of those complex and subtle freehand curves that look beyond the reach of mere mortals, but there is also a second category of curves that are plainly the work of simple geometry and compass arcs. Here, then, lies the key to this mastery of curvature and where this gets really exciting: From the small details of a moulding profile to the sweeping curve on a bow-front dresser, the artisans generated curved layout lines by striking simple arcs or sections of circles with a compass. And in doing so, they employed just a small handful of simple curved sections that help the eye to clearly visualize boundaries and transitions. These simple compass curves are a gateway to allow your mind and hands to explore curvature in an entirely new light.

The ability to deconstruct a curved line with a compass equips and allows the inner eye to step through the veil and begin drawing (and imagining) free-flowing

FIG. 2.3.11. Simple sections of circles are embedded in the traditional tool set. Hollow and round planes all cut a 1/6 arc of a circle.

curves with a genuineness. It hinges on something so simple that I tripped over it a dozen times before seeing it. They utilized an imaginary chord to govern the curved line. The chord allows you to clearly imagine the starting and ending points of a curve or a series of curves. A chord makes it simple to manipulate curves slower or faster, or to divide them into simple proportional sequences. I'm not saying you can lay out a lively cabriole leg with simple arcs from a compass, but after drawing those simple arcs with a compass your eye crosses a bridge into a world you never before saw. It frees the hand and eye to express with greater confidence and execution at the bench. Don't underestimate your own ability to absorb the lessons these simple compass layouts have to impart. Oh – and we can't forget this also: Not every design project requires a complex sculptural curve. Often you simply want a pleasant curve that hits the sweet spot. Our simple compass arcs provide a tool to quickly lay out simple curves with confidence.

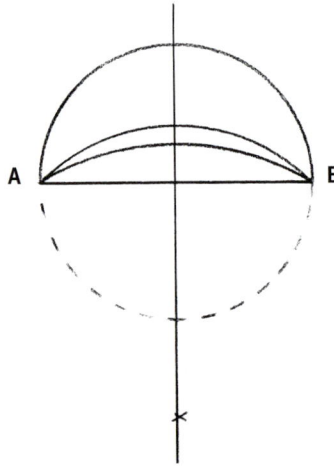

FIG. 2.3.12. This simple drawing is a key that contains three curves that unlock the artisan-age approach to curvature.

INCORPORATING CURVES

A DRAWING EXERCISE

Curved Notes on the Visual Scale

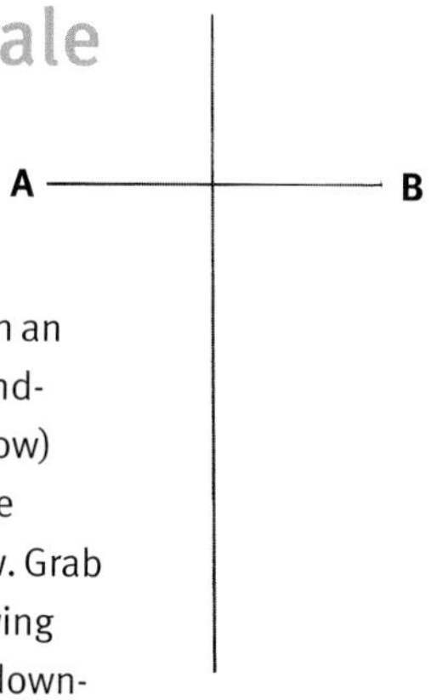

Let's take a step back to the handful of rectangles that make up our visual scale (Section I, Chapter 2). Recall that a small series of rectangles act like visual building blocks to govern a form. In the same way, you might not be able to envision an infinite number of curves, but it is possible to imprint a small handful of curved notes in your mind's eye. Drawing 2.3.12 (at left below) illustrates three curved sections that are all drawn using a simple chord to govern the curve and represent a range from fast to slow. Grab your compass and let's walk through this and unpack it in a drawing exercise. Locate the midpoint on A,B and draw a perpendicular downward nearly to the bottom of a piece of paper. Place one leg of your compass at that midpoint and set your pencil to A then scribe a solid arc to B. Continue the arc below the chord but make that arc a dashed line. It should be self-evident that you have drawn a half-circle using one-half the chord as a radius. This is the fastest regular curved section you can generate between chord AB. Next, set your compass point where the perpendicular crosses the dashed-line semi-circle you drew beneath the chord. Set your pencil to A and scribe a second arc to B. This slower arc just happens to be a perfect quarter-section of a circle. Now set your compass point on A and set your pencil to B. Swing down and place a mark where it intersects the perpendicular. Switch the point over to B and swing down and make a mark on the perpendicular from the other side. Use this intersection to set your compass point and scribe a third arc from A to B. This gentle arc is a perfect one-sixth of a circle. Note that these three curves are like notes that span a range from fast to slow. This section of a circle is most intriguing because of the tool set built around it. Traditional hollows and rounds are always based on one-sixth of a circle. The smallest hollow is based on a chord that's 1/8" across. Cyma curves incorporated into moulding designs are made up of sections of circles based on one-sixth. Don McConnell, from Old Street Tool (makers of traditional moulding planes), shares that a section of circle much greater than one-sixth becomes problematic from the standpoint of cutting geometry. Yet aside from those practical considerations, our moulding profiles trace back to ancient archetypes based on one-sixth of a circle. Did the designs give birth to the tools or was it the other way around?

At the most basic level, these three simple curved sections are ubiquitous in traditional furniture designs and architecture. You might even conclude that they are the beginnings of a visual scale of curves.

FIG. 2.3.13. AB is our chord to generate three curved notes.

Making Adjustments with Chords

One of the exciting aspects about using this method to visualize and generate layouts is that by using the chord as an increment you can creep up on a curve that looks right to your eye. If one-sixth of a circle is still too fast for your eye, you can adjust the radius of your curve based on simple increments of the chord to gradually creep up to the sweet spot your eye is searching for. Jim shares some practical methods for making these layouts and adjustments to curves in Section III.

What floored me when I stumbled onto this is that a huge amount of curved layout in hundreds of historic furniture designs used just three sections of circles: one-half, one-fourth and one-sixth. How could three curved sections account for the amazing legacy we see in artisan-age design? Back to our music analogy, it's just a small number of notes that offer infinite creative potential.

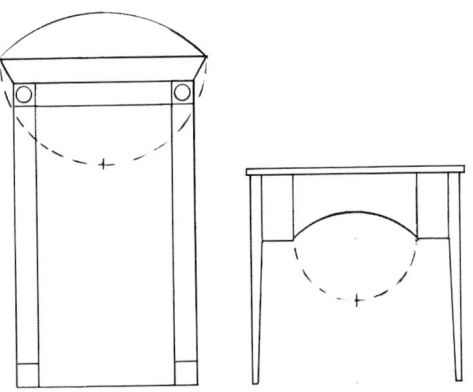

FIG. 2.3.14. The same simple quarter-section of a circle that generates the curved pediment on a doorway shows up often in traditional furniture forms.

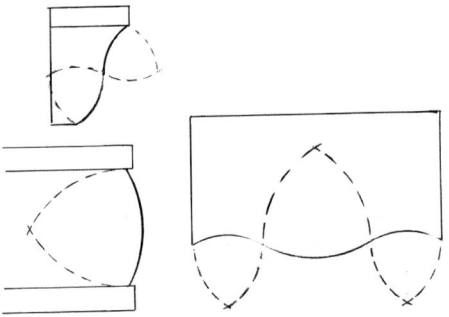

FIG. 2.3.15. One-sixth of a circle weaves its way into the cyma curve on a crown moulding, a pulvinated frieze on a table apron or the contoured front on the top of an oxbow chest.

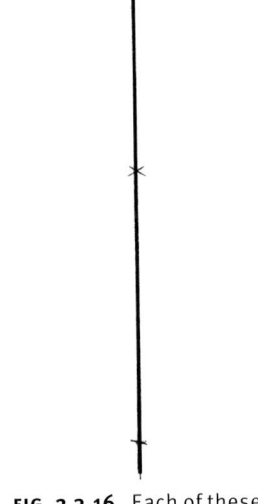

FIG. 2.3.16. Each of these sections of a circle is a multiple of the chord. The faster curve is 1/6 of a circle and uses one chord as the radius. Doubling the chord slows the curve. Using multiples of a chord you can tweak a curve slower.

Creating Visual Music with Our Notes

Now that we have established a small series of curved visual notes based on simple chords, how do we combine them in lively compositions? The good news is that many of the same concepts apply to curves that apply to straight lines and rectilinear spaces. Just as a grid lacks rhythm and appears static, a series of identical curves has a similar if not jarring effect. Here are some graphics to illustrate how curves can complement or clash in a composition.

We can use punctuation when combining curves. One way is to create a small curve as a transition point at the end of a large curve. We can also create points of rest between curves by placing a small fillet or bead at the transition points where larger curved sections join together.

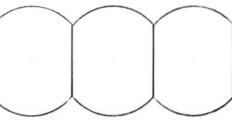

FIG. 2.3.17. *(above)* These repeated curved sections are a great turning exercise on the lathe, but they do little for the eye.

FIG. 2.3.18. *(right)* This profile is organized vertically using contrast and punctuation. Curves add additional layers of interest by contrasting concave vs. convex, large vs. small and fast vs. slow.

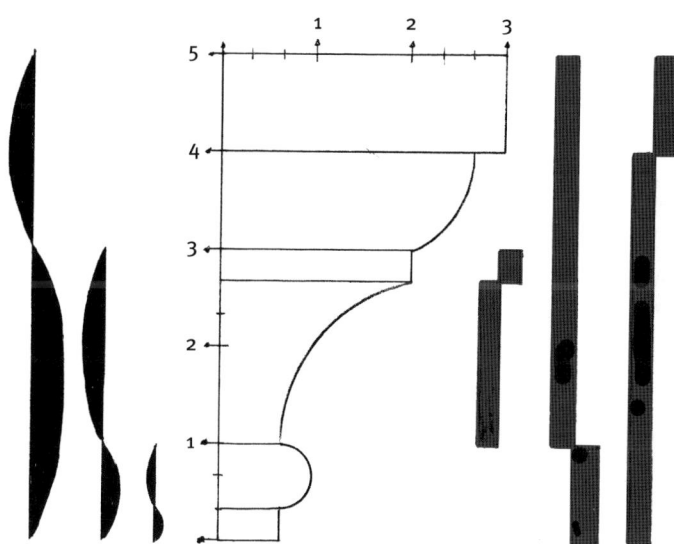

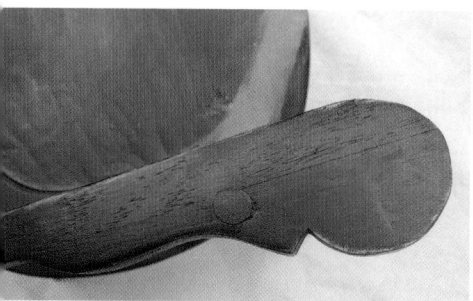

FIG. 2.3.19. Small points of rest link these flowing curves and mimic how our muscles transition to tendons where they attach to bone.

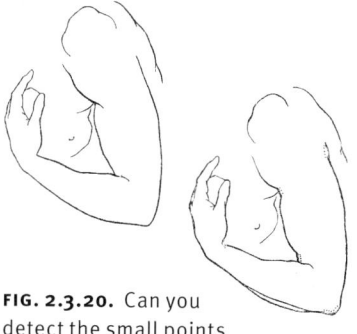

FIG. 2.3.20. Can you detect the small points of rest that gives the arm on the right more life and "spring?"

CHAPTER 4

FIG. 2.4.1. The classic orders dominated pre-20th-century furniture-design books. Above is shown a Corinthian capital.

Classic Orders

Which seems more odd: A 21st-century book on furniture design that devotes a chapter to the classic orders, or an 18th-century design book that excludes them? The majority of the nearly 200 design books published in English in the pre-industrial era paid homage to the classic orders. In fact, many of them consisted largely of an exhaustive treatise on the classic orders and their application. Quite a few no doubt included the orders because the authors knew they wouldn't garner the respect of the artisan class without them.

The lifeblood of craft has always depended on knowledge passing from one generation to the next, and I struggle finding words to convey the importance that classic orders played. This is an opportunity to walk in the footsteps of thousands of artisans gone before you, a chance to learn things that cannot be put into words, because this leads into a room in your imagination. The classic orders aren't about memorizing some nifty proportional recipes. In fact, it's the furthest thing from recipes. It's about learning to see. The physical act of drawing challenges the mind to reshuffle and see things anew. Try not to approach this like you're learning a task or skill; instead just immerse yourself in this rite of passage. Have some fun with it, and let the ancients knock down the cobwebs and pry open some windows in some long-forgotten play space in your imagination.

Grab a clean pine board about 8" wide and 3' long for a canvas. If (when) you botch the first attempt, simply plane or sand to reveal a new surface for another go. Pencil in all your lines then, after the entire drawing is complete, go back over your pencil lines with a marker. Think of it like a maze or a puzzle that will change the way you think and make new connections in your imagination. I encourage you, as always, to do this with pencil and not a computer to make sure you get the most direct connection between the portal of your hand and inner eye.

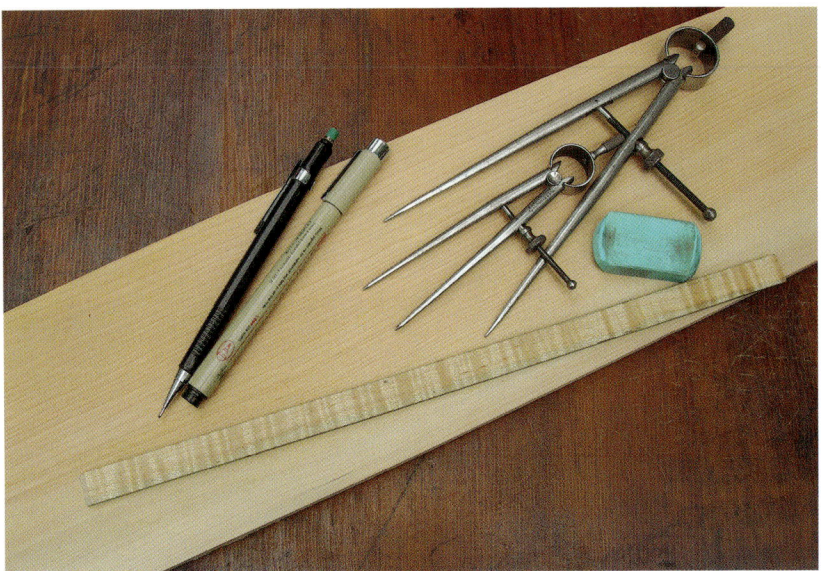

FIG. 2.4.2. You'll need a sharp pencil, an eraser, several dividers, a straightedge and a couple fine-point markers to make your pencil lines permanent at the final step.

Disclaimer: Drawing the classic orders can cause the following side effects: Minor accidents and traffic violations while gawking at architecture in public spaces, spousal abuse while driving and committing said gawking. It's also known to cause a malady called "classic order neck" that results from standing for prolonged periods looking up. Proceed with this drawing exercise at your own risk. The authors, George Walker and Jim Tolpin, and the publisher, Lost Art Press, take no responsibility for any resulting injuries, fines or calamities resulting from your participation in this drawing exercise.

A word about scale. Because you will be drawing a relatively small image, some of the details will be too awkward to draw with a compass. For elements such as moulding profiles or the finer points on the capital, draw a separate detail sketch in larger format with a compass. Once you have completed the larger sketch, go back and hand sketch those details in. You'll be pleasantly surprised by how well you can freehand sketch once you have the boundary of the form established and a little practice on the larger detail drawings. This has real value in furniture design, also. For example, a volute is a delightful form to work into a design, yet because of scale, almost always requires drawing freehand. Generating a volute with a compass will inform your freehand attempts. Also because of scale, don't attempt to use geometry to draw the entasis (slight convex bulging) on the upper two thirds of the column, just draw a straight taper.

In this drawing exercise you will render a Roman Doric order based on James Gibbs' "Rules for Drawing the Several Parts of Architecture" (circa 1732). There are five orders – Tuscan, Doric, Ionic, Corinthian and Composite – that exist in an almost endless number of versions and varieties to draw and explore. This Doric order is your doorway into this ancient way of seeing and thinking. In the bibliography I list some references to learn more about the nomenclature, history and application of the orders, but for the sake of this exercise I've purposefully kept details as simple as possible.

A few points about communicating proportions using arcs. One common way to show how a proportion relates to another element is to use a half-circle or quarter-circle to indicate a connection. Typically, a half-circle extends a mirror image proportion along the same line. Conversely, a quarter-circle mirrors a proportion from one element to an adjacent element but from horizontal to vertical (or vice versa).

Start by organizing the form (Doric order) into its major vertical parts: the beginning, middle and ending, better known as pedestal, column and entablature. Draw a vertical centerline and establish the top and bottom of your drawing with a pair of horizontal lines, leaving yourself a few inches of margin above and below. Use dividers to step off these major elements and indicate their boundaries with horizontal lines. Once you establish the height of the middle (column) you can determine the module. In the case of the Doric, divide the column height into eight equal parts. That's the diameter of the shaft near the base and also, therefore,

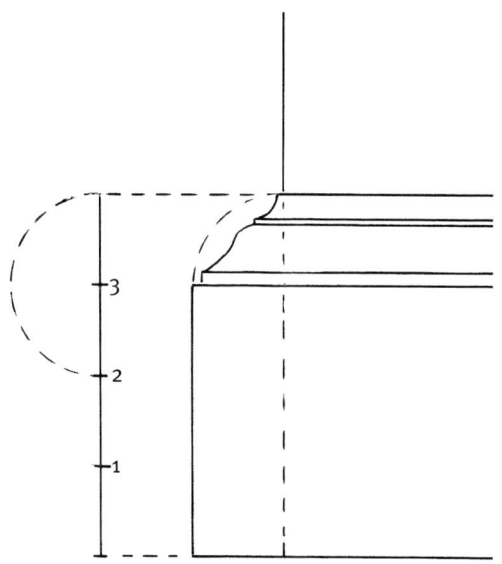

FIG. 2-.4.3. The moulding at the top of this base is a proportional extension of the base below it. The half-circle indicates that it's one-third of the base's height. The quarter-arc shows the linkage between the height of the moulding and the projection of the base.

Module Key

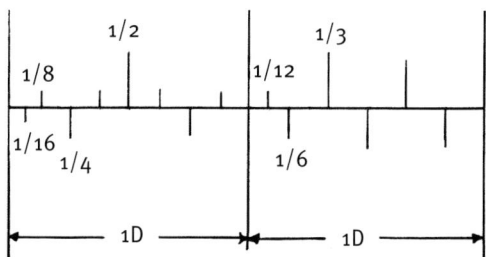

FIG. 2.4.4. On this Doric order the diameter of the column at the base is the module. That is, one-eigth the overall height of the column. Once you find the module, step off a key with simple divisions of the module. You can then use the key to quickly reset your dividers as the drawing progresses.

your module. Now – and this is important – draw a small module key in the space below your drawing. Many of the elements that follow will be simple divisions of the module, for example, the column-base height is a one-half module, so having this key handy will speed up the drawing process. To create a key, draw a horizontal line and mark off two modules end-to-end using vertical hash marks to highlight them. Then use your dividers and, through trial and error, step off one module into halves, quarters and eighths. Then step off the second module into thirds, sixths and 12ths.

Start with the largest divisions and work down to the smaller details. Once you have established the overall column height and diameter of the shaft at the base, there are a couple reference lines to pencil in. Note that the column height is divided into thirds and that the lower third's shaft diameter remains constant while the upper two-thirds curve in gradually – an effect the Greeks called entasis. (As I mentioned earlier, however, at this scale you may want to just render the entasis as a slight taper rather than as a curve.) Also note the use of reference lines: One extends the outside diameter of the shaft above the column while a second extends the outside of the column base below into the pedestal. These lines allow you to step off the horizontal projection of elements in the pedestal and entablature.

Once you've established the overall vertical organization, draw in the details of the pedestal. Start by stepping off the vertical organization and then establish the horizontal projection for each part. Most are a function of the module or pulled from an adjacent proportion. Move up to the column and then the entablature.

For certain, you will take a wrong turn or two and have to backtrack and rethink it. It's all part of learning to see proportionally. When your drawing is completed, you'll not only have some studies to hang on the shop wall, but you'll also have created an important mile marker on your journey to becoming an artisan designer.

VERY IMPORTANT: Once the drawing is complete, go back and set your dividers to some of the simple divisions from your module key and probe the entire drawing for relationships. You will be pleasantly surprised to see how many simple proportions you wove into this without realizing it. Go back through and jot down how many layers of contrast, symmetry and punctuation occur. Congratulations. You have just rendered a standard of visual music from the artisan age. It stands silent before your eyes no longer.

CLASSIC ORDERS

A DRAWING EXERCISE

Drawing a Doric Order

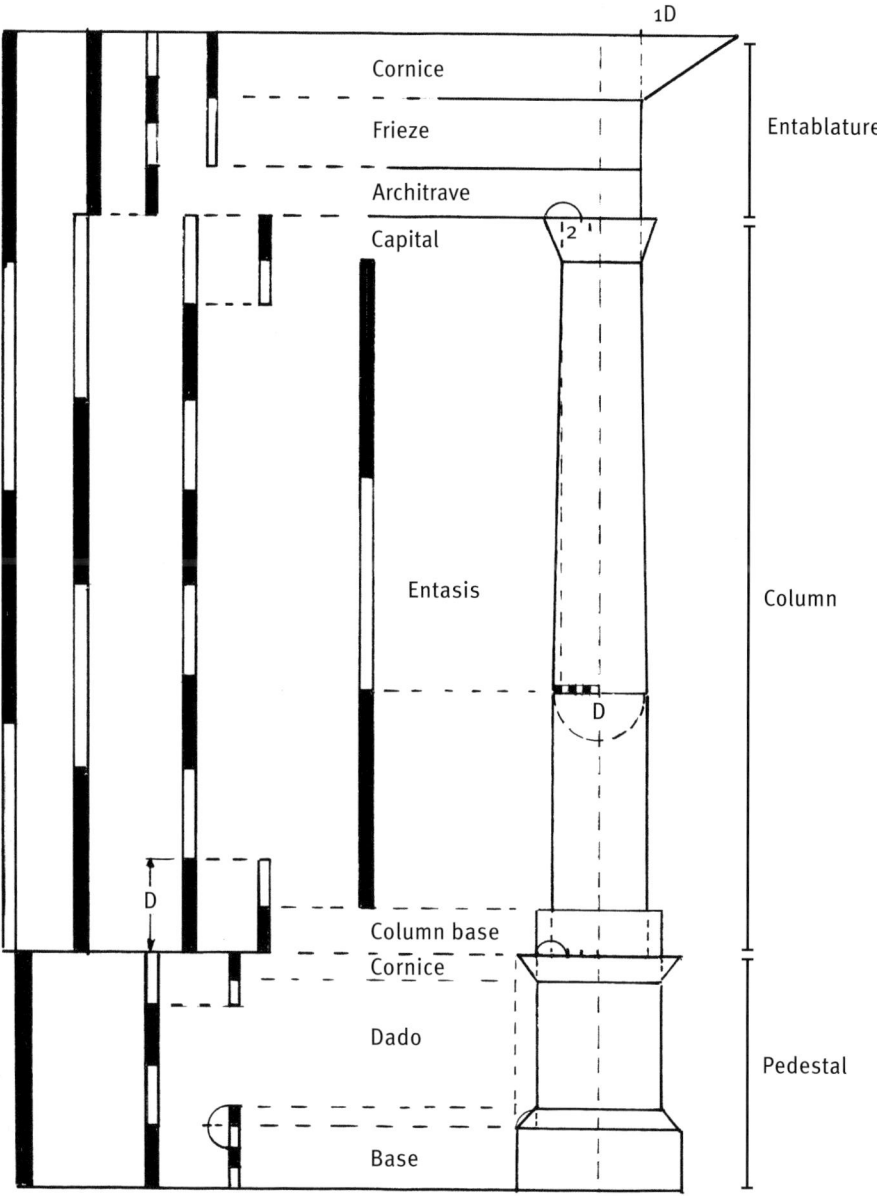

FIG. 2.4.5. Step off elements, working from largest to smallest.

(CONTINUED ON NEXT PAGE)

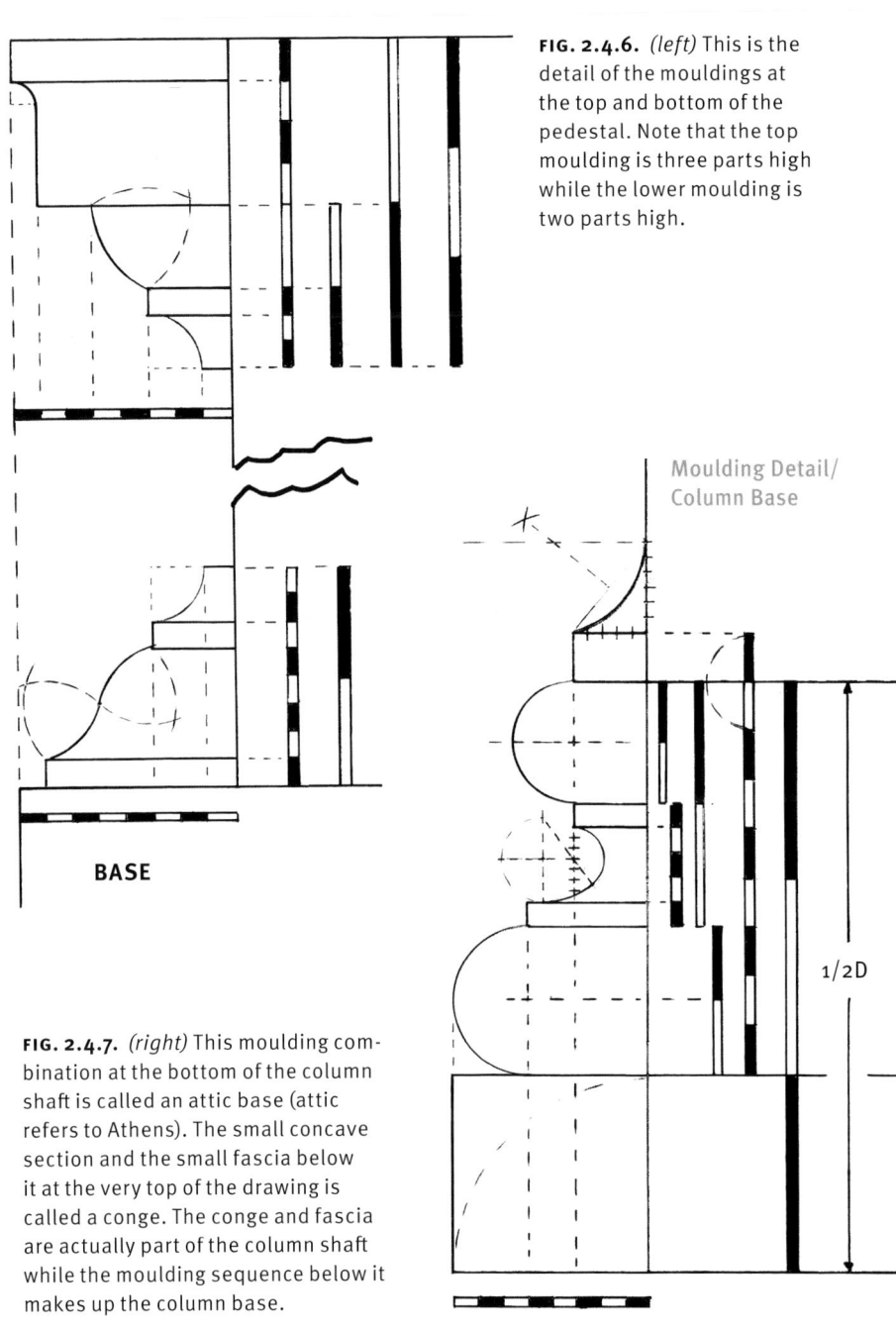

FIG. 2.4.6. *(left)* This is the detail of the mouldings at the top and bottom of the pedestal. Note that the top moulding is three parts high while the lower moulding is two parts high.

FIG. 2.4.7. *(right)* This moulding combination at the bottom of the column shaft is called an attic base (attic refers to Athens). The small concave section and the small fascia below it at the very top of the drawing is called a conge. The conge and fascia are actually part of the column shaft while the moulding sequence below it makes up the column base.

CLASSIC ORDERS

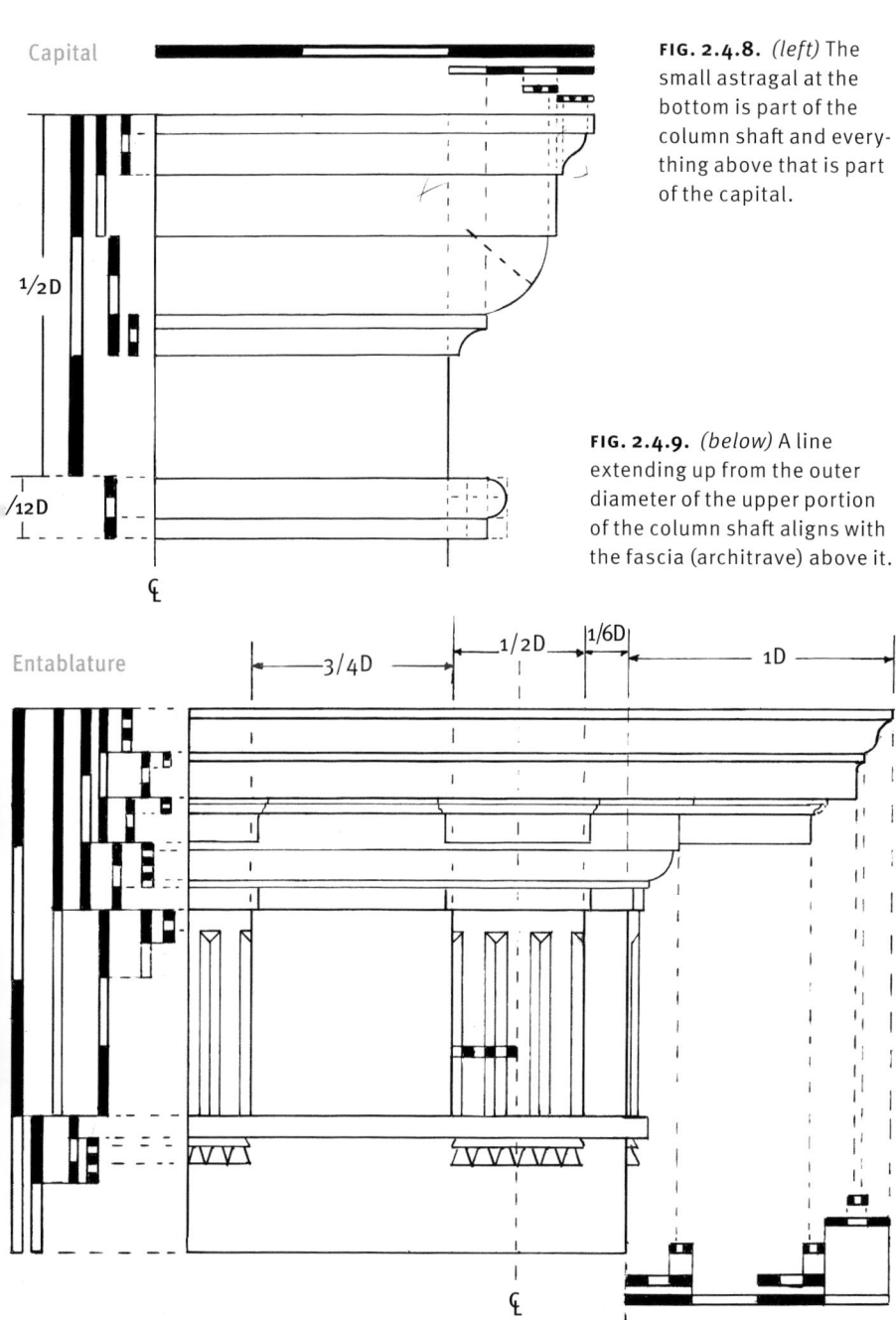

FIG. 2.4.8. *(left)* The small astragal at the bottom is part of the column shaft and everything above that is part of the capital.

FIG. 2.4.9. *(below)* A line extending up from the outer diameter of the upper portion of the column shaft aligns with the fascia (architrave) above it.

SECTION III

Artisan Geometry

1
Traditional Tools

2
Basic Geometric Constructions

3
Generating Shapes

4
Generating Curves & Tapers

5
Developing Moulding Profiles

CHAPTER 1

FIG. 3.1.1. This 13th-century manuscript illumination depicts God using a compass to create the universe following geometric principles.

Traditional Tools

As George has spoken to in the preceding chapters, "Artisan Geometry" is what we are calling the form of geometry employed by pre-industrial craftsmen, using the simplest of instruments and strategies to proportion spacings, draw lines at certain angles and to create a wide variety of shapes that underlie the form and decorations of their traditional designs. Their geometry was not concerned with proving Euclidian theorems or solving or expressing algebraic equations, but rather with finding the most efficient ways to design and lay out their work. For the artisans it was all about straightforward spatial relationships and not about arithmetic and number theory. In other words, it was a tool of the trade – and that's how I present it to you here.

"God forever geometrizes."
— Plato

You might be aware that the tools and techniques of the artisan's pre-Euclidean, generative geometry could not (and still can't) produce certain polygons, generate a square of equal volume to a circle (the infamous "squaring the circle") or trisect an angle to finite mathematical precision. (See the "Rabbit Holes" page at georgewalkerdesign.com.) Artisan geometry can, however, do these tasks (as well as most any other "rule-and-compass" construction) to a margin of error well beyond the discernment of the human eye. Which is, of course, well beyond practical necessity when creating tangible objects made from wood. If you haven't fooled around much with a straightedge and compass, you will likely be amazed at what you can accomplish with these "primitive" tools that essentially do just two things: establish a straight line and swing a circle.

I'll start with an introduction to the traditional tools of the artisan geometrists, including one you may not have heard of: the sector. You can't buy this tool (currently), but you can easily build one of wood and I'll show you how. In teaching you the various constructions, I try to avoid rote rules. Instead I show what's actually happening when you intersect circles and lines in various ways – and how this creates certain shapes, develops specific curves and produces whole-numbered ratios and spacings. Note that the "why" of how these constructions work is presented here in the text while the step-by-step how-to is demonstrated via animations you can download at lostartpress.com/geometry.

The Tools

In this chapter, I present the basic instruments that you'll need both to draw constructions on paper and to do layouts on the stock itself. There is a difference in scale and workload between these tasks and that is reflected in the size and sturdiness of the tools. In either case, this equipment is not that expensive even when new (though you do get what you pay for, which means you might want to consider the premium offerings from Starrett) and most can also be readily found through dealers of used woodworking and drafting hand tools. The majority of the layout tools – the straightedge, the sector, the try square and the bending battens – can be shop-made.

Dividers

There are a number of different types of dividers to choose from, depending on the work expected of them. For light work where dividers are primarily used to step off spaces, a very simple set that depends only on friction at the pivot to

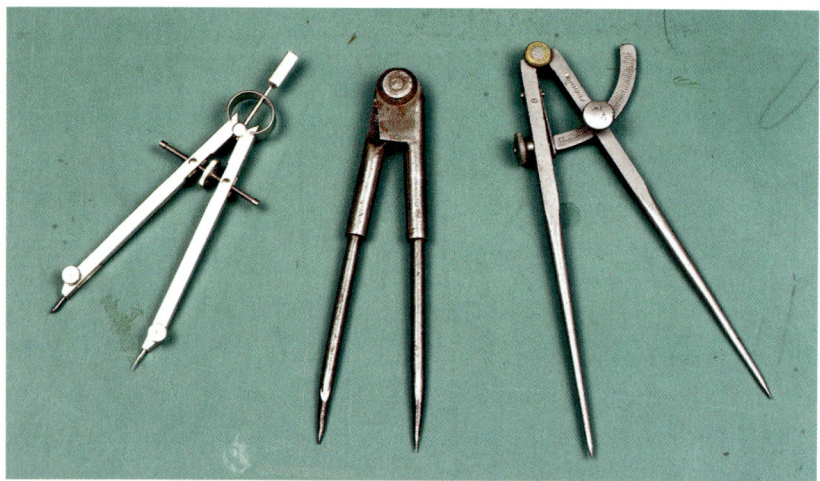

FIG. 3.1.2. Dividers come in different styles, offering various means of fixing the arms. The divider in the middle depends on friction and lacks a vernier adjustment.

FIG. 3.1.3. Tap the head of a divider with a ball peen hammer to take out slop.

FIG. 3.1.4. Use a file to sharpen the points of a divider.

maintain the setting is the traditional choice. For drafting work, a divider with more moving parts is the norm: A spring steel band holds the legs apart while a screw precisely adjusts the setting against the spring's constant compression. This "spring" divider is the tool of choice for creating scale drawings, but it isn't sturdy or generally large enough for layout work. For the latter, choose a traditional workman's "winged" divider that locks down with a set screw. Even when handled somewhat roughly, these dividers will usually hold their setting. For making fine adjustments to the setting after the wing is locked, better versions provide a second knob that can be loosened or tightened against a spring, allowing the leg to move in a fine-adjustment range of about 3/16".

Tuning up a Pair of Dividers

Most new dividers of good quality are ready to use right out of the box. Used and cheaper versions, however, may need a bit of tuning up to work properly. There's not much you can do for the spring types, but you can do quite a bit for the tradesman's wing-types. Start by checking for play in the pivot point, taking out any slop by lightly tapping on the pin with a ball peen hammer while resting the pin's opposite end on a small anvil. Next, check to be sure that the points are even in length; you'd be surprised how even a 1/8" deviation can make it difficult to accurately walk out short steps. Finally, use a file to hone the tips to a fine point. (Note: A second cut mill file is good for honing, but drop down to a bastard file if you need to first reshape the tip.)

Using Dividers

While it wouldn't seem that you'd need much skill to use a pair of dividers, it does take some to use them accurately and efficiently. Let's start with how to set the dividers to "walk out" a certain number of spaces between two points. Referring to the drawing below, first approximate the setting by eyeball (or with a sector) and then step out the required number of divisions. Unless you have a great eye (or are lucky), the last step will either under- or over-shoot the limit point. If this is the case, divide (by eye again) the discrepancy by the number of steps you walked out and then tighten or back off the vernier to reset the dividers to the first of these tiny divisions. (The drawing should make this clear). With a little practice, you often get it dead-on in this second go around.

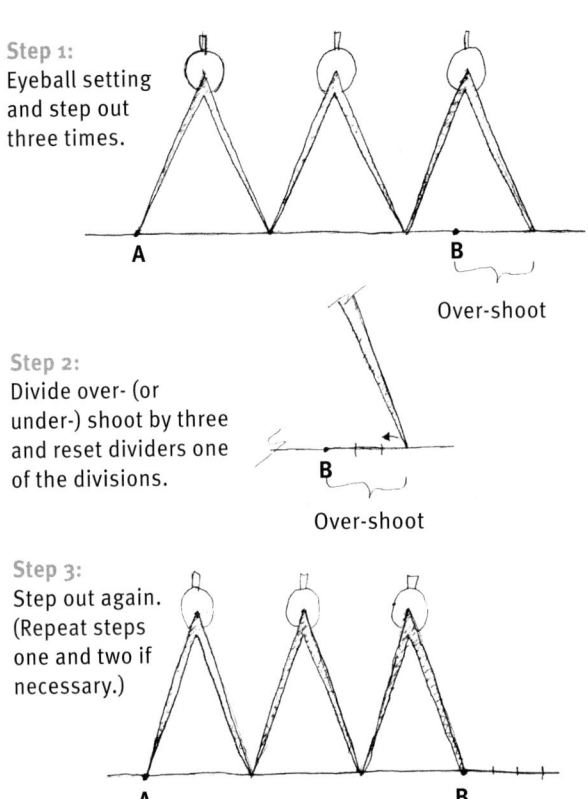

Divide AB into three parts:

Step 1:
Eyeball setting and step out three times.

Step 2:
Divide over- (or under-) shoot by three and reset dividers one of the divisions.

Step 3:
Step out again. (Repeat steps one and two if necessary.)

FIG. 3.1.5. Technique for walking out even spacings.

Another common use of the dividers is to transfer a known dimension (such as copying a dimension on a full-scale drawing to the stock, or transferring an existing condition such as a mortise to the stock to be tenoned). The transfer is a simple matter of setting the divider points to the known dimension and then setting the points on the stock to be laid out. What's neat (literally) about dividers is that the

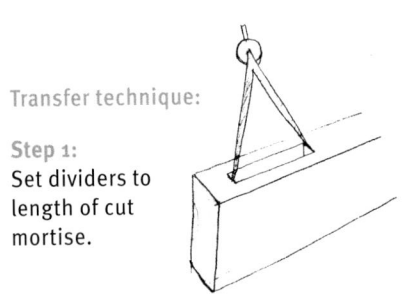

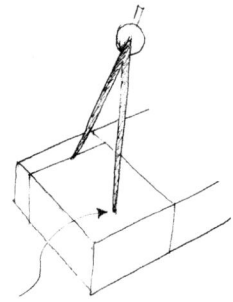

Transfer technique:

Step 1:
Set dividers to length of cut mortise.

Step 2:
Set one leg of dividers to fixed cutline; mark length.

FIG. 3.1.6. Transferring a mortise length to a lay out a tenon.

registration marks it produces are very fine pinholes to which you can precisely register a knife blade. (You don't even have to look; you can feel when the blade tip drops into the hole.) The potential level of accuracy of these "primitive" layout tools is in the ten-thousandths of an inch range.

If you want to keep a particular transfer setting for use later in the project, I suggest you do one or both these things: First, make a referral board for resetting the dividers and second, mark the dividers to alert yourself that it has a dedicated setting. The referral board is simply a short piece of wood on to which you've transferred the setting and drawn a circle around each pinhole. The marker is a piece of masking tape (with an optional symbol noting what it represents) affixed to one leg of the divider.

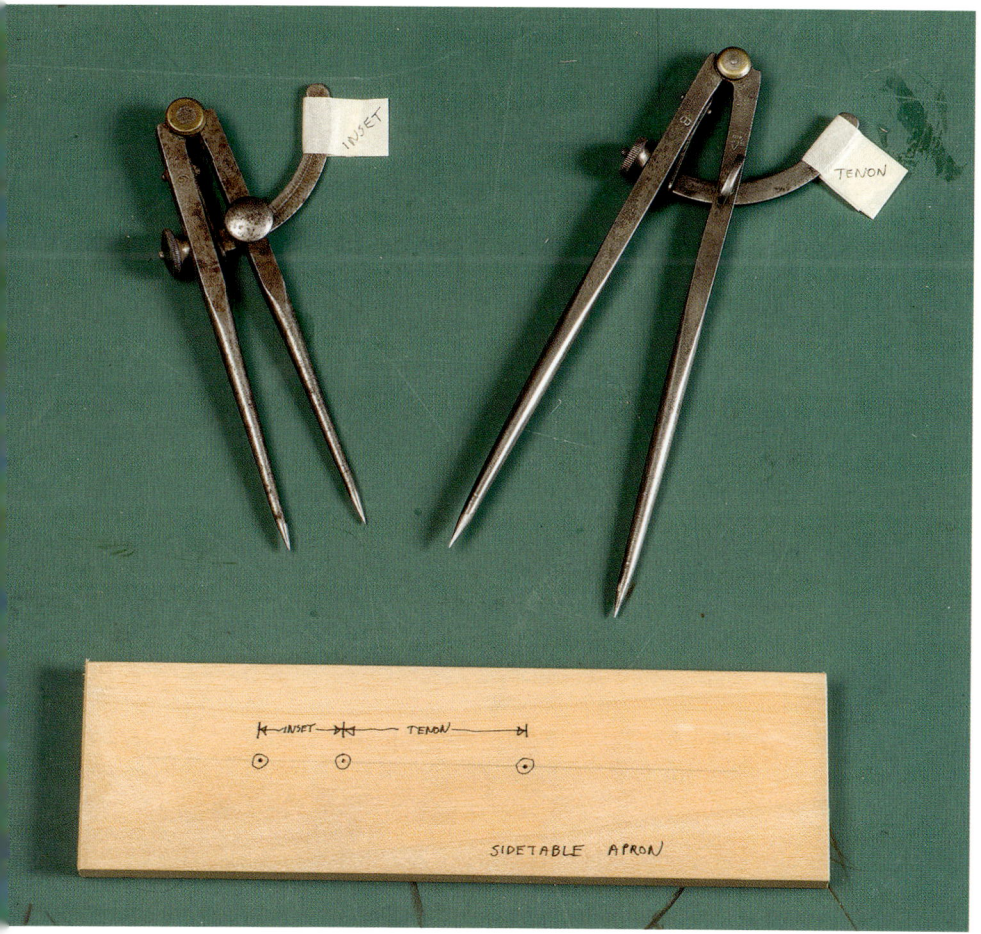

IG. 3.1.7. Referral board and a marked pair of dividers.

The Compass

There are two basic types of compasses that I use in my work: one for drawing and the other for doing layouts. For the lighter-duty and generally smaller-scale work involved in drawings, I use a spring-bow-type compass with a center wheel adjustment and changeable points. For layout, I use the lock-wing type with a pencil grip. I usually come up with a mechanical pencil to fit the grip; otherwise I use an HB (hardness scale) drafting pencil. Better versions of these compasses include a vernier adjustment. For larger-radius circles I use a set of trammel points affixed to a straight stick for layouts and a beam-type compass for drawings.

Tuning up a Compass

There's generally not much to tuning up a compass other than sharpening the metal point (as I discussed earlier for the dividers). You may, however, need to file the pencil grip on your layout compass a bit larger in diameter to allow it to grasp a mechanical pencil. On your drawing compass, sharpen the lead insert by rubbing the point across very fine sandpaper (#600 grit) at a 45° angle.

Using the Compass

When using a compass on paper, avoid drawing on a stack of paper because that readily causes the focal point of your compass to slip. Instead, use a sheet of thick, single-layer cardboard from a drawing pad or bite the bullet and buy a "self-healing" rubber pad that can be found at most office supply stores or online.

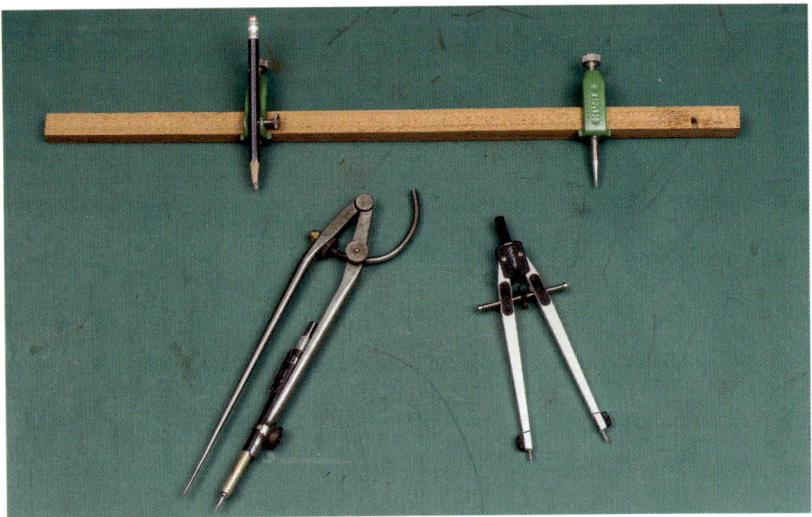

FIG. 3.1.8. Tools for drawing arcs come in a variety of sizes. The trammel points at the top of the photo can be mounted to a stick of any length to create large arcs.

 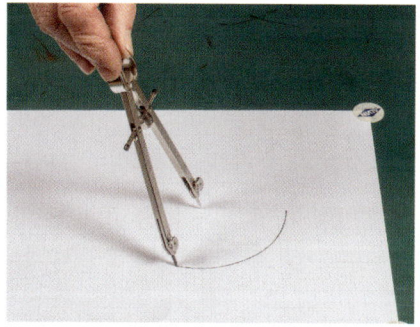

FIG. 3.1.9. Sharpening a stick of lead on fine sandpaper.   **FIG. 3.1.10.** Holding the compass to draw a circle.

As you may have already discovered in grade school, there is a trick to smoothly drawing a circle with a compass. If you've forgotten, here it is: Place one hand on the top grip and position the point with the other hand to the desired focal point. Prick through the paper into the drawing board or mat. Now, with only one hand on the compass, lean it in the direction of travel and, while keeping about two-thirds of the force down on the point, swing the compass completely around in one fell swoop. It takes a bit of practice to make a continuous swing – and it requires that you keep the focal point sharp. You may also find it helpful to use a sharp awl to prick the focal points during the drawing process.

The Secret of the Sector

The sector was originally a mathematical instrument (possibly invented by Galileo) composed of a pair of hinged sticks engraved with a variety of scales that – coupled with a pair of dividers – allowed medieval navigators to calculate trigonometric functions and to thereby derive bearings. We know that simple versions of the sector were used by Sheraton (he recommended them in his landmark book on furniture design, "The Cabinet Maker's and Upholsterer's Drawing Book," and we can assume they were likely in wide use by the late 18th century) to apply whole-numbered proportions to his designs.

Here I will show you how this was done. You'll see how to divide a board's dimension (or the dimension of a space to be filled) into equal parts, how to lay out hardware locations and how to change the scale of a design up or down without losing its proportions. With a sector, you'll accomplish these tasks within a matter of seconds and without having to crunch fractional numbers. All you need do is take the sector up in one hand, a pair of dividers in the other and calculate a handful of whole-number fractions of 12. That's the magic of it…and that's no secret!

I'll also show you how to build a sector because you cannot, as far as I can tell, buy one from any catalog or online tool dealer. Refer to the "Rabbit Holes"

Suggested Tool Set
Drawing Tools

- **Dividers/compass:** One 6" spring-bow type with interchangeable points (including lead)
- **Squares:** Plastic drafting square with at least an 8" leg
- **Straightedge:** Architect's rule (not for scales – but because it's easier to pick up)
- **Flexible edge:** Commercial version for larger curves; strip of rubber for small, tight curves
- **Drawing surface:** "Self-healing pad" or a piece of sheet stock – at least 2' x 3' in size
- **Graph paper** (to underlay vellum)
- **Pencil:** Mechanical 5mm
- **Pencil sharpener,** drum type
- **Eraser:** White gum type – block form and pencil
- **Eraser shield:** Thin metal with a variety of hole sizes and shapes so you can isolate the area to be erased
- **Brush:** Soft paintbrush for sweeping away eraser particles – never use your hand or you'll create smudges
- **Paper:** Vellum (or to save money, but harder to erase, banner paper). Use commercial "drafting dots" or light-duty masking tape to hold down corners

FIG. 3.1.11. Drawing tools.

Layout Tools

- **Compass:** One 8"-wing type with vernier adjustment. (You may be tempted to save money by buying a combination divider/compass, but you'll soon find it a hassle to constantly be changing out the points.) Add smaller and larger sizes as needed
- **Dividers:** At least one 6"- and one 10"- wing type with vernier adjustment
- **Try square:** Commercial or shop-made: one with 4" and one with 12" tongue
- **Straightedge:** One 3'- to 4'-long in wood or metal. I also often use the project's story stick to double as the layout straightedge
- **T-pins:** Use these as locator pins for the straightedge and battens
- **Bending battens:** Make from clear, straight-grain wood. Make one of uniform thickness for constant curves and another tapered for bending to a changing radius – both about 3' long, and longer for larger projects. Mine have a bowstring to hold their shape while I draw the line
- **Chalk line** (Note: I replace the typical thick cord with a thinner string so it will produce a finer line.)
- **Trammel points**

IG. 3.1.12. Layout tools.

FIG. 3.1.13. An antique sector.

NOTE: These two lines, when intersecting a circle drawn from the intersection, define a sector of the circle.

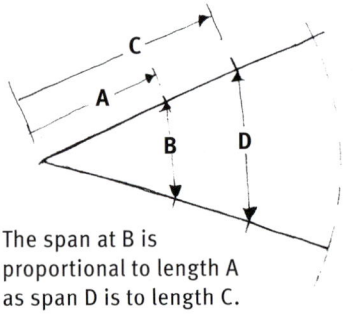

The span at B is proportional to length A as span D is to length C.

FIG. 3.1.14. The geometry of the sector.

page at georgewalkerdesign.com for illustrated building instructions. Once you start working with this tool of the Renaissance, you'll wonder how you ever made do without it.

How the Sector Works

The sector works on this basic axiom of geometry: The third side of a triangle having two other sides of equal length (an isosceles triangle) will always be in proportion to the third side of another isosceles triangle having the same base angle. Because the sector is simply two lengths of wood (called the arms) connected at a hinge point, it produces an infinite number of isosceles triangles along its length, all with the same base angle. So as we move along the length of the two sticks in evenly spaced steps, the third legs will be in a whole-number ratio to each other.

Using the Sector

What the geometric niceties of the sector mean at the bench is that if you set your dividers to hit the 10th notch on each arm, the spread of the dividers will be exactly twice the distance between the fifth notches (see Fig. 3.1.15 at bottom left). Likewise, if you set your divider

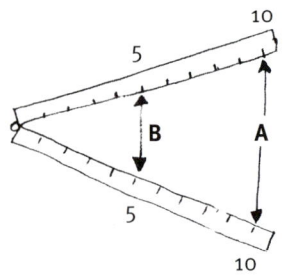

Span A is twice that of span B.

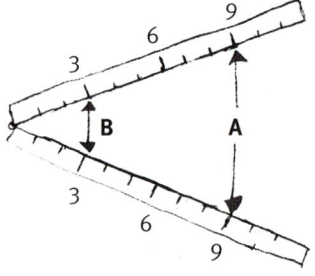

Here, span A is three times longer than span B.
NOTE: At the sixth division line, the span would be 2/3 that of the span at the ninth division.

FIG. 3.1.15. Deriving proportions on the sector.

at the ninth notch, you now have a dimension that is three times the distance between the third notches. This wonderful state of affairs opens up, as you will see below, a world of possibilities in both refining and speeding up your layout work. Best of all, you no longer have to deal with crunching fractional numbers or, for that matter, division or multiplication work outside of single digits. The sector generates physical dimensions that can be "lifted" and transferred with a set of dividers, making it unnecessary to generate numbers that must be recorded and transferred with numbered measuring devices (i.e. rulers). I don't know about you, but I find that to be an enormous boon for my eyes, my mental health and, perhaps most important of all, my ability to avoid mistakes.

Sector Layout Task 1: Dividing a Dimension Into Equal Parts

Let's say we want to make a plank door for your rustic-design cabinet – and we would, of course, like the four panels to be of equal width. Instead of measuring the width of the opening and then dividing that number by the number of planks (Quick: What is 17 $^{15}/_{16}$ divided by four?), you can get the answer from the sector nearly instantaneously – with the bonus of setting a layout device to mark this width out at the same time. If you are ripping the stock by hand (that is, you don't need a number to index the machine to), you don't even need to find the measurement for this span; you can simply lay it out from the dividers right onto the stock to be ripped. Refer to the drawings below to see this sequence of steps.

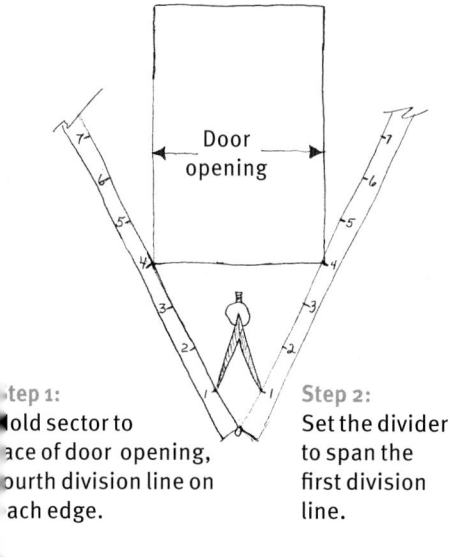
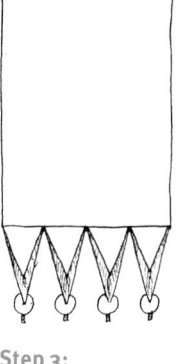
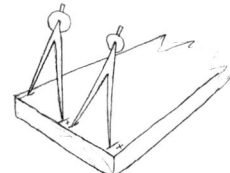

Step 1: Hold sector to face of door opening, fourth division line on each edge.

Step 2: Set the divider to span the first division line.

Step 3: Step out the divisions on the rail of the cabinet with dividers.

Step 4: Lay out the cutline on the stock from the dividers.

FIG. 3.1.16. Laying out a plank door.

Section Layout Task 2: Maintaining Proportional Divisions From One Station to Another

Now let's say the door opening is wider at the bottom than the top. How are we going to generate planks of equal width from top to bottom? As you might guess, the sector comes to the rescue. We simply set the sector as described above to get the individual plank width for the span at the bottom and mark this on one end of the board. We then repeat the process at the top and mark the other end of the board.

For the sake of aesthetics, however, let's not assume we can lay out the taper from the edge the mill gave us to work with. As you can see in Fig. 3.1.18 at right, this can result in an awkward (read: ugly) grain pattern. Instead, we'll begin by ripping and truing one edge parallel to the centerline of the cathedral, then we'll lay out the width of the plank's top and bottom from there. Another way to ensure

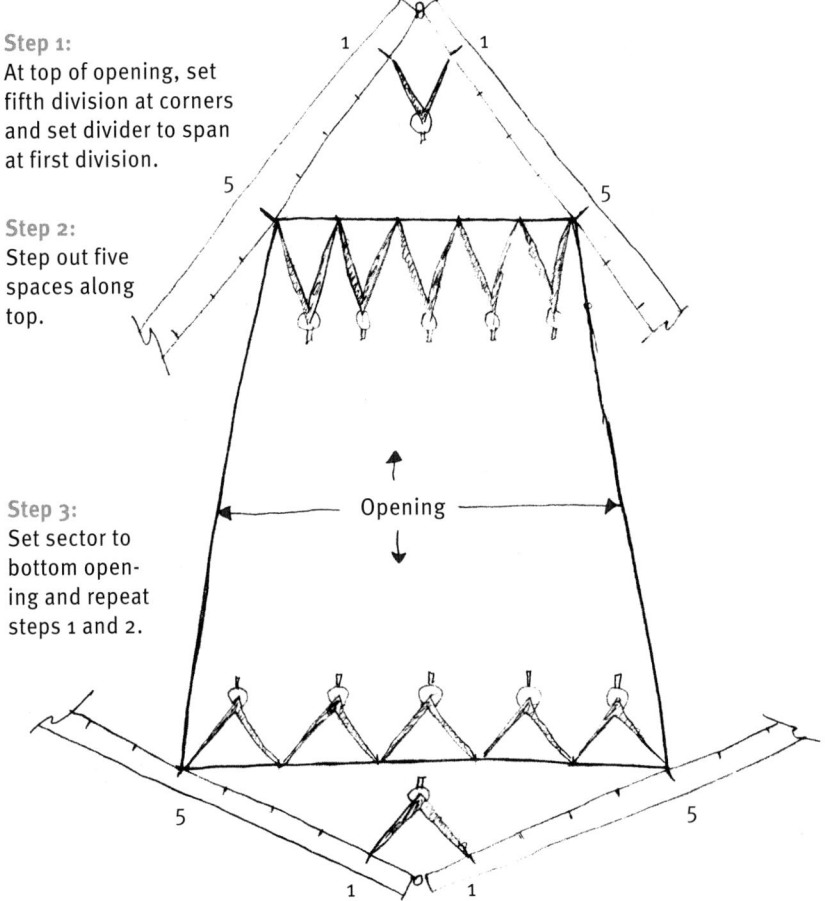

Step 1: At top of opening, set fifth division at corners and set divider to span at first division.

Step 2: Step out five spaces along top.

Step 3: Set sector to bottom opening and repeat steps 1 and 2.

FIG. 3.1.17. Layout of tapered planking.

that the cathedral is centered on the plank is to draw a centerline first, then lay out to either side of it. But wait, our divider is set to fifths of the span top and bottom. The solution: We'll reset the sector to give us 10ths and then use this dimension to lay out on either side of the centerline. The drawing should make this clear to you.

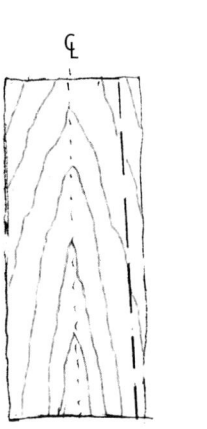
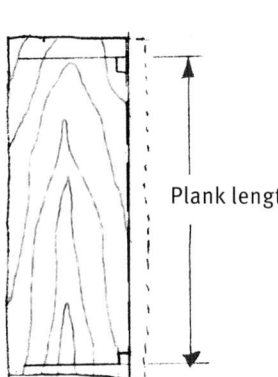

Step 1:
Make first edge cut roughly parallel to centerline of cathedral. Cut.

Step 2:
Mark end cuts perpendicular to edge cut.

Step 3:
Lay out top and bottom spans with dividers. Connect marks and cut.

Alternative Method:

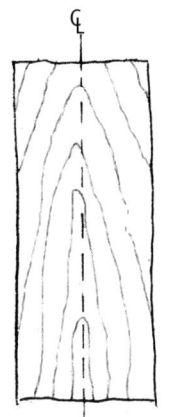
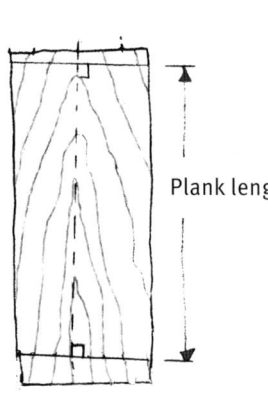
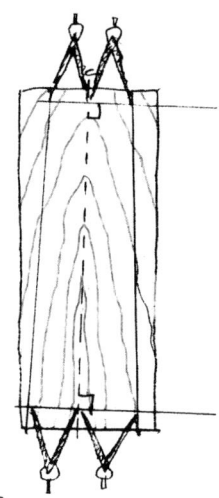

Step 1:
Draw centerline through cathedral.

Step 2:
Lay out end cuts perpendicular to centerline.

Step 3:
Lay out half-spans to either side of centerline top and bottom. Connect and cut.

FIG. 3.1.18. Layout of taper on stock.

Section Layout Task 3: Laying Out Hardware Locations

Now let's use the sector to quickly lay out hardware locations (such as drawer pulls) in pleasing, whole-number ratios that relate to the overall span of the component to which they are mounted (and to each other if in pairs). For example, in the drawing below, the sector instantly finds the vertical centerline of a drawer face for mounting a pull; we simply open the arms of the sector so that an even number falls on each end of the face (in this case 8) and then set the dividers to half that number (4) on the arms. We've located the center as ⁴⁄₈, which reduces to ½. We'll then set one leg of the divider to the edge of the drawer face, make a pinpoint mark with the other leg, and extend a vertical line with a pencil. The pull will install somewhere along this line. If you want it centered, you just repeat these steps, setting the sector across the width of the face. If, however, you want it offset toward the top a bit (commonly done because we are usually looking down on a

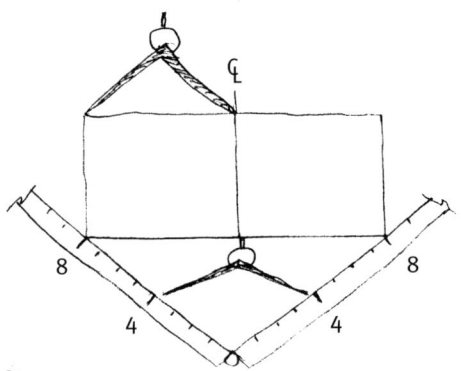

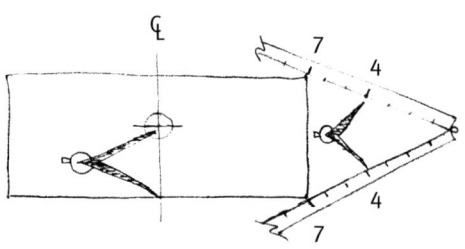

Step 1:
Place sector to eighth division and set dividers at fourth division.
4/8 = 1/2 so dividers will mark center.

Step 2:
Place sector to seventh division across width and set dividers to fourth division. Lay out 4/7 from bottom on centerline.

FIG. 3.1.19. Locating a single pull in center.

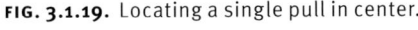

Step 1:
Place sector to tenth division and pick off span with dividers at the second division.
2/10 = 1/5

Step 2:
Lay out 1/5 inset from either end with dividers.

FIG. 3.1.20. Locating a double pull.

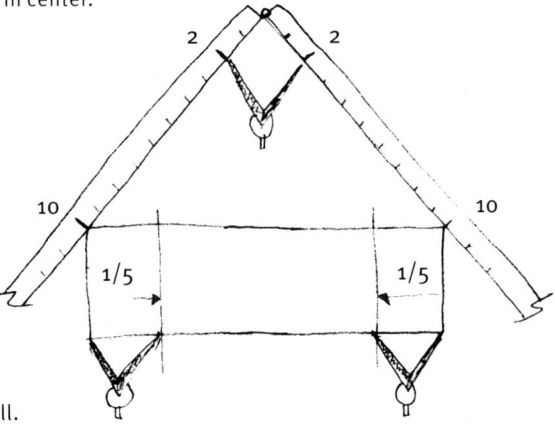

chest of drawers), a good ratio is $4/7$ up from the bottom. To find this, we orient the sector on its seventh division lines across the width and then set the divider to the fourth division line. This, as I'm sure you've guessed by now, is four-sevenths the width of the face.

In a similar fashion, if we are laying out two pulls, we may choose to set them in $1/5$ of the way in from each end – a common choice (along with $1/4$) in traditional casework. We'll get this spacing by setting the sector so that the fifth division falls to either end and then pick off the span at the first division. If the face is too long for the sector's fifth-division marks to reach, we'll set the sector divisions at 10 and pick off the inset at the second division marks ($2/10$ equals $1/5$).

Straightedges

For drawing and for doing small-sized layout work, architect's scale rules are the norm and work just fine. My favorite straightedge for this work is a K&E two-sided rule that features an overhang that makes it easy to lift off the paper. Triangular-shaped rules also work well.

FIG. 3.1.21. Collection of straightedges.

You should be aware that I do my drawings without using T-squares and drafting squares by using an underlying grid of graph paper as a guide. These aren't engineering drawings after all; instead, they are generally scale views of the project that act as guides for stepping out the actual dimensions to the indicated ratios on tick sticks.

For larger-scale drawings and layouts, I generally use the tick sticks themselves. I plane a straight edge on one edge or use dedicated, shop-made wooden straightedges – see my book "The New Traditional Woodworker" (Popular Woodworking Books) for instructions on how to make one. I have several sizes for larger-scale work and a smaller one for testing surfaces and edges for true. I sometimes add a thin strip of leather on one face of my wooden edges to prevent it from slipping off the work. For creating really long straight lines (such as a cutline for a long rip cut on stock), I find that a chalk line is much easier to work with than a straightedge.

Notes on Using Edges

Using a straightedge to accurately create a straight line can be a little tricky. This tool is a template (rather than a generator of a straight line like a tensioned string or a laser beam) and as such is subject to error if it shifts during the tracing process.

FIG. 3.1.22. Using pins to locate straightedge.

To prevent that from happening, a non-skid surface on one side of the tool is a big help – as is using a straightedge long enough to avoid having to slide it over to complete the line.

To set the edge accurately on long lines, I mark the locations of the line with a tiny hole (usually from the compass or divider point – which is often how the line is established anyway from stepping out or as a transfer). I then place a common pin into each hole and slide the edge up against both, then draw out the line with a sharp pencil.

Checking & Truing an Edge

To check an edge for true, lay it down on a flat surface and draw a line along its full length. Now flip it over on its opposite side and draw another line, being sure that the ends of the lines touch precisely. If there is any gap in the line, the edge is either convex or concave. If your straightedge is made from wood, you are in luck – you can true it in less than a minute with a true, sharp and finely set handplane.

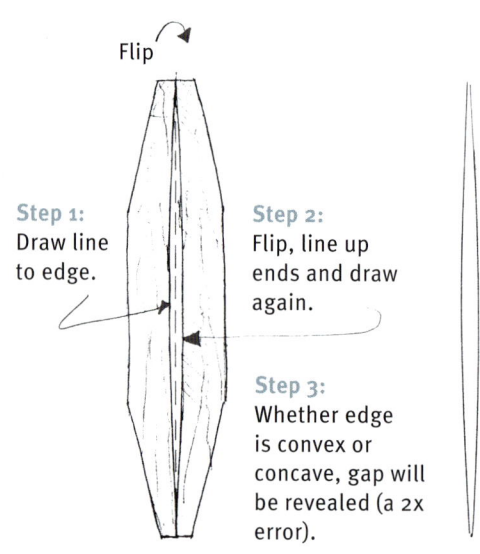

Flip

Step 1: Draw line to edge.

Step 2: Flip, line up ends and draw again.

Step 3: Whether edge is convex or concave, gap will be revealed (a 2x error).

FIG. 3.1.23. Checking an edge for true.

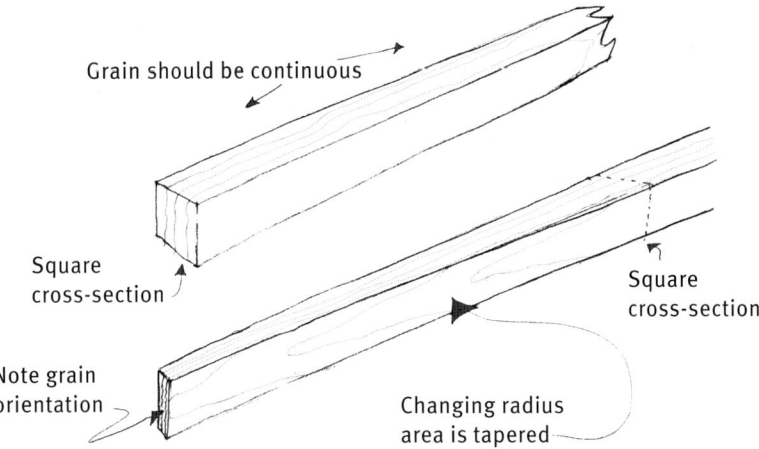

FIG. 3.1.24. Constant radius and changing radius battens.

Battens & Sticks

I use battens that I make from clear straight-grained cedar or spruce (because I can get old-growth stock with tight, straight grain locally) for laying out curves to station points, for generating curves of constant radii (i.e. arcs) and for laying out the changing radii of an ellipse. To produce fair and accurate curves (boatbuilders call them "sweet") I choose batten stock with consistent grain density and run. I look for evenly spaced growth rings and for grain lines that run uniformly from one end of the stick to the other.

To draw fair, curved lines to any set of station points you'll need a batten perfectly square in section and as long as necessary to reach the end points of the curve – plus at least another 20 percent of that length. I find that a 4'-long batten should be about ¼" square to produce a sweet curve. As the length increases, so should the cross section. At 8', for example, the cross section should increase to twice that area (a ½" square). This is, of course, just a rule of thumb; you may need to adjust the cross section due to the density and resilience of your particular stock and to the tightness of the curve. You are looking for the sweet spot where the stick bends fair and without kinking or breaking.

Creating Arcs with Sticks

To draw arcs of a constant radius (i.e. a segment of a circle) to station points you can use sticks in three different ways. The first two methods are useful if you can't easily work from the focal point of the circle whose segment you are trying to capture between the two end points. The third method does make use of the focal point, and can draw out a circle to any radius – all you need is a stick slightly longer than the radius (and a clip-on tool that we'll discuss).

FIG. 3.1.25A. Setting up parallel line with dividers to align two joined sticks for drawing an arc to three points.

FIG. 3.1.25B. Drawing the arc by holding the pencil at the junction of the sticks.

Step 1:
Set one stick to rest at C and B.

Step 2:
Orient a second stick of at least the same length to be parallel to line A-B at height of apex C.

Step 3:
Screw sticks together.

Step 4:
Hold pencil at juncture of sticks and move construction, bearing against points C and B. Repeat from C to A.

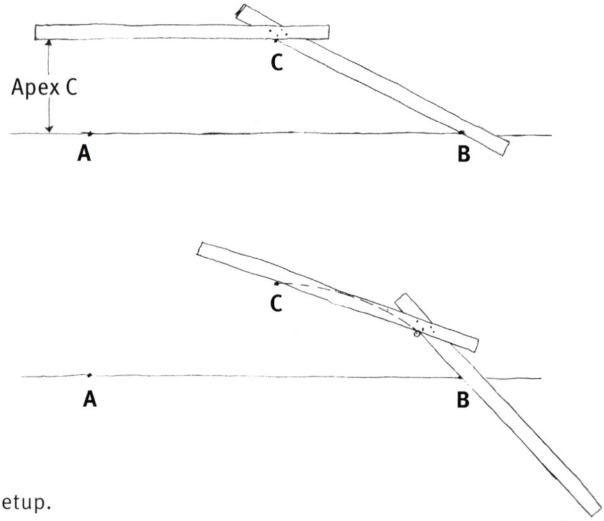

FIG. 3.1.26. Illustration of arc sticks setup.

FIG. 3.1.27. Using a batten to draw an arc to station points.

Here's the first method of drawing an arc: Overlap two sticks so that one touches the end of the arc's chord and the other its apex while the second stick runs parallel to the chord at the distance of the apex. (Fig. 3.1.25A at left should make this clear). Physically tie the sticks together with pins, small screws or strong double-sided tape. Place pins to act as bearing surfaces at the three points. Now put your pencil at the juncture of the two sticks and move the assembly along the arc, carefully keeping the edges of the sticks against the pins.

The second method is to simply bend a batten so that it touches the apex and the two endpoints. You then eyeball the curve as you adjust the position of the battens where they extend past the end-point pins. Remember: To make the curve fair the stick needs to be of the appropriately sized cross section and be at least 20 percent to 30 percent longer than the arc segment being drawn. (If it's too short you'll discover that the stick tends to flatten out between the pins.)

When the curve looks fair, hold the extensions (past the end points) in place by setting pins against them or, as shown in the photo above, resting lead weights on them. For increased accuracy, especially on large project layouts (say the edge of a conference table), you can create more station points for the arc through a geometric construction.

A third way to draw an arc assumes you can access the focal point. (You can find the focus via geometry from your end and apex points as shown at right). The trick is to simply create a large compass by attaching trammel points to a long, straight stick. You set one point at the focus and the second trammel point (fitted with a pencil) at one end of the proposed arc, then swing the arc to the other endpoint.

FIG. 3.1.28. Stick set up with trammel points.

Making an Ellipse

To lay out an ellipse – which is, for our purposes here, essentially an arc with a changing radius – you can create a series of station points (see page 142) and then bend a batten to the points to draw the curve itself. The trick, though, is to get the batten to make the typically quick bend at the end of the long axis. The solution is to plane a taper into the batten so the wood becomes thin enough to accept the tight radius required. Its crucial that this batten has perfectly straight, continuous

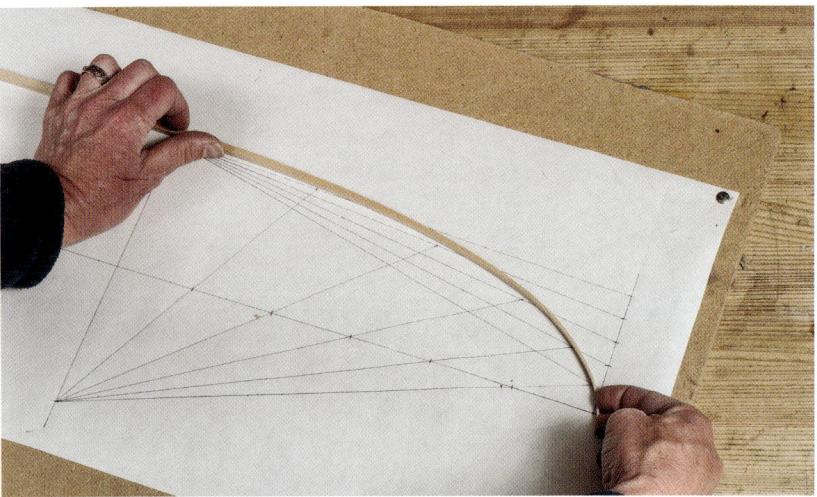

FIG. 3.1.29 . Bending a batten to ellipse station points. Note the taper of the batten.

FIG. 3.1.30. Using a stick (fitted with two set pins and a pencil) with a square to draw an ellipse.

TRADITIONAL TOOLS

grain or it is more liable to break. For creating small-sized ovals (as when making scale drawings or decorative layouts) you will find it easier to use one of the two geometric constructions as shown on page 143. (See also the animations available at lostartpress.com/geometry.)

Alternative methods for laying out an ellipse don't require station points and battens. Instead you can use a string and pencil – though a stick in conjunction with a square makes a more reliably precise construction. The stick and square method is also the way to go if you are going to be laying out more than a few of these shapes – then it's worth taking the time to make the stick with its required pins and pencil holder. You can set it up with a variety of pin locations for quick setups for your other commonly needed ellipses.

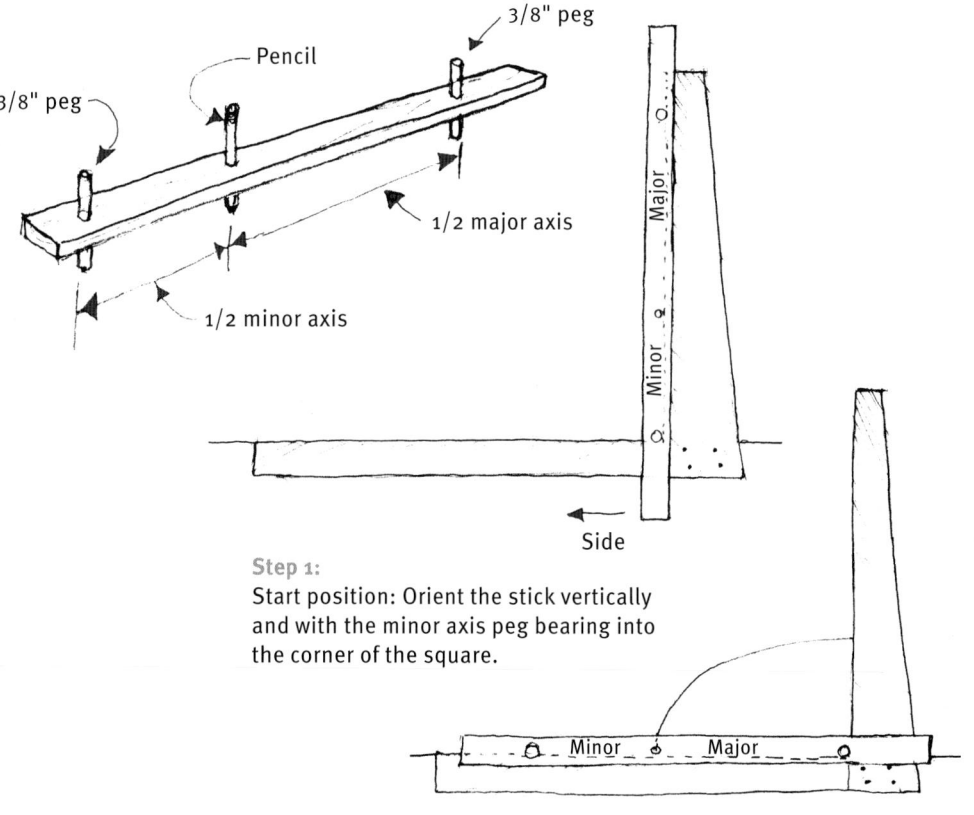

Step 1:
Start position: Orient the stick vertically and with the minor axis peg bearing into the corner of the square.

Step 2:
Slide the stick so the minor axis peg bears against the horizontal leg while the major axis peg slides down along the vertical leg. The pencil automatically draws one quadrant of the ellipse.

FIG. 3.1.31. Making an ellipse stick.

You'll also need a square to run the stick against, which can be a standard carpenter's 2' framing square clamped in place, or just two boards temporarily screwed or clamped in place at a right angle to one another. You may, however, want to build your own layout square for this and many other purposes.

Squares

For doing smaller-sized drawings, plastic drafting squares (which are simply templates of a right angle) in combination with a T-square are a quick way to draw a right angle – though I find it much easier to simply trace over the right-angle lines of the graph paper I lay under the drawing vellum. For the larger angles encountered in making full-scale furniture drawings, I'll either construct the right angle through geometry (explained later in this section), or I'll use a large shop-made square. This square also guides the ellipse stick for generating those shapes.

I make my layout square from relatively thin (about ⅝" thick to keep the weight down), straight-grained, clear cherry. The base is 3" wide by a little more than 3' long (a 1:13 ratio). I join the legs with a bridle or half-lap joint, being sure to make the shoulder cuts perfectly square to the trued edges of the legs. I bolt rather than glue the joint together because I want to be able to disassemble the square to true a leg if necessary.

FIG. 3.1.32. Large layout square; try square.

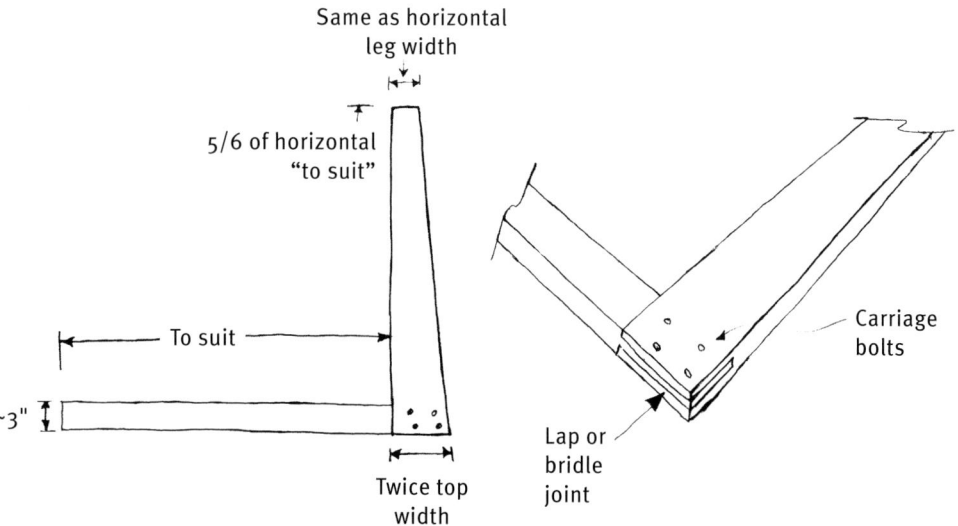

FIG. 3.1.33. Square for full-scale drawings (and for guiding an ellipse stick).

It's always a good idea to check to see if the square you are using is, in fact, square. The test for true is similar to that of the straightedge – you reverse the blade and check for deviation in the line, which doubles any error. The drawing below should make the process clear to you. Note that a metal combination square is difficult to fix while a wooden-bladed square is easily adjusted with a finely set handplane.

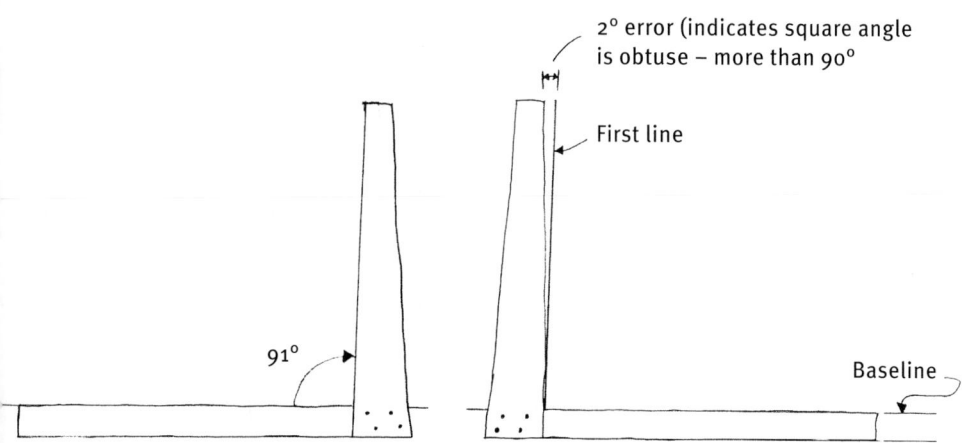

FIG. 3.1.34. Checking a square for true.

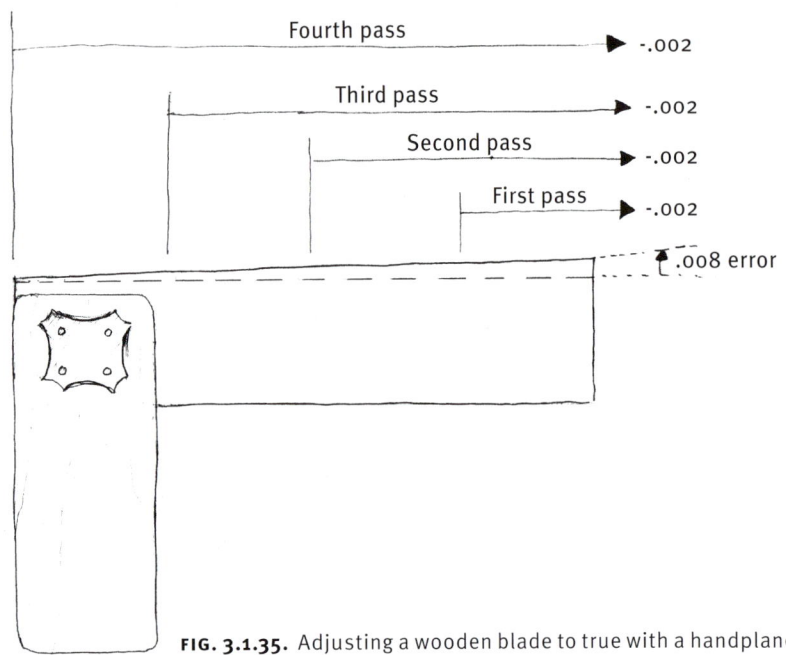

FIG. 3.1.35. Adjusting a wooden blade to true with a handplane.

Using a Square

When using a square, you generally need some way to index one of the legs to a baseline so you can trace a right angle to that baseline. Drafting squares are usually set against a T-square or other parallel support arm while layout squares index to the edge of the stock. A strip of wood fixed along one arm of the large layout square serves this purpose as does the thicker (than the tongue) handle of the try square when laying out cutlines.

Speaking of cutlines: To ensure you make them accurately (when it's appropriate and necessary to do so), always use a knife to mark the line and always fix the blade at the cut mark before moving the square into position. The cutline will then be exactly where it's supposed to be, and the knife line will serve as an indexing "tool track" for either the saw teeth or chisel edge. As our woodworking school's shop motto states: "Cut to the Line and You'll be Fine."

FIG. 3.1.36. Layout squares index the trued edge of the stock to mark a right angle.

TRADITIONAL TOOLS

121

FIG. 3.1.37. Marking cutline location with an awl referenced to story stick.

FIG. 3.1.38. Setting knife into awl point.

FIG. 3.1.39. Sliding square up to knife blade.

CHAPTER 2

FIG. 3.2.1. The square and compasses (the insignia of Freemasons, of which some period joiners were members) carved into stone. This is part of the foundation stone on a Masonic hall situated in the center of Lancaster in the United Kingdom.

Basic Geometric Constructions

I use simple, "rule and compass" generative geometry to create full-scale drawings for most of my projects. (As mentioned earlier, I use the stick and batten methods for doing larger layouts and other special cases.) As you get familiar with these ancient, artisan methods you will likely find, as I have, that they are as fast and accurate (if not more so) than working with numbered angles (via protractors) and dimensions (via numbered rulers). I admit and caution you up front, though, that it takes a bit of practice – and your full attention – to get these tools to work to the precision they are capable of. Assuming your points are sharp, we are talking about the potential for precision falling within one or two thousandths of an inch.

The constructions in this and the following chapters accomplish most of the tasks you will need to do when producing lines (and segments of lines) for scaled drawings. They are especially effective if you are designing to whole-number proportions rather than to measurements. Most of the constructions presented below are also shown as step-by-step animations you can download so you can observe in real time how they are produced.

Bisecting a Line Between Two Points

This construction not only finds the midpoint of a line between two points, but it produces

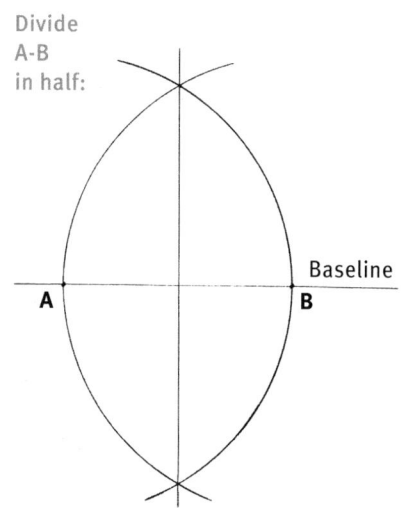

FIG. 3.2.2. Bisection.

a centerline at a right angle above and below the line at that midpoint. All you are really doing in this process is simply intersecting two circles and joining the intersection points. You'll use this technique for finding midpoints, for creating centerlines of symmetrical structures and as a step in creating a number of other more complex constructions.

Dividing a Line into Equal Segments Between Two Points

While you can always divide a line into equal segments by stepping off with dividers, it is a trial-and-error process that can sometimes take four or more tries to get right. This construction gets it right on the money in a short amount of time – no matter how many divisions you need to make. You'll use this construction for such tasks as laying out repetitive fastener and hardware spaces, evenly spacing decorative features and for laying out certain types of joints such as dovetails.

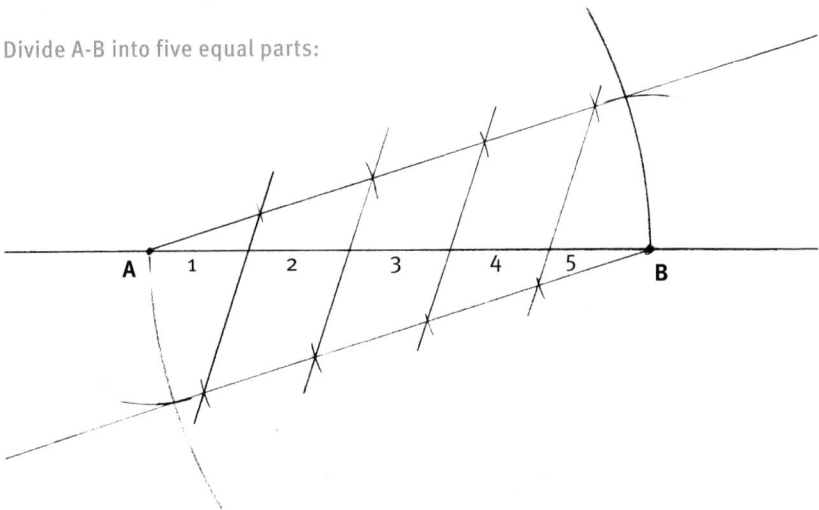

FIG. 3.2.3. Equal divisions.

Dividing a Line into Segments of a Specific Ratio

In the last construction, you saw how to divide a line into equal parts. In this variation, with hardly any additional effort, you can divide a line into different ratios. This makes quick work of laying out the relationship of components such as a line of drawer faces, locating hardware placement on door stiles and drawer faces and making decorative exposed joints.

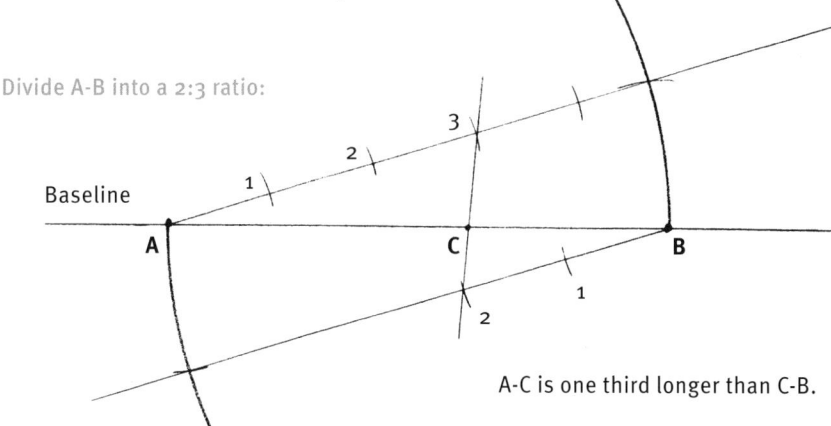

FIG. 3.2.4. Divisions to a ratio.

Erecting a Perpendicular from a Point on a Line

This is the first construction I do with almost every drawing because nearly any rectilinear object needs a right angle from its baseline. This method assumes you want to start from a fixed (rather than an arbitrary) point along the baseline. It's not deceptively simple – it really is simple. In essence all you do is swing a circle from above the line so that its circumference passes through your start point. You then draw a couple of lines through certain intersections. These lines form a right angle within the circle, with the corner at your set point. This bit of geometric magic is the product of the first-known mathematical proof in recorded history.

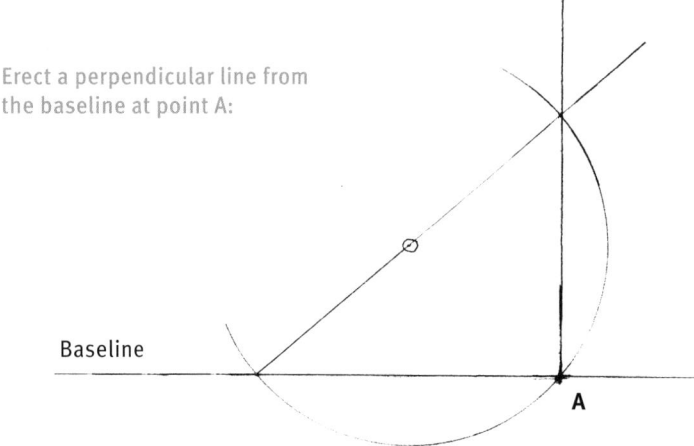

FIG. 3.2.5. Perpendicular from a line point.

Dropping a Perpendicular from a Point Above a Line

In certain instances, you may find it necessary to erect the perpendicular from a point away from a baseline. This construction shows one method that is simple and quick to execute.

Drop a line down from point P that will intersect the baseline at a right angle:

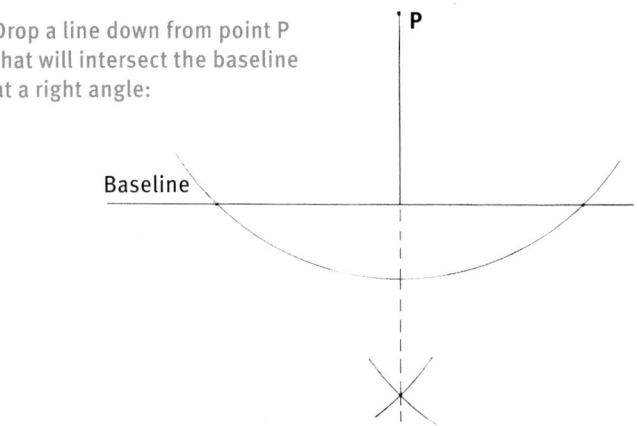

FIG. 3.2.6. Perpendicular from a point away from baseline.

Erecting a 45° Angle from a Point on a Line

By the time you carefully position a protractor or drafting template to draw out a half-right angle (i.e. 45°) you could just as easily (and with probably more accuracy) use geometry to accomplish the same task. You'll use this construction for laying out everything from angled case sides (think New England corner cabinet) to the cutlines of miter shooting boards and boxes.

Erect a 45° angle from a point along a baseline:

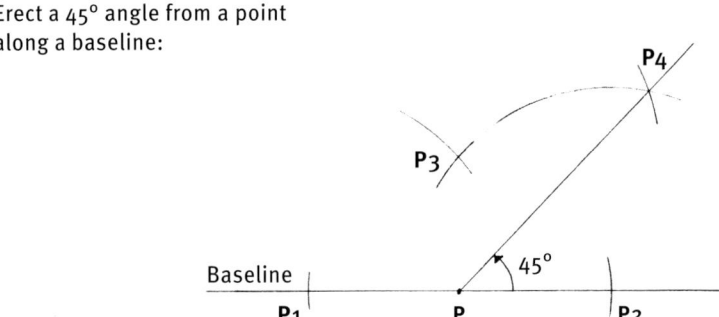

FIG. 3.2.7. A 45° angle from a line point.

Bisecting an Angle

Whenever you need to know the bisected angle (not necessarily the number, but the actual angle itself) of two intersecting lines, this construction is the way to quickly produce it. The most common application is to find the miter angle for the framework that will conjoin to the full angle. Think picture frame but without right angles.

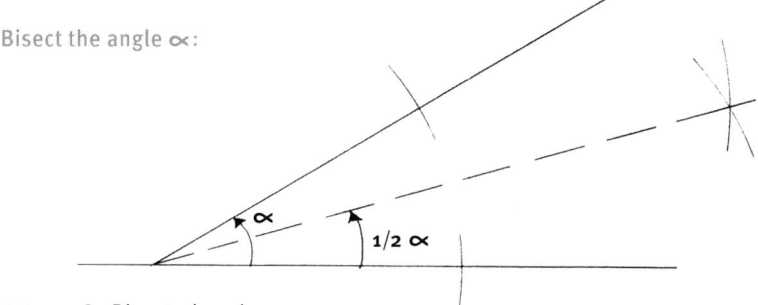

FIG. 3.2.8. Bisected angle.

Trisecting an Angle

Yes, it is impossible to derive to finite precision a trisected angle using traditional rule and compass construction. However, it can be done to real-world, practical accuracy using a "neusis" trick from Archimedes (see the "Rabbit Holes" page at georgewalkerdesign.com). I've also devised an even easier method that is just as accurate for our purposes – though it does require stepping out with the dividers. This method not only works to trisect the angle, but to divide it into any number of equal angles. You may occasionally use this method for laying out decorative patterns, but mostly you'll use it to impress your friends and confound your enemies.

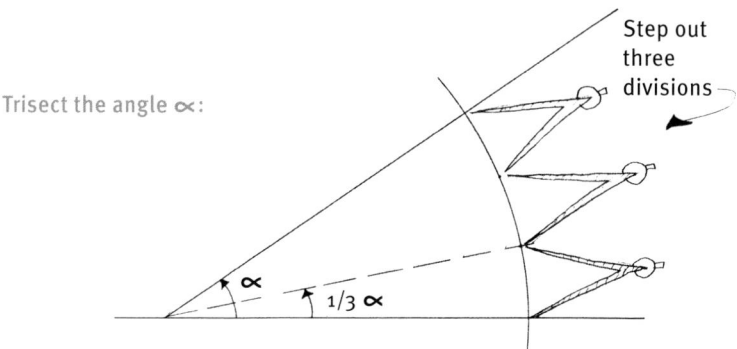

FIG. 3.2.9. Trisected angle.

CHAPTER 3

FIG. 3.3.1. Geometric shapes within a highboy.

Generating Shapes

Once you've gotten down the basic geometric constructions of lines covered in the last chapter, it's not much more of a leap to generate shapes from those lines. In this chapter I'll show you how to generate squares and their stretched-out iterations (i.e. rectangles). Then we'll move on through a very simple triangle into polygons of five and more sides. You can make any type of polygon, within reasonable accuracy, with a single construction. There are, however, simpler constructions for generating a hexagon (six-sided) and octagon (eight-sided).

Erecting a Square from Two Points on a Line

When you have a baseline (and who doesn't?) and you intersect that baseline with a circle to create a perpendicular line as shown earlier, you are less than a stone's throw away from generating an actual shape. I'll start you off with the second-most basic shape (after the circle) I can think of: the square. In this construction, we'll generate a square by connecting the intersection points of four circles. We'll assume you have already established a baseline and two points that define the width of the square you wish to generate.

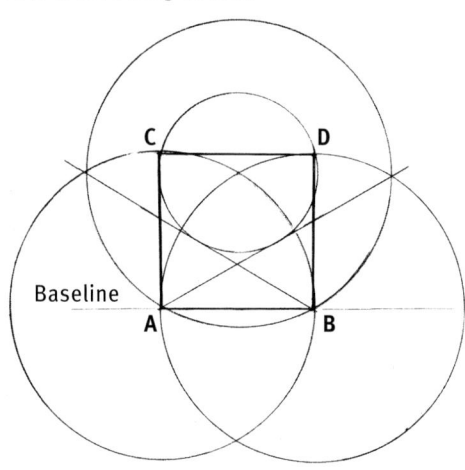

Four intersecting circles:

FIG. 3.3.2. Erect a square from line A-B.

An Alternative (Slightly Quicker) Method Of Generating a Square

This is a bit simpler way to make a square because it involves intersecting only three circles. I find it more intuitive, and if that's true for you it may become your preferred method.

Harmonic Expansion Of a Rectangle

As George showed you earlier in the book, artisans developed rectangular forms from squares – and in fact categorized these rectangles as a function of the square. A "square-and-a-half," for example, was a rectangle that was one-and-one-half times longer than its width – which works out to a 2:3 ratio. "Two square" was simply a rectangle twice as long as its width – and therefore a 1:2 ratio. Many of the ratios were considered by early builders to be "harmonic" – that is, they were musically tonal ratios as proposed by Pythagoras for use in creating shapes (i.e. 1:2 equals an octave, 2:3 equals a fourth,

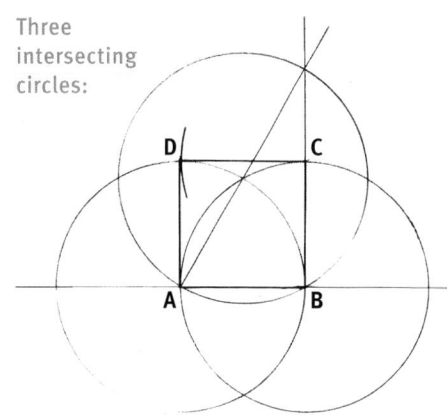

Three intersecting circles:

FIG. 3.3.3. Alternative erection of a square.

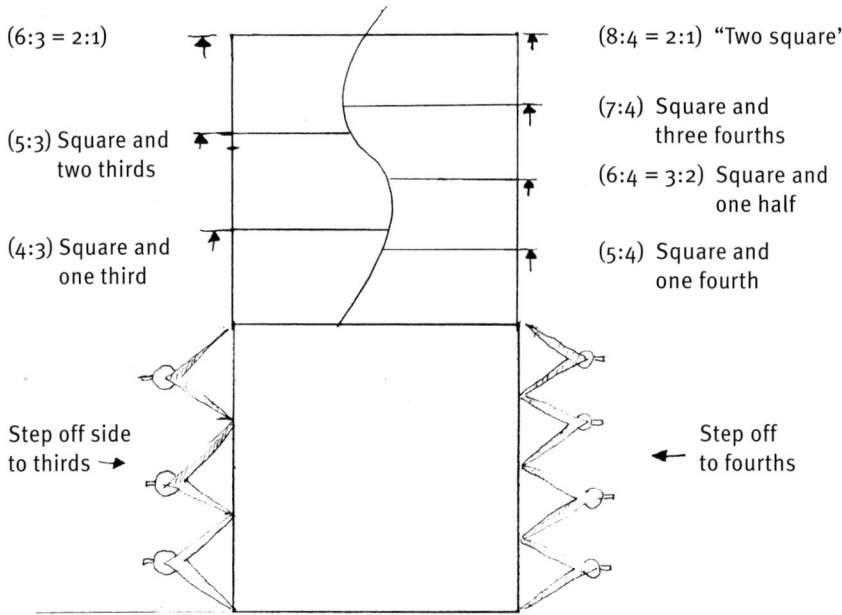

FIG. 3.3.4. Harmonic expansion of a rectangle.

and 3:4 equals a fifth). We humans like the sound of these ratios, and we seem to like the look of them as well. Using dividers (and, optionally, a sector to speed things up) you can, as shown in the drawing and animation, quickly produce a rectangle at any whole-number ratio to its square base.

Graduated Rectangles

This geometric construction develops an arithmetic proportional relationship (i.e. each unit grows by a certain, fixed amount) amongst a stack of rectangles. You'll find it extremely efficient and useful to lay out graduated drawer faces. In this example, we'll add the width of the blade that will separate the drawers: none to the first face, one to the second, two to the third etc. Because for practical reasons we are assuming the stack has to fit in a certain vertical space (i.e., between the top and bottom of the dresser) we start by determining the height of the first drawer face, choosing in this case, one-sixth of the height of the opening.

Lay out a bank of drawers with a progression equal to the intervening blade given the top drawer face is one-sixth the height of the opening:

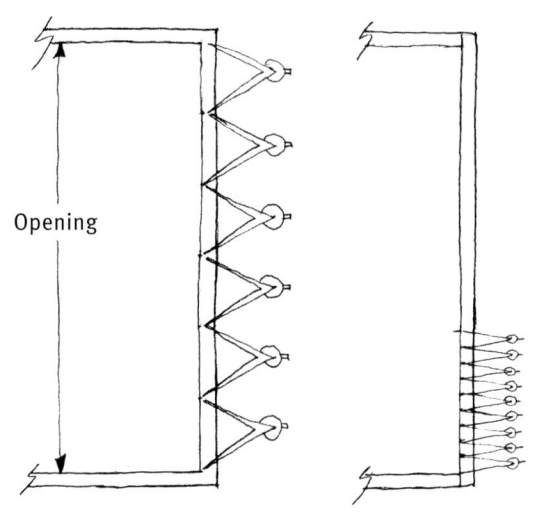
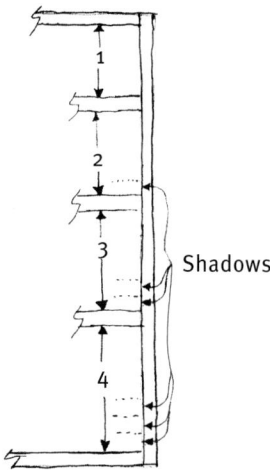

Step 1:
Step out six divisions of the available opening.

Step 2:
Step out nine divisions of bottom two sixths. (Three of these divisions represent the intervening blades; six are the "shadow" blades added sequentially to each drawer face.)

Step 3:
- Step out a sixth, add an intervening blade.
- Step out a sixth, add one "shadow" blade and second intervening blade.
- Repeat, adding two shadows and one intervening.
- Remaining space will be a sixth plus three shadows.

FIG. 3.3.5. Laying out a bank of drawers.

Generating a Geometric Expansion of a Rectangle (Expanded From one Corner of a Square)

In nature, geometric expansion (which is also called "diffusion" symmetry) is ubiquitous throughout the known universe – from the structure of the atom to that of galaxies. It's also the way many living things grow: expanding out from a single point with all dimensions maintaining a proportional relationship with one another. (In other words, the shape stays the same no matter the size.)

The drawing below shows you how incredibly simple it is to expand a rectangle by simply extending a diagonal line. Also note that because proportions also stay the same within the shape, you can easily maintain harmony between internal elements such as rails and stiles. You'll see how I applied this convenient truth in several of my projects in the next section of the book.

Expand a rectangle geometrically (example, by one third):

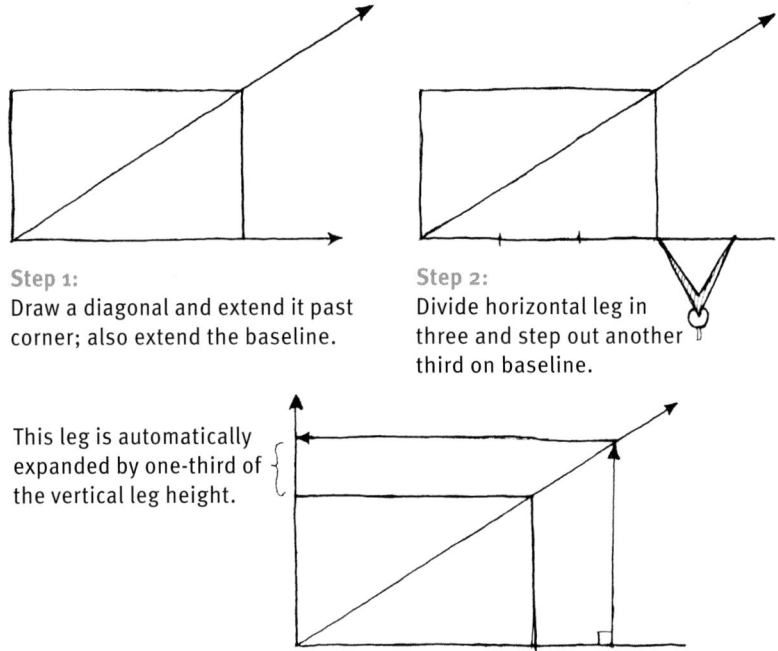

Step 1:
Draw a diagonal and extend it past corner; also extend the baseline.

Step 2:
Divide horizontal leg in three and step out another third on baseline.

This leg is automatically expanded by one-third of the vertical leg height.

FIG. 3.3.6. Geometric expansion of a rectangle.

Geometric expansion in a Fibonacci series (see Figs. 3.3.7a and 7b) is found throughout nature. This expansion process allows leaves on a branch to achieve the best spacing and orientation possible for capturing sunlight, it arranges seeds to maximize their number in the smallest amount of space and it allows our own bodies (specifically, the spacing of our joints and limbs) to move efficiently whether walking or building furniture. Also notice what happens when we trace the effect of the expansion by swinging a quadrant of a circle from each corner of each square. Look familiar?

Each expansion is the sum of the two prior numbers:
1 → 1:1 → 1:2 → 2:3 → 3:5 → 5:8

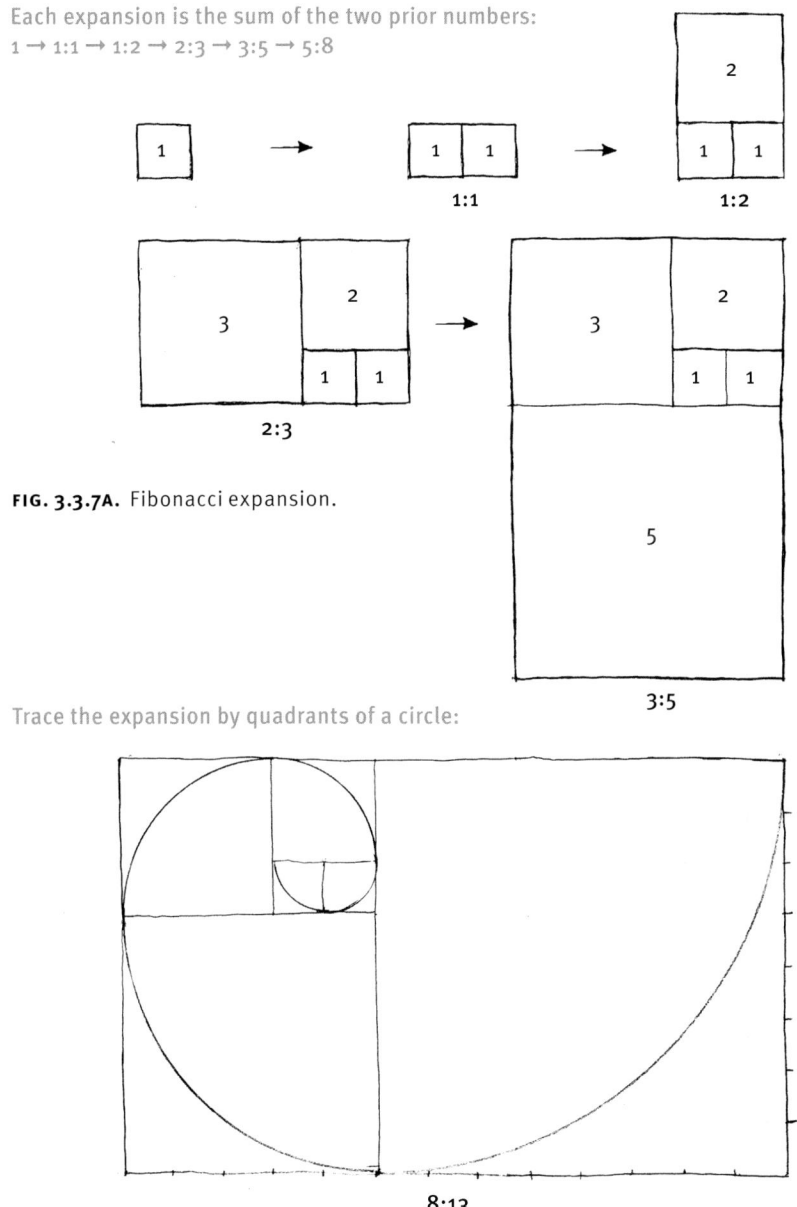

FIG. 3.3.7A. Fibonacci expansion.

Trace the expansion by quadrants of a circle:

FIG. 3.3.7B. Expansion in quadrants of a circle.

Erecting an Equilateral Triangle from Two Points on a Line

Need to make an equilateral triangle (a shape in which each corner angle is 60°)? This construction is an amazingly quick and fun exercise to do. All you need is a line with two points that define one leg of your triangle and a compass set to that spacing. Basically, you're just going to intersect two circles and draw lines to that intersection point. Later in this section, you'll see that because an equilateral triangle inscribes one-sixth of a circle (because 60° is one-sixth of 360°), the length of the legs is also the radius of that circle – and that allows you to quickly generate certain curves.

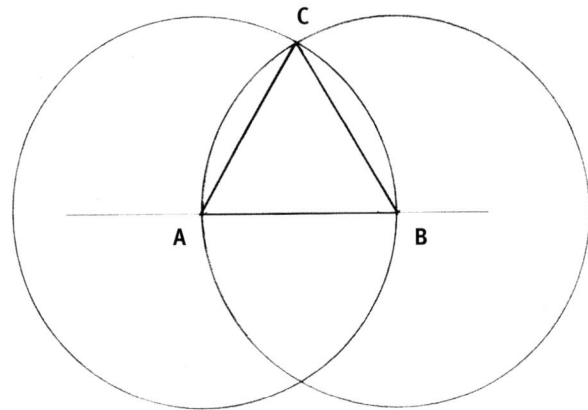

FIG. 3.3.8. Erection of an equilateral triangle.

Generating Polygons of Five or More Sides

This is an old artisan trick for creating polygons with any number of sides. Certain polygons (seven- and 11-sided, for example) cannot be produced to finite accuracy with this method but, again, they will be close enough for us woodworkers. To use this construction to draw other polygons (the example shows a pentagon), you simply step out the number of segments equal to the number of sides desired. You will always lay out the first facet to the second segment. Notice that any line drawn from a vertex to the center of the polygon provides the miter angle for building a framework to form that polygon.

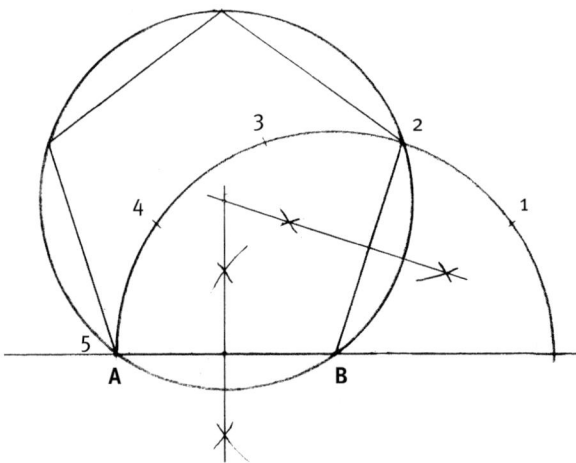

FIG. 3.3.9. Polygon generation (this example is a pentagon).

Special Case: Hexagon

Six-sided polygons, because their facets equal the radius of the circle that inscribes the form, can be drawn using a simpler construction as shown at right. Basically, what's happening is the fitting of six equilateral triangles into the inscribing circle.

Note that you can also work backward to find the radius of a circle by creating a hexagon: With a pair of dividers, step out along the circumference of the circle until you achieve six equal divisions. Connecting the division points produces a hexagon – and the facet length is equal to the radius of the circle.

Construct a hexagon from points A-B on a line:

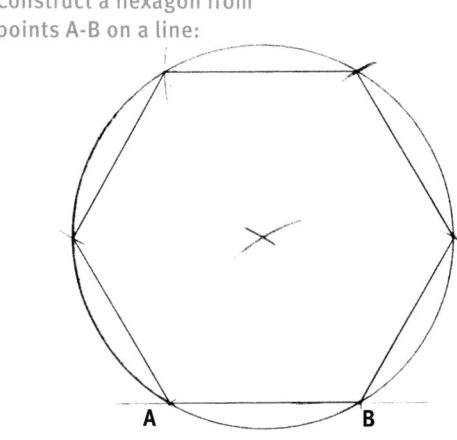

FIG. 3.3.10. Hexagon generation.

Special Case: Octagon

To develop an octagon, you can either segment a circle into eight parts, or you can truncate the corners of a square. The drawings below show both methods. Either are a bit faster to execute than the generic polygon method shown earlier.

Construct an octagon within a circle:

Construct an octagon within a square:

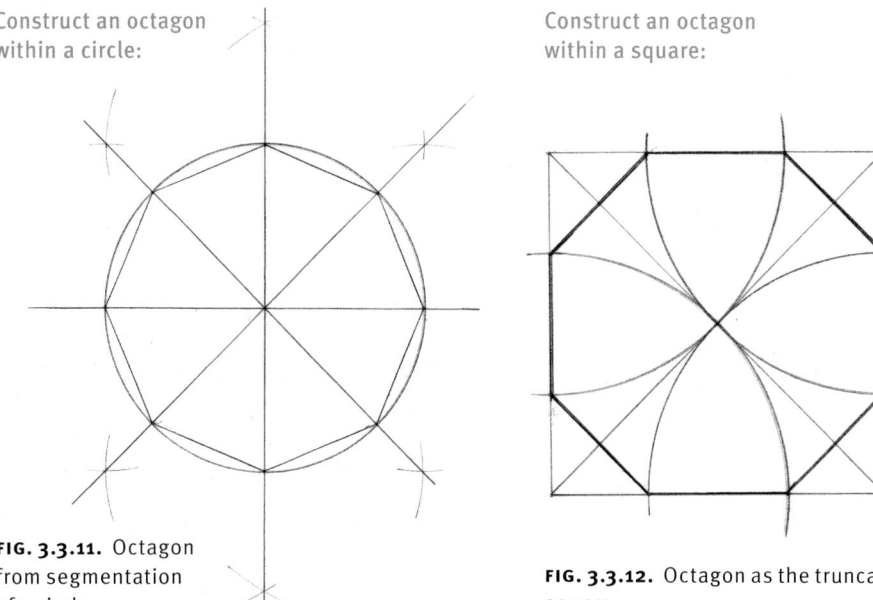

FIG. 3.3.11. Octagon from segmentation of a circle.

FIG. 3.3.12. Octagon as the truncation of square.

CHAPTER 4

FIG. 3.4.1. This furniture piece beautifully blends arc forms with the shape of the hardware and the natural swirls of the drawer face graining.

Generating Curves & Tapers

So what's this "thing" we have about arcs? We seem to love them. Not surprisingly they are, as I'm sure you've noticed, one of the most common design elements applied to our built world – from the lofty entryways of cathedrals to the sweeping supporting structures of bridges to the raised "eyebrow" of a cabinet door. Once again, we have to go with conjecture for an explanation for this love affair, but I think most people agree that they make a structure look inherently strong – and in fact, the arc generally does make them stronger. Consider these natural examples: the supporting swelling under a tree branch or the arched opening of a cave. Both of these elements are essentially curb appeal in that they provide us with the visual cue that we will be safe taking shelter beneath or within them.

Arc from Station Points

We use this type of geometric construction (in which we are essentially generating a proportional expansion of a circle) to establish a number of station points to which you can bend a batten. You'll find this method useful for producing large

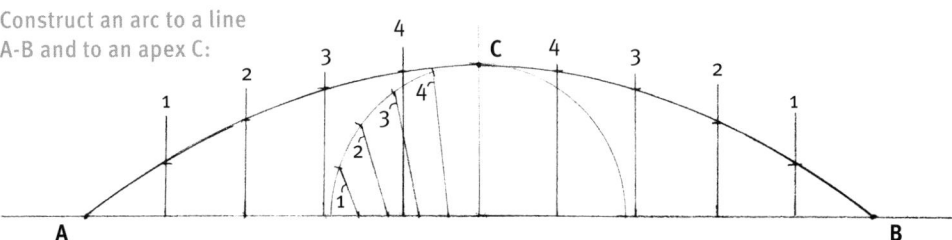

FIG. 3.4.2. Expansion from circle to arc.

arcs (again, like the edge of a conference table or in architectural work) where it would be unwieldy, if not impossible, to generate the arc with either joined sticks or a trammel point set to a focal point. Note that you aren't limited to the four station points shown in this example; the more you choose to use, the more accurately you can make the arc.

Arc Relative to Chord

In this construction we are drawing an arc to our choice of curvature between two fixed points. We don't care about the height of the apex, but rather the degree of curvature. (Gentle curves were traditionally referred to as "slow," while more dramatic bends were called "fast.") I came up with this construction to allow me to not only quickly change an arc's radius, but to do so at a certain proportion – that is, to a defined segment of a circle. My friend, Dr. Francis Natali, worked up a spreadsheet (see the "Rabbit Holes" page at george walkerdesign.com) that shows the amount of error between radius and segment produced by this construction. I was gratified to see that for segments between one-sixth and a one-twelfth (which are perfect), the error was less than 1 percent. When you go below a sixth, however, the accuracy is severely compromised with this method.

The drawing and animation show a ninth-segment generation. To change the segment to another value, simply set the focal point to another one-sixth of the chord division point along the bisector.

Why might this be important – or at least useful? My experience indicates that choosing a specific value segment gets you very quickly to an appropriate degree of curvature for the overall shape of the structure. I think you'll see this clearly in the way I arrived at curvatures in a number of my projects that we review later in the book.

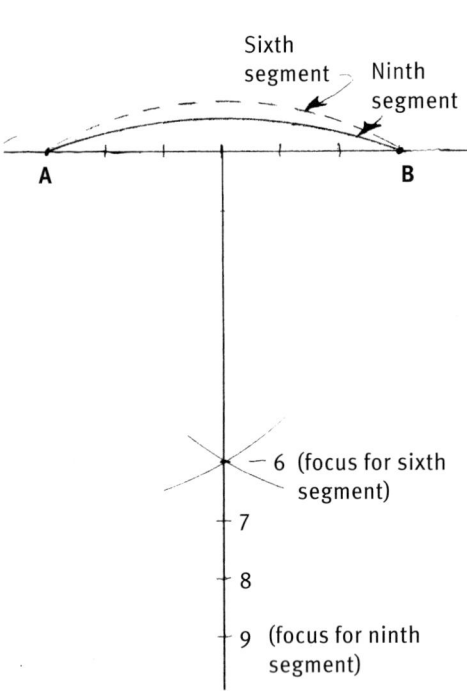

FIG. 3.4.3. Arc to chord construction.

Locating a Focal Point

Let's say you know the endpoints of the arc you want to draw, and you know how high (i.e. the apex) you want it to reach. You also want to draw it out with either a compass or a set of trammel points on a beam. What you need to know next, then, is where to put the focal point of the compass or trammel point – which is, of course, the focal point of the circle that will generate the arc segment you are looking for. This simple construction reveals that point.

Generating a 'Gothic' Arch

Are you into Goth? Or do you forgo the white face powder and black capes and just appreciate the brooding design? If so, then this construction is for you. It's simple, it's easy and it makes a very pretty double arc. I'm

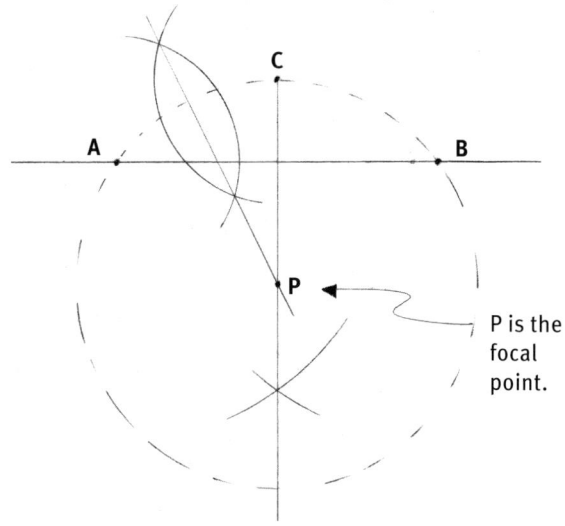

Find the focal point of the circle that passes through points A and B on a line and through the apex C:

P is the focal point.

FIG. 3.4.4. Finding an arc's focal point.

Construct a Gothic arch:

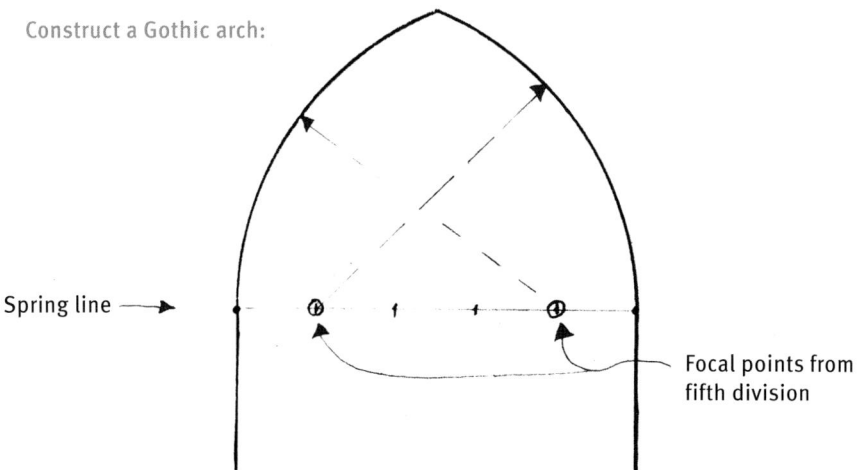

Spring line

Focal points from fifth division

FIG. 3.4.5. Gothic arch construction.

FIG. 3.4.6. This magnificent secretary employs Gothic arches atop its divided-light doors.

showing the traditional version in which the height of the arc's intersection is made lower than the width of the opening – specifically, to a focal point set to one-fifth of the width at the "spring line."

Generating a 'Lancet' Arc

Or maybe you have a thing for Sir Lancelot…or perhaps you just like arcs with a bit more reach. In either case, you will be well-met to learn this construction, which is only slightly more difficult to execute than the already easy Gothic arc. The traditional Lancet arc is always higher than it is wide, which means the focal point of the arcs are set outside the opening. Traditionally, the focal point was set to plus $1/5$ of the span at the spring line, which is why the Lancet arc was also called a "pointed fifth." The apex of the arc is, as a result, in a 4:5 ratio with the chord (span).

FIG. 3.4.7. This contemporary church furnishing is based on a Lancet arc.

Construct a Lancet arch:

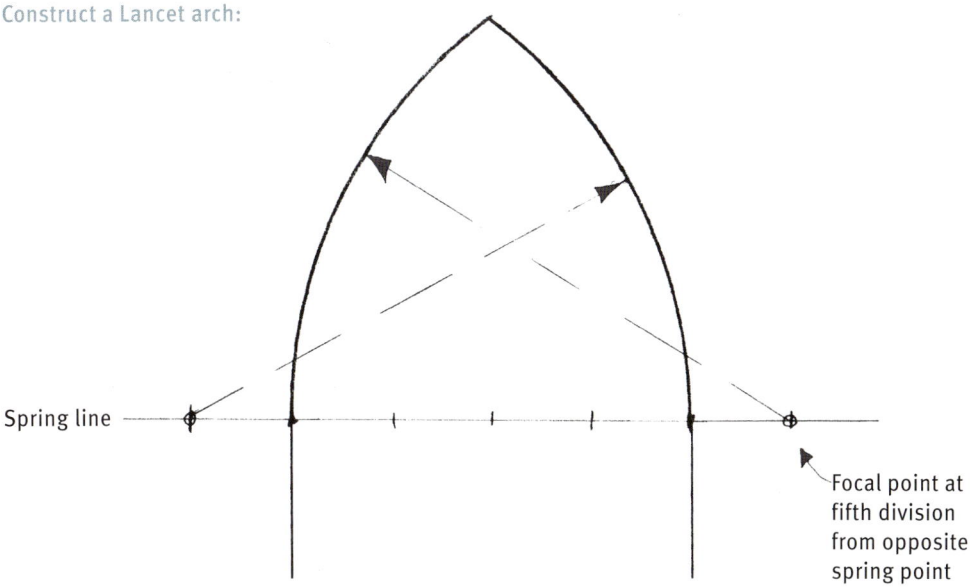

Spring line

Focal point at fifth division from opposite spring point

FIG. 3.4.8. Lancet arch construction.

Ellipse

If you like arcs, you probably really like the ellipse. It's a common furniture element found everywhere, from traditional moulding profiles to primary styling elements such as those seen in Thomas Moser's contemporary furniture line. They are also relatively easy to generate as I showed you earlier, using the pegged stick and square method. Here, though, you'll see how to execute various geometric constructions. The first is appropriate for creating large ellipses that would be too cumbersome for the stick and square. The next two are best for smaller-scale drawings and can be readily executed using only a compass and straightedge.

FIG. 3.4.9. The ellipse is often used as a decorative element.

An Elliptical Arch from Station Points

This construction produces a series of station points generated from intersections arising from lines drawn from equal divisions along the major and minor axis of the desired ellipse. The more divisions you step out along the axis, the more numerous – and potentially more accurate – the resultant stations points. If you are careful in using the dividers and straightedge, you can make a very large and accurate ellipse (or a portion thereof).

Construct an elliptical arch from points A-B on a line and to an apex point C:

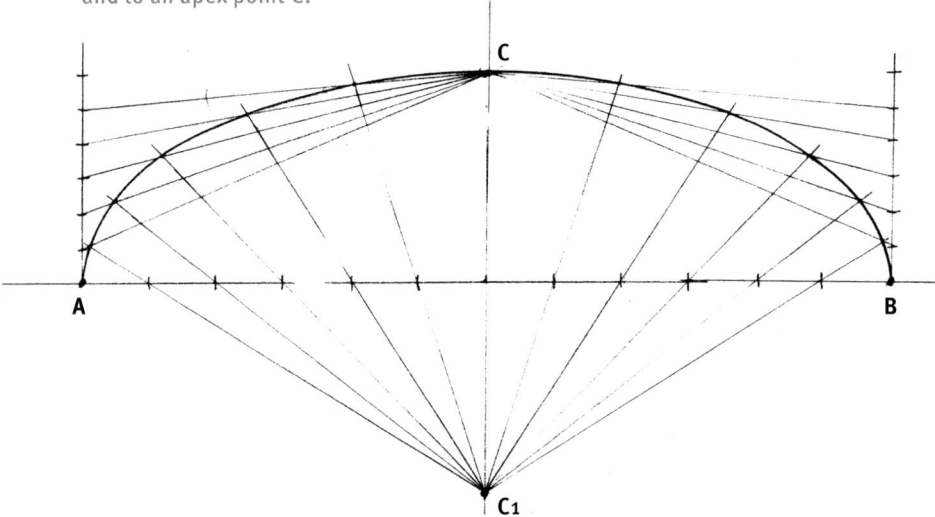

FIG. 3.4.10. Semi-ellipse station point generation.

An Oval from Melded Circles

In this construction you will find four focal points for a pair of different-sized circles. The melded intersections of the two large circles with the two smaller circles produce a visually acceptable ellipse – especially at the size of scaled drawings. (Technically, the form is an oval because a true ellipse has a constantly changing radius.)

This version assumes you want to form the ellipse to a set width and height (i.e. major and minor axis). The apex-to-major-axis ratio must range from between 1:3 to 2:5 for this construction to work.

An Oval to a Fixed Width

This version of the melded circle construction assumes you are only concerned with the width of the ellipse and can let the height (or the apex in the case of a

Construct an oval to a fixed width and apex:

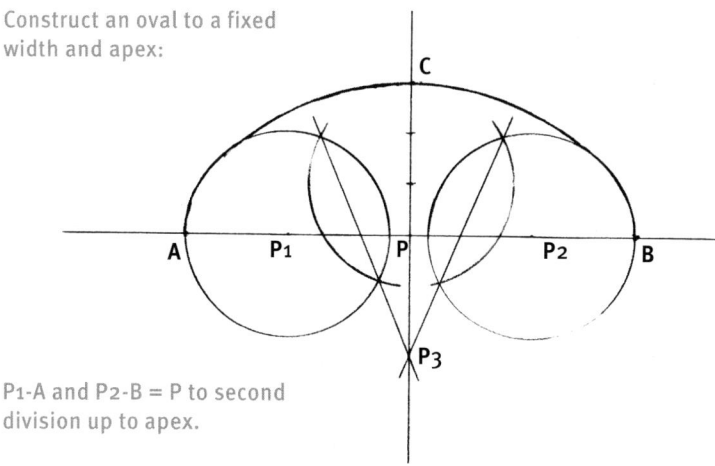

P1-A and P2-B = P to second division up to apex.

FIG. 3.4.11. Oval generation from melded circles – fixed width and height.

Construct an oval to a fixed width; "floating" apex:

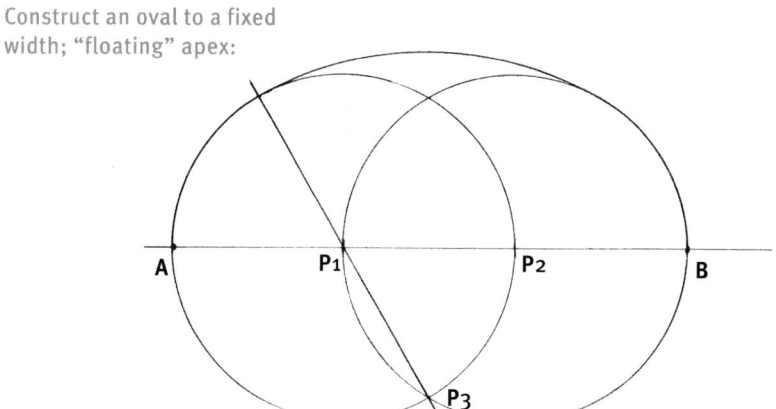

FIG. 3.4.12. Developing an oval from melded circles – fixed width only.

semi-ellipse) float. The apex-to-major-axis ratio automatically comes out to about a 1:3 ratio.

Volutes

It looks pretty complicated at first, but for creating large-sized spirals all it takes is four nails and a pencil tied to a piece of string to create a visually acceptable form. The starting radius is adjusted by the length of the string while the rate of change in radius as the string swings around and bears against a different focal point is determined by where you place the four nails in a grid. Basically, all you are doing is creating a sequence of quarter-circles of diminishing radii. For scale drawings

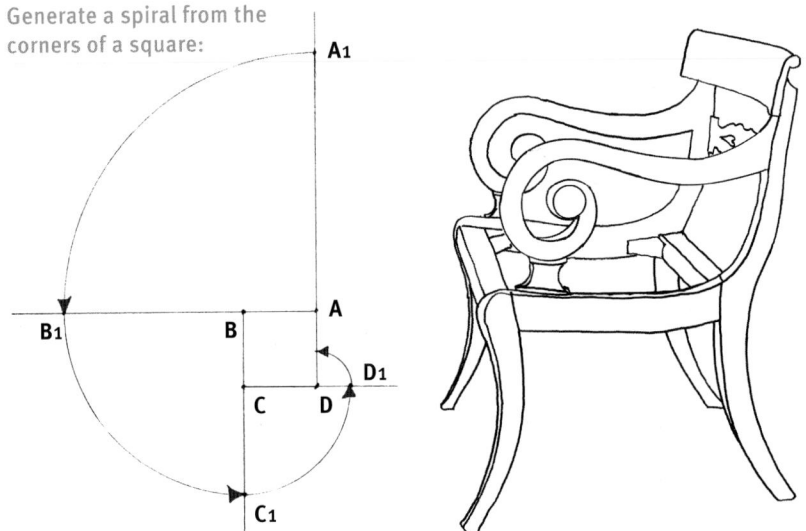

FIG. 3.4.13. Volute in furniture piece.

FIG. 3.4.14. Volute generated from a gridwork of focal points.

and smaller layouts you can, more practically, forgo the string and use a compass as illustrated in the animation (download at lostartpress.com/geometry).

After doing at least one drawing using a grid of focal points set at the corners of a square as shown above in Fig. 3.4.13, play around with the grid layout. Try a rectangle pattern and notice how it "quickens" the spiral in two of the quadrants (because the longer side of the rectangle increases the radius' rate of change). You can also experiment with other grid patterns such as a hexagon, or even an ellipse. You'll notice that the greater the number of focal points, the more tedious it becomes to use a compass – so in this case revert back to the string and pencil technique.

Tapers

Earlier, I introduced you to the sector and to a simple way of laying out tapered planks between two spans (see: "Task 2: Maintaining Proportional Divisions from One Station to Another" on page 108). This method works fine for straight lines, but what if you would like to make the taper curve slightly outward (for reasons I'll get into below)?

To do that, we'll reach back into antiquity for the simple geometric method that the ancients developed to create this convex taper (which the Greeks later named "entasis"). For millennia, artisans used this method to lay out everything from the pyramids in Egypt to the Parthenon's columns in Greece, to the radiator grilles of a Rolls Royce.

But why did they bother with this subtle – and obviously labor-intensive – curved tapering? The answer is aesthetics and therefore subjective. What happens is that long vertical objects with straight sides – and even straight tapered sides – tend to look concave to the eye because of parallax. For most people, this concavity tends to make the object – especially columns that are obviously supporting massive weight – look less sturdy. After all, when we see a person holding up a heavy object, we are used to seeing the muscles strain and bulge. Our entire musculature is, from one point of view, a study in entasis. There may be other reasons entasis is ubiquitous, but I'm going with this one.

As you can see in the drawing at right, developing entasis is, once again, a simple matter of choosing and laying out whole-number ratios. In this example, I decided to apply the entasis to the top two-thirds of the column shaft and to reduce the shaft's width by ⅙. Note that I chose to use just two station points which to spring the layout batten for drawing the curve. You can develop more points if you wish by simply increasing the number of divisions of the upper two-thirds of the column.

FIG. 3.4.15. Note the curved taper of the legs of this demilune table – an application of entasis.

Lay out a convex taper where one end is one-sixth narrower than opposite end. Start the taper at one-third of the overall length.

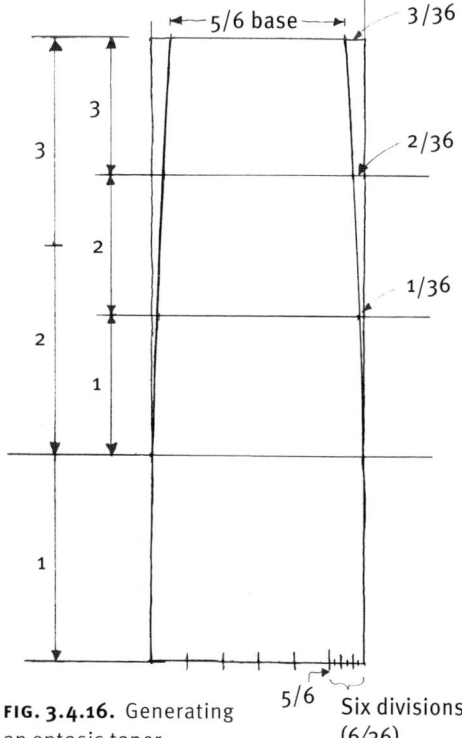

FIG. 3.4.16. Generating an entasis taper.

CHAPTER 5

FIG. 3.5.1. Moulding profiles.

Developing Moulding Profiles

When you understand – which means when you put into practice – the practical geometry of the artisans, you experience how it really is quite straightforward to generate elegant moulding profiles. Earlier in the book George talked about the proportions commonly found in classical mouldings that related the shapes to one another. Here in this practicum of applied constructive geometry, I'm going to illustrate a few of the more basic constructions for developing the curves found in many of the profiles.

Generating a Sine Curve

One of the more common (and appealing) family of moulding profiles incorporates a reversing curve – which I believe is reflective of the forces being transitioned from a vertical to a horizontal surface. The cyma recta – which calls to mind the spreading out of a tree's root system just above the ground – is often used to cap baseboards or the aprons of larger furniture pieces. The

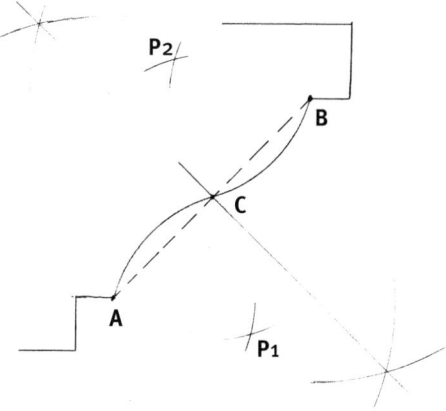

Develop a sine curve along a line A-B:

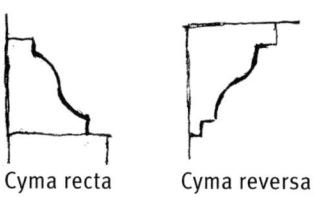

Cyma recta   Cyma reversa

FIG. 3.5.2. Sine curve generation.

cyma reversa – which you can imagine as a reflection of the under-swelling of tree branches where they join the trunk – often underlies (and indicates support of) overhangs.

The reversing curve of these profiles is a simple sine waveform that you can easily create between two points using only a compass and about one minute of your time. As you'll see in the animation, you're simply going to bisect the line to find its midpoint, then swing out one-sixth sector of a circle – one convex and one concave – to either side of this point. Again, a round of applause for the hexagon in which the radius equals the facet length.

Tweaking Curves Faster

If you would like to make the curves a bit more dramatic (what was traditionally called "faster") then you make a proportional adjustment to the radius of the curves so they describe a larger segment of the circle. In this example, the radius has been lessened by one-sixth of the span between the endpoints (i.e. the chord of the circle being segmented). This produces a one-fifth sector, and therefore a tighter radius curve between the points.

Changing Proportions of a Sine Curve

Another tweak: The opposing curves do not necessarily have to be equal in length. In Fig. 3.5.4 below, I divided the generation line span into five parts and made the upper curve three divisions long. The curves are thus in a 3:2 ratio to one another.

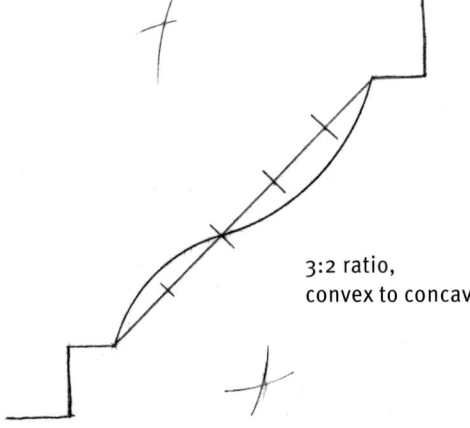

"Tweak" the curve "faster:"

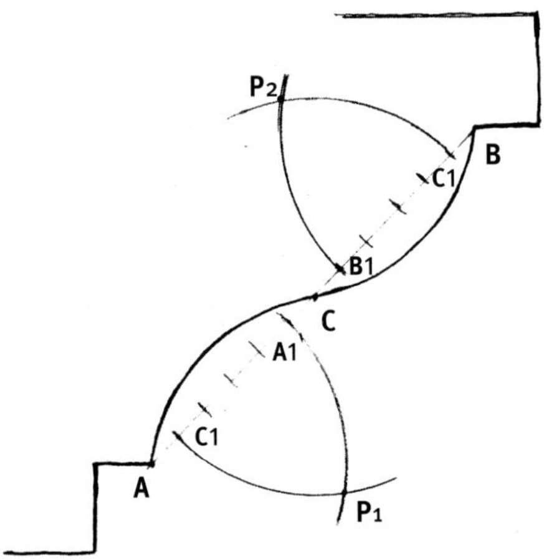

Make the convex section one-third larger than the concave section:

3:2 ratio, convex to concav[e]

FIG. 3.5.3. Tweaked curves.

FIG. 3.5.4. Changing proportions of sine curve

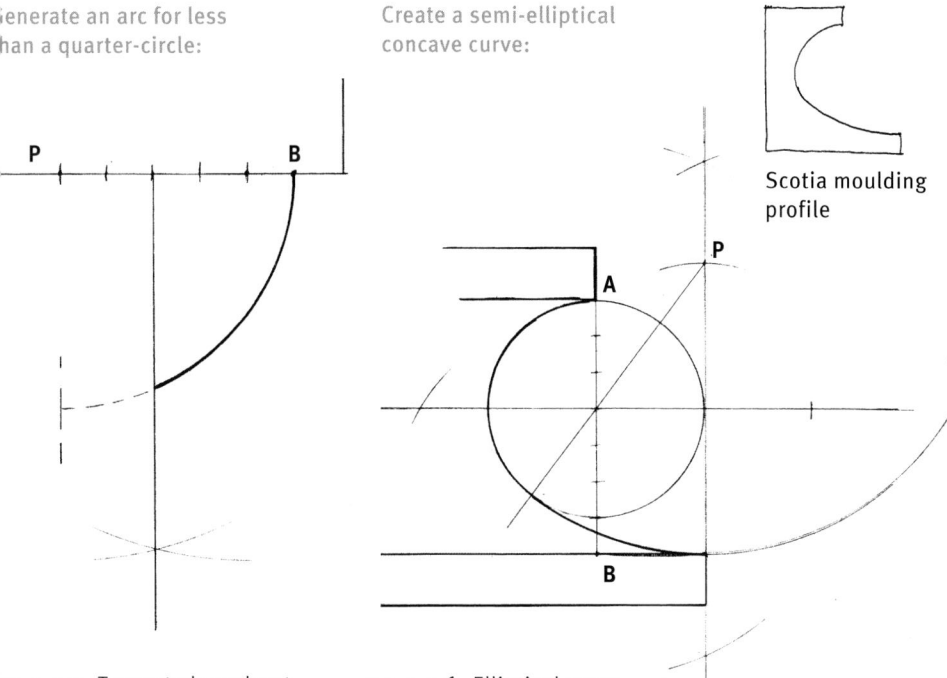

FIG. 3.5.5. Truncated quadrant.   FIG. 3.5.6. Elliptical curve.

Developing a Truncated Quadrant

A quarter of a circle in a moulding profile is actually somewhat rare – they are almost always not quite a quadrant. Why? I think because the truncation produces a more graceful – and less boring – curve. It's also quick and easy to execute as you can see in the animation (download at lostartpress.com/geometry).

Developing Semi-elliptical Curves

Now if you really want to get fancy – and have a bit of fun doing so – try adding a bit of an elliptical curve to the profile. As you can see, this is how the ubiquitous scotia moulding is laid out. It looks a little complicated at first, but it actually quickly becomes intuitive after a few run-throughs. You'll also notice that the construction not only produces the curve, but it tells you where to start and stop it.

Conclusion

With a bit of practice, you will become adept at developing these curved profiles with your straightedge and compass. When you do it enough, you get a grasp of just how the geometry of the circle is being applied to the overall form – and at that point you'll likely find that you can fairly accurately draw the profiles freehand.

SECTION IV

Projects

1
Step Stool

2
Candy Box

3
Lap Desk

4
Tool Tote

5
Boot Bench

6
Coffee-for-two Tray

7
Cup Cabinet

8
Side Table

9
Vanity

CHAPTER 1

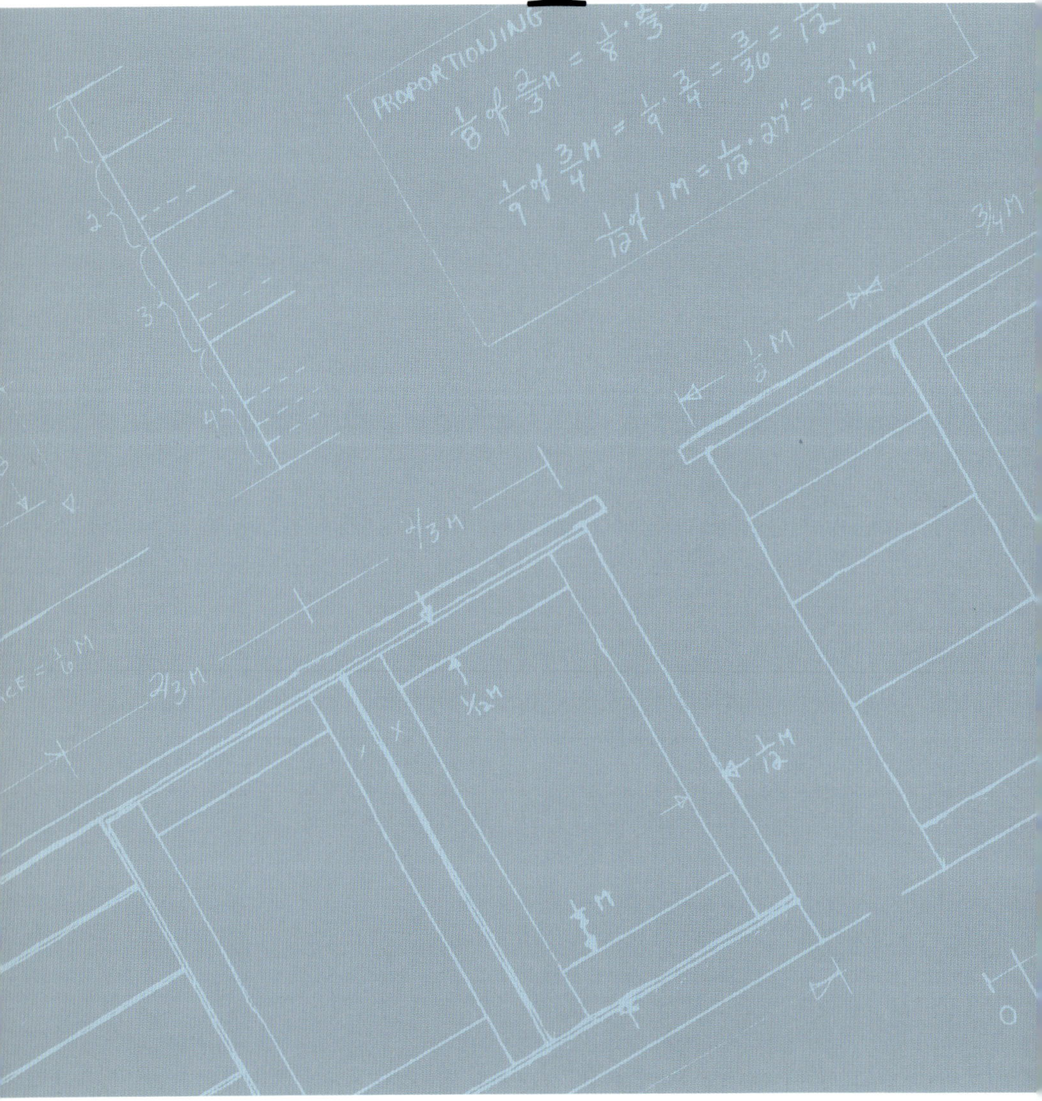

FIG. 4.1.1. It's time to show how the principles in this book can be applied to all your furniture designs.

About the Projects

In this section, I'm going to present some projects I built over the course of working on this book. (No electrons were harmed in the making of any of them, by the way; all were produced with hand tools.) The fundamental design strategy for each of these projects is right out of the ancients' playbook: I developed all the dimensions, as well as the radius of the curves, by trying and then applying simple ratios to a "base one" module. Sometimes this module was a dimensional starting point for the project while other times it would arise later as the most convenient way to develop the various ratios for the overall form and its internal details.

It is important to understand, however, that the module itself need not be a whole number. In fact, most of the modules in these projects were not based on a numerical measurement at all. Instead, they were derived either from an anatomical dimension such as the span of my own hand, or from a material or functional constraint. The fact that the module's actual dimension is not necessarily a whole number (for example, my handspan is $8^{11}/_{16}$") does not introduce any more complexity to the layout process, because this number essentially resolves to one as it serves as the base number for all the subsequent ratios used throughout the design.

> "It is good to think, better to look and think, best to look without thinking."
> — Johan von Goethe

I arrived at the various proportional relationships through intuition and the strategy of: "If it looks good, it probably is good." In other words, trial and error. Just as my son composes original songs on his keyboard – making notations when he likes what he hears – I tried out combinations of whole-number ratios between the sizes, spacings and curvatures of the various components until I liked what I saw. Amazingly, and probably predictably, I discovered that the commonest and simplest ratios almost always tended to look the best. It doesn't surprise me that I also tend to like songs that are composed of simple notes, chords and progressions. And like my son, I also enjoy more time and freedom to devote to the creation process due to the fact that I don't need to make up any of the "notes" from scratch.

The primary reason why I reach an appealing form quickly through whole-number ratios is that each and every part automatically ends up being proportionally related to one another. In my side table project, for example, I chose to make the aprons one-sixth the height of the legs. My eye quickly decided that the height of the drawer face looked perfect at two-thirds of the apron height – which, by geometric progression, turns out to be one-ninth of the leg height. The drawer faces, aprons and legs all relate to one another in simple ratios – in other words, they play well together. I didn't have to think all this through; these harmonious relationships just seem to happen.

The Design & Layout Process

The way I arrive at the final form of the project goes something like this: I start with some concept sketches and then, when I find an iteration that intrigues me, I draw up an accurately proportioned drawing of at least one elevation – more if the project is asymmetrical. It's only necessary to make the drawings of large pieces full-scale if you need to create layout templates for curved components or if you need to understand the layout of a complex joint. Because the design is based on ratios rather than dimensions (and this is an extremely important and useful distinction), you can scale the project up or down by simply changing the dimension of the base-one module. For example, if you want to scale down the furniture piece 33 percent for a child, you simply divide the module into three parts and use two-thirds as the module.

If I have trouble visualizing the design beyond the concept sketches and elevations, I'll take the additional step of mocking up the piece at full-size in cardboard. This invariably confirms (or denies) the visual appeal of the proportions when seen from a variety of typical viewing angles.

As you'll see in my discussion of the design process for each of the projects, I generally use harmonic expansion to develop the overall form of the piece and then switch to geometric expansion (actually "contraction" in this case) to proportion internal parts such as the rails and stiles of doors. I develop curvatures to whole-number ratios relating to the length of their span, usually choosing ratios of 1:1, 2:1 or 3:1 (refer to Section III, Chapter 4). I have found that these simple strategies make the design process amazingly intuitive and efficient. In fact, it often feels to me as if these designs evolved by themselves as I picked various notes and progressions and then just nudged them in the right direction.

FIG. 4.1.2. Simple ratios and modules can be used to create pleasing forms.

In my hand-tool woodworking process, I don't bother to make a cutlist. Instead, I lay out the project's components on the stock using a tick stick. On smaller projects rendered in full scale, I simply hold the stick to the drawing to make the layout marks. If the drawing is scaled down, I make up a full-sized module scale and step off the dimensions with dividers, following the ratios indicated on the drawing.

So follow along in the coming pages, then try out a design for yourself. I think you'll be absolutely astonished to discover how quickly it will come together for you. And remember: There isn't any one rule of proportions and progressions that must be revered and followed here. The whole-number ratios are just the notes; you choose the amount and the sequence by what your eye informs.

It's your design to build – your song to sing in wood.

PROJECT ONE
Step Stool

FIG. 4.1.3. Both of these alder step stools were built around the anatomical module of one handspan.

Design Parameters & Process

- I chose my handspan as the height of the stool because a person's handspan is typically equal to their normal (i.e. comfortable) stepping height. (You may find it interesting to learn that a person's handspan is typically one-eighth of the full span of their body, which is equal to their height). My handspan (about 9") then serves as the "base-one" module for all the other ratios that form this step stool.
- The width of the stool is one module plus one-seventh of that module, which makes it about equal to the length of a person's foot – an obviously perfect width for a foot stool.
- The length of the stool is two modules, which is also, by definition, two handspans. Two handspans happens to be the width of our shoulders, which also means that the stool will be stable side-to-side, even if stood upon with both feet. Notice that as the form takes shape we start with a rectangle that is one handspan high by two in length, a simple ratio of 1:2.
- I made the width of the cross beam support three-sevenths of the module, finding that dimension to be wide enough to provide diagonal stability. I spaced the beam evenly from top to bottom, two-sevenths of a module to each end. This spacing also creates visual contrast, breaking up the vertical space into a sequence of 2:3:2. Note that the cross support may look a bit too beefy in this side view – but you never view it this way. Seen from standing height, parallax corrects it to

a pleasing proportion. I confirmed this, by the way, by making up a cardboard mock-up and setting it on the floor.

- I laid out the dovetails with seven pins, sustaining the theme of "sevenths."
- I inset the elliptical foot cutout two-sevenths from each end and proportioned the ellipse to a 1:4 ratio of semi-minor to major axis. Notice how this echoes that little 2:3:2 contrast sequence used earlier in the layout of the brace.
- This echo repeats yet again in the placement of the wedges, which are inset one-seventh in from the ends of the through-tenons that secure the ends of the cross brace to the end boards. This placement is partly necessitated to ensure that the wedging action will work, but the wedges also act as visual punctuation (as do the tenons themselves relative to the width of the end wall).

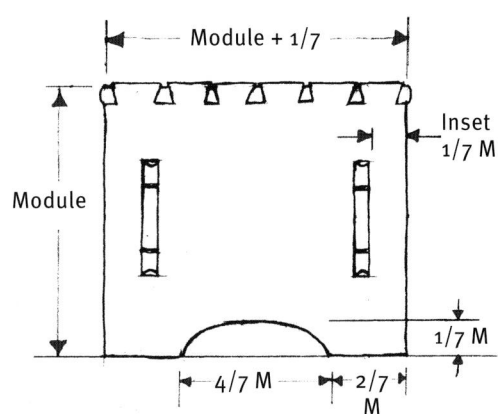

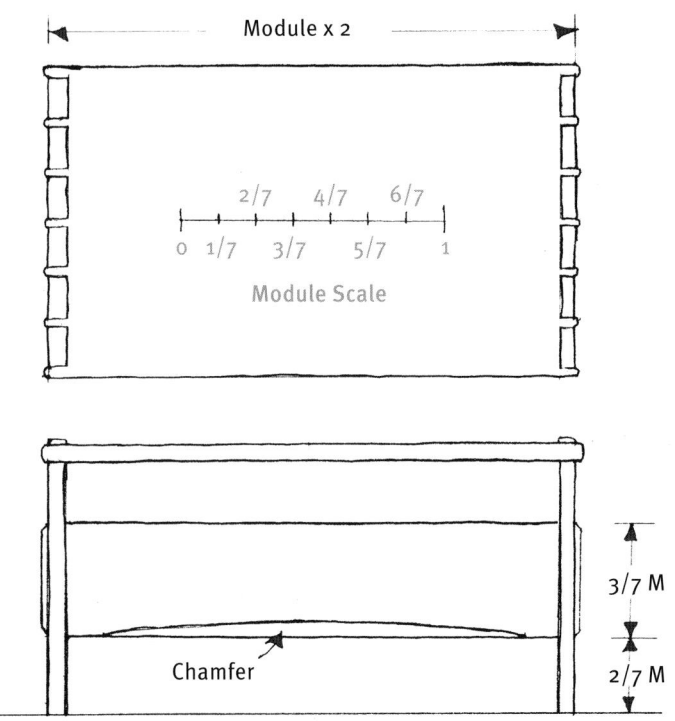

PROJECT TWO
Candy Box

FIG. 4.1.4. This "candy" box was designed from the inside out, based on the size of the intended contents – in this case, rock "candies."

Design Parameters & Process

- In this project, I proportioned the form from the inside out, using the size of the stone "candies" that must fit in each cubby. So the module became the internal side dimension of one square cubby.
- The height of the cubby is one-half of the module.
- By sizing the interior dividers to one-eighth of the module and the sides to one-fourth, the sum total of sides and dividers equaled one module (see the detail in the drawing). The result is that the box is four modules wide by four modules long – a square just like the interior cubbies. The large square is echoed by the symmetry of the smaller squares. Also notice how the dividers punctuate each cubby space while the sides produce a border that punctuates the entire interior volume.
- The box height at the apex of the crowned lid panel is two modules high, making the overall proportions of the box a cuboid in a 1:2 ratio.
- The lid is two-thirds of a module thick and is located one-and-one-third modules up from the bottom, establishing the height of the box relative to the side length as a simple 1:2 ratio. This often happens when making simple divisions of a module. We end up generating layers of simple ratios without having to even think about it. Notice that the curve of the lid panel comes down one-third a module from the apex.

PROJECTS

1/4 + 1/8 + 1/8 + 1/8 + 1/4 = 8/8 = 1 Module

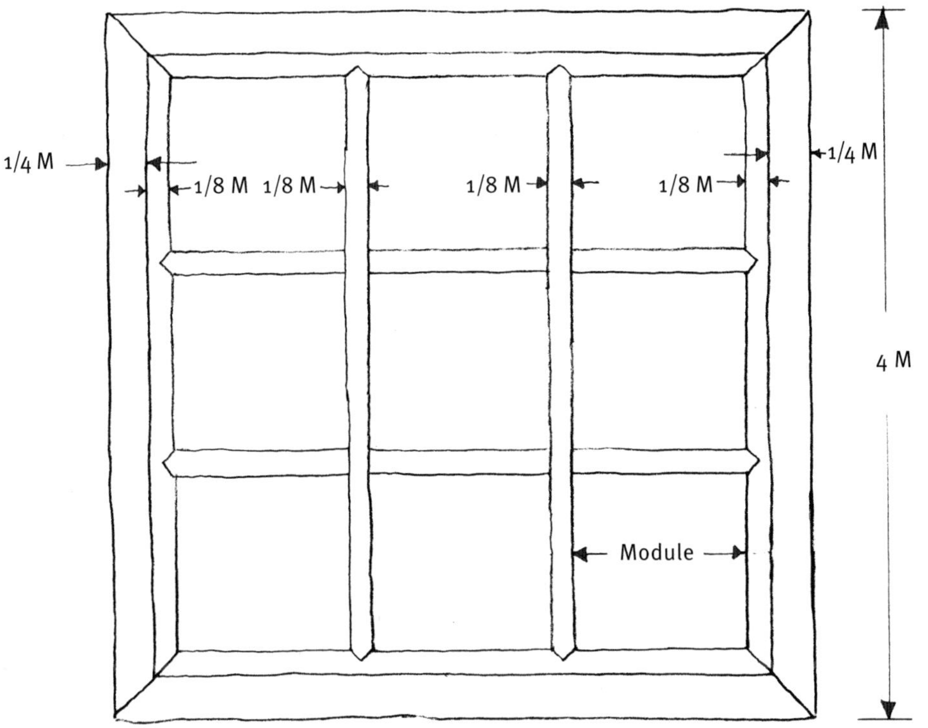

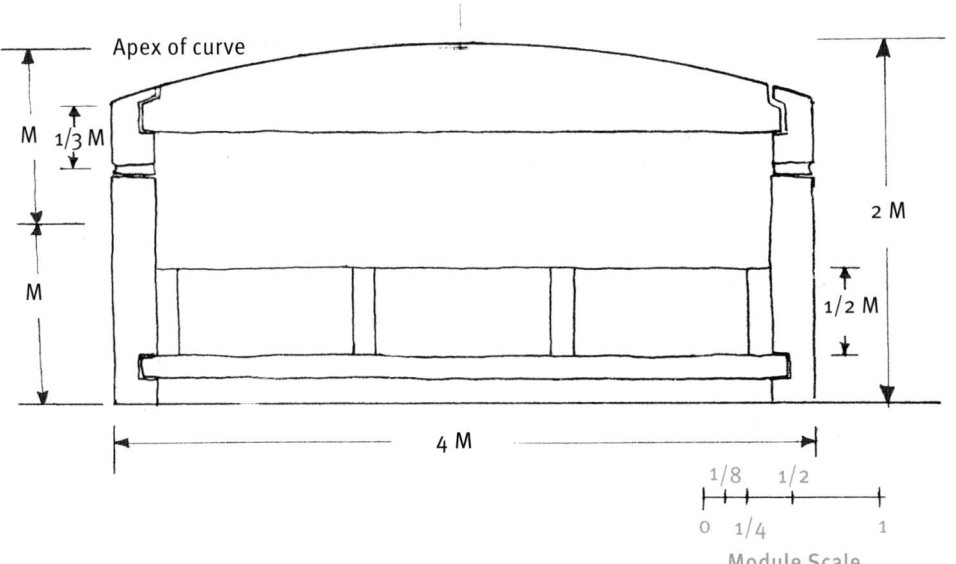

> PROJECT THREE

Lap Desk

FIG. 4.1.5. I chose a proportion based on the intended use of this lap desk as the starting point for my design.

Design Parameters & Process

- The only starting parameter for this Shaker-style lap desk was the requirement that it provide a writing surface for note cards (about an 8" x 11" rectangle) so I chose this proportion (8:11) for the overall plan view of the lid.
- I then made the width of the top and bottom lid frames one-eighth of the overall frame height. By selecting 1¼" as the frame width (which would also serve as the module length), the internal panel/writing surface is six modules wide (and therefore 8") and is more than 11" long. Drawing a diagonal intersects the inside edges of the top and bottom frames at exactly one-eighth the length of the lid (thanks to the magic of geometric expansion), establishing the width of the side frames.
- I added a two-module-wide extension to the angled frame lid to increase the internal capacity of the desk.
- To angle the lid to a 2:1 ratio, I made the sides one module high at the front rising to two modules high at the back.
- The lid and extension overlap the desk box by one-eighth of a module along all sides.

- I chose butt hinges that were close to one module in length, and I inset the hinges two modules.
- Note that the frame of the lid acts as a border around the writing surface and thus punctuates that space. If your eye chooses to make the frame lighter or stouter, remember that those framing elements are tied proportionally – if you make them stouter, the writing surface shrinks in both directions. Also note how the small ebony stops at the top and bottom act as another layer of punctuation.
- While the layout of the internal dividers is sized for paper and writing utensils, it also creates a pleasing division of major and minor spacings.

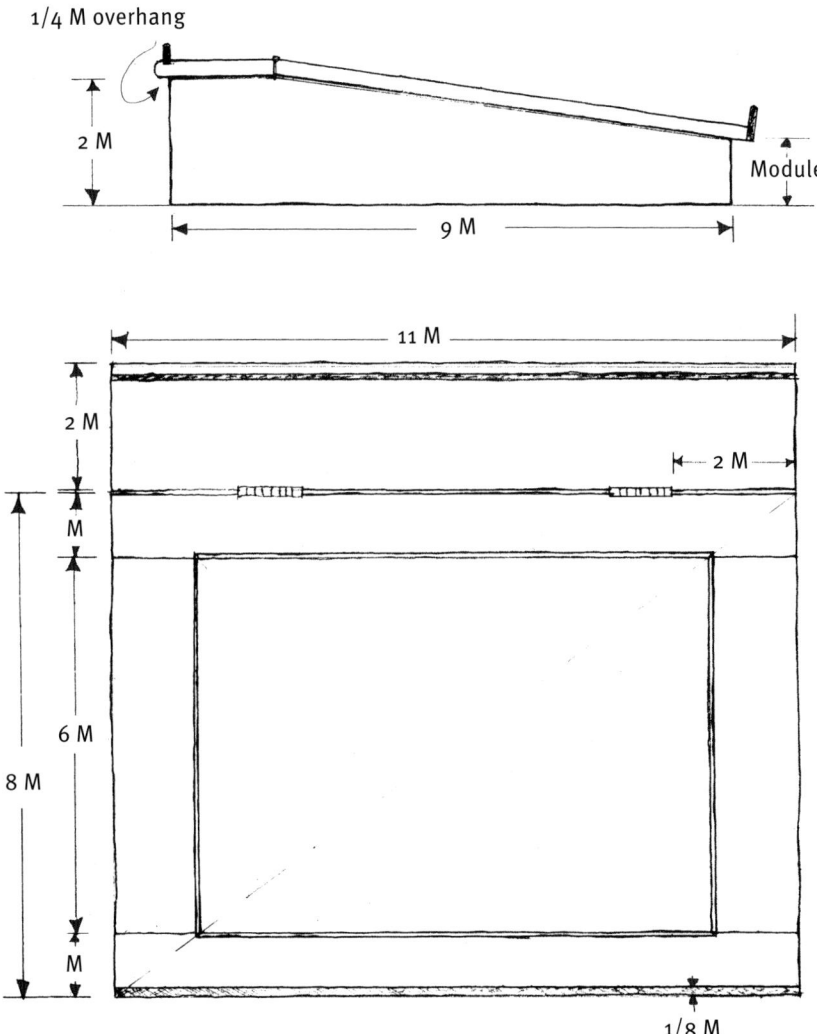

PROJECT FOUR

Tool Tote

FIG. 4.1.6. I chose my handspan as the module for this tool tote, because that's about as wide as a tote can be without hitting your leg as you walk.

Design Parameters & Process

• Like the step stool, I choose my handspan as the module for this project. For a different reason though: I used the width of my handspan for the width of the tool box as this is about as wide as a tote can get without it constantly bumping up against your leg as you carry it. (Swing your arm by your side with your fingers outspread and see for yourself.) This width also (fortuitously) provides enough internal width to contain a bench plane and a handsaw side by side with a divider in between. (Why is that? Because these tools are less than a handsbreadth (closed hand) wide, and your handspan is two handsbreadths.)

• At three modules in length, the tote will contain up to a 24"-long try plane and a panel saw. If I wanted it to hold a full-sized handsaw (whose length is three handspans long for the blade, plus a bit less than a third for the handle), I would extend the tote length another one-third module as indicated in the drawing. (Why is a handsaw blade three handspans long? Use one at a proper knee-high sawbench and you'll find out.)

- A removable box for layout tools sits on the side boards and between the ends, and is sized one-fourth a module in height – tall enough to contain the tools under a sliding lid.
- The overall height of the tote at the ends comes to one-and-two-thirds modules. I tried to simply double the module, but it made the whole box look thin and tippy, and added unnecessary weight. Again, here's a case where function is driving the design, yet by using simple ratios of a module, simple harmonic ratios emerge. In this case the height is broken into a major and minor with the lower section four parts and the

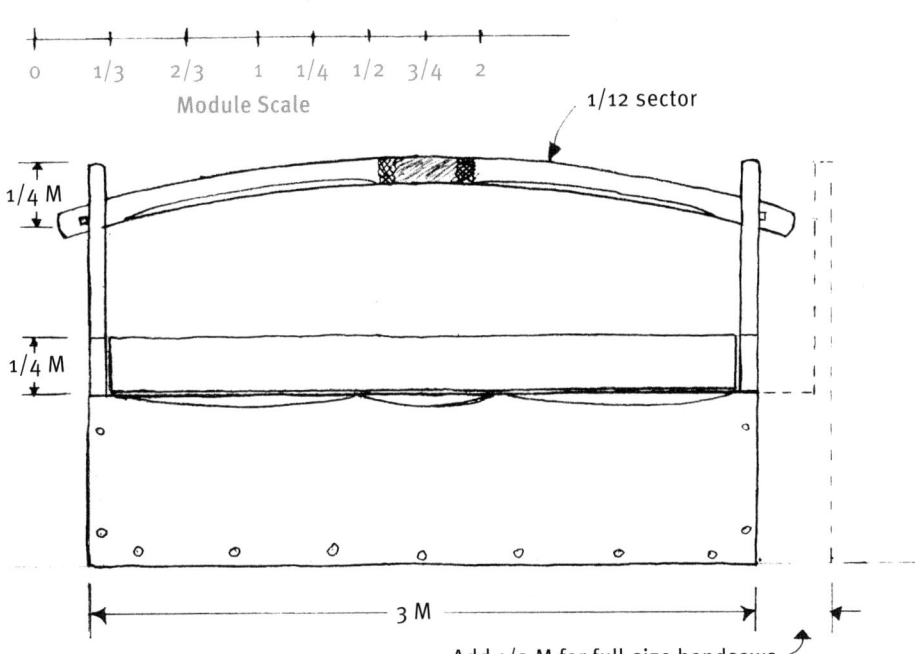

upper section three parts. The ratio of the rectangle governing the end panel is therefore 4:7.

• For fancy (and to cut down the weight) I shaped the edges of the end boards with a curve (a one-sixth sector of a circle) and joined them with a semi-circle sized to one-third of a module. I also carved in some chamfers on the top edge of the side panels – not just for show, but to provide an inset for your fingers when lifting out the removable box. The long chamfers are one module long while the middle is two-thirds of a module. Why? Because they look right and were simple to lay out.

• To carry the tote, I designed a curved handle – not just for looks, but to stabilize the tote when carried. Trial and error revealed a simple one-twelfth sector of a circle provided a functional and just-right-to-the-eye curve.

• The drawing below shows how I found the one-twelfth sector focal point by stepping off the width of the chord (which is the overall length of the tote) along a bisector.

• I laid out the four dovetail centerlines on one-quarter module intervals. If I weren't so lazy, I would have laid out seven dovetails to reflect the 4:7 ratio of the end boards.

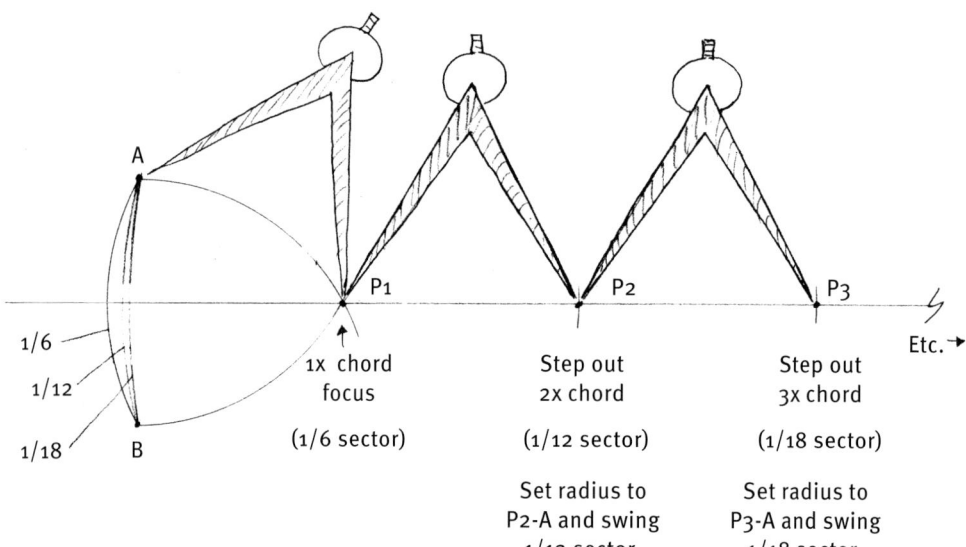

FIG. 4.1.7. Laying out multiple chord to radius.

PROJECT FIVE
Boot Bench

FIG. 4.1.8. The first design parameter for any seating project, such as this boot bench, is the height.

Design Parameters & Process

- The first parameter of a sitting bench is its height; it has to be comfortable (or at least functional, in this case) to sit on. The typical comfortable seating height for most people is two handspans (check that biometric for yourself right now) and that's what I chose here. (Note that to ease the layout process, I laid out to the underside of the top, letting the top thickness float.) The seat height also serves as the module for all subsequent proportional relationships.
- The width of the end board is two-thirds of the module, resulting in a 2:3 width-to-height ratio.
- Because of space constraints at the client's site, the length of the bench needed to be limited to about 60". Because the seat height is about 18", I laid out three-and-one-third modules to arrive at the length. Because the width of the seat at the ends is two-thirds of a module, this results in a length-to-width ratio of $2/3:10/3$ or 2:5.
- I decided to curve the front edge of the seat not only for aesthetic reasons, but to make the seat deeper and therefore more comfortable to sit on. The curve is a one-18th sector (in which the radius equals three times the span). I also cut a slight curve at the ends of the seat board, using the length of the seat as the radius.

- I used the one-18th sector value to curve the top edge of the backboard, setting the apex at two modules. Notice how simple ratios sneak in again: The height of the seat back at one-third module is half of the two-thirds module seat width at the ends, presenting a subtle but nice contrast.
- The twin cyma curves laid out (symmetrically) at opposite ends of the curves punctuate the ends of the backboard. Also note that those cyma curves are linked proportionally to the smaller cyma braces below in a ratio of 1:2.
- The support crosspiece also received a one-18th sector radius curve; the width at each end is one-third the module.
- All the exposed edges of the boards were shaped to a one-sixth sector radius (i.e. the thickness of the board equals the radius of the profile).
- The small cymas under the seat overhang at each end, and in addition to acting as a structural brace, serve to punctuate the leg and signal the transition to the seat. The height of the brace is equal to the spacing of the boot shelf above the floor, lending a subtle symmetry to the front elevation.

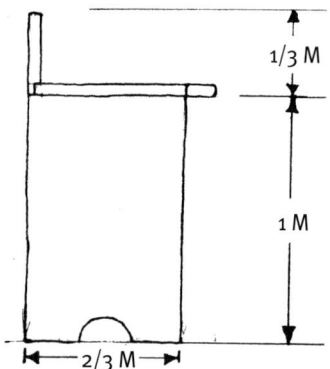

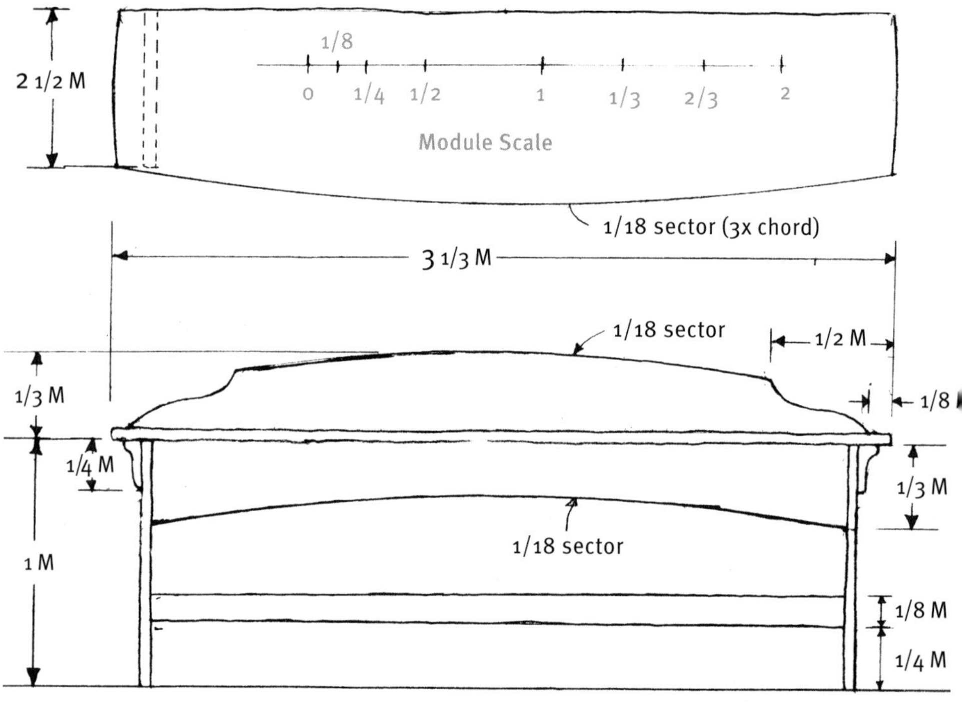

PROJECT SIX
Coffee-for-two Tray

FIG. 4.1.9. The curves and overall dimensions of this little coffee cup tray create a harmonious composition of simple ratios.

Design Parameters & Process:

- The single parameter for this little serving tray was the demand that it be able to contain two coffee cups and a pair of small pitchers for cream and sugar. I found the required dimensions by mocking up the tray in cardboard around these items.
- To keep the ratios simple, I decided to make the tray twice the length of its width, and the height of its side pieces one-third its width (and therefore one-sixth its length).
- I canted out the ends and sides in a 1:3 ratio.
- The top edge of the end pieces curves to a one-sixth sector, and the edge of the side pieces to twice that: a $1/12$ sector.
- Again, all exposed edges are shaped to a one-sixth sector profile (a simple job with a spokeshave, by the way).

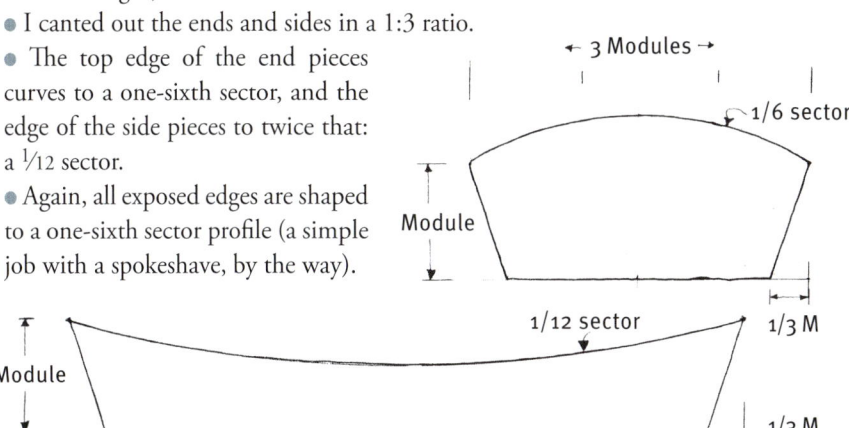

PROJECT SEVEN
Cup Cabinet

FIG. 4.1.10. The modules for this cup cabinet are based on the size of the cups.

Design Parameters & Process

• When done with the coffee, I needed a place to put the cups. So the parameter for this coffee cup cupboard is again worked around the size of the cups. It needed to be wide enough to contain a single row of three or more cups. After mocking-up, I sized the side of the cabinet to be a certain depth (around 5"). I found it convenient to use this dimension (the cabinet side) as the module.

• The face of the cabinet is a simple ratio of 3:4 (three modules wide by four high). This size accommodates three shelves (four counting the bottom). Note that the ratio applies to the door rather than to the overall height and width of the cabinet.

• To add some elegance (and a lot of extra work, to be sure) I decided to bow the front face and door of the cabinet to one-12th sector.

• To create a border and punctuate the door itself, I chose one-third of a module for the width of the door stiles, which means they come to one-ninth (one-third multiplied by three modules) of the door width. Using a diagonal to generate geometric expansion (actually, in this case, contraction), I laid out the rails to one-ninth of the door height.

• I sized the cabinet side thickness (and the internal top and bottom pieces) to one-ninth of the module. To provide more dramatic punctuation, I thickened the top and bottom mouldings to one-sixth of a module with an overhang of one-12th a module. (That means the overhang is half the thickness of the stock – a good rule of thumb for the minimum amount of aesthetically pleasing overhang.)

• As seems to be my thing, I shaped the edges of the mouldings to a one-sixth sector.

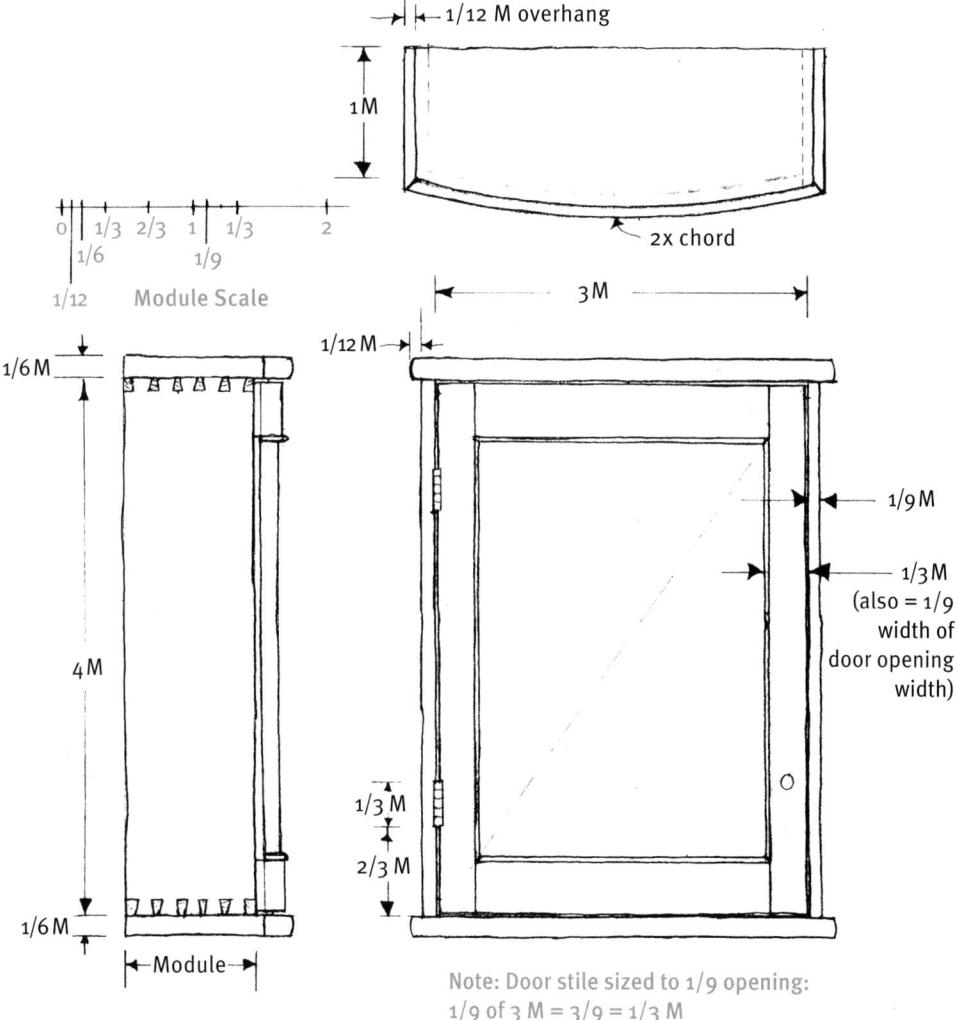

Note: Door stile sized to 1/9 opening:
1/9 of 3 M = 3/9 = 1/3 M

PROJECT EIGHT
Side Table

FIG. 4.1.11. This Shaker-inspired contemporary table is a simple 2:3 ratio.

Design Parameters & Process

• This little side table is my interpretation of the ubiquitous Shaker-style side table. As on most of these tables, the front elevation (and side elevation in the case of a square-topped version) is a simple 2:3 width-to-height ratio. I chose the width to be 18" because this brings the top of the table to about 28" (depending on the thickness of the top) – a perfect height for a bedside table. I also found that the width dimension would serve well as the base-one module for the internal component ratios.

• I punctuated the overall height of the form by sizing the height of the drawer face with its upper and lower blades (and also the aprons) to be one-sixth of the table height (a nod to the classic orders). This ratio also works out to be one-fourth of the module. (One-sixth of the one-and-one-half module leg height is one-sixth x one-and-one-12th equals one-fourth a module.)

- The blades are one-sixth of the apron height and add another layer of punctuation (and correlation of ratios) to the apron.
- To size the legs to appear delicate, I made them one-12th of a module (which resolves to 1½" because the module is 18"). I tapered them down from just below the apron to one-half that amount at the foot.
- The top overhangs the aprons and the curved drawer face and blades by one-12th a module – a typical Shaker convention (in which a table overhang equals the thickness of the legs). As a nod to the leg shaft taper, I tapered the top edge to half its thickness.
- The curve of the drawer face and the top is one-12th of a sector. Interesting how this seems to pleasantly correlate with the 1:12 ratios occurring elsewhere on the piece.

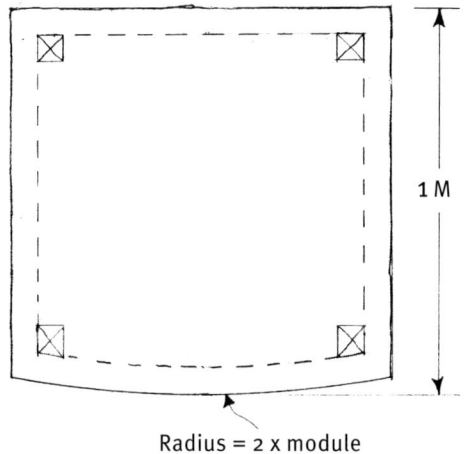

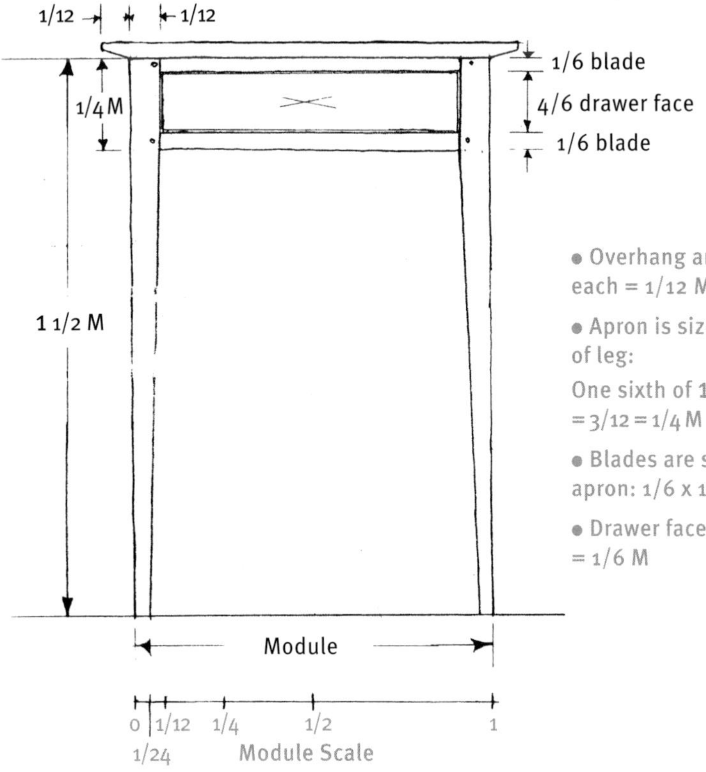

Radius = 2 x module

- Overhang and leg width each = 1/12 M
- Apron is sized to 1/6 height of leg:
One sixth of 1 1/2 M = 1/6 x 3/2 = 3/12 = 1/4 M
- Blades are sized to 1/6 of apron: 1/6 x 1/4 = 1/24 M
- Drawer face is 2/3 of 1/4 M = 1/6 M

PROJECT NINE

Vanity

FIG. 4.1.12. Using ratios to design this vanity was a major change from my earlier approach to cabinet design.

Design Parameters & Process

- In a dramatic departure from the way I developed dimensions for cabinetwork in my 25 years in the trade, I decided to use simple ratios to lay out the overall shape and internal components of a bathroom vanity (rather than standard-issue numerical dimensions). I did start with a standard vanity height of 31" and then subtracted 1" for the countertop and 3" for the base frame to arrive at 27". I found that this dimension would serve well as the base-one module to develop the rest of the dimensions. I made the length of the cabinet two modules, producing a horizontal rectangle (of the casework itself) with a simple 1:2 ratio.
- In the first version (at top on the next page), I equally divided the width of two doors and the bank of drawers (each are two-thirds of a module). In the sec-

PROJECTS

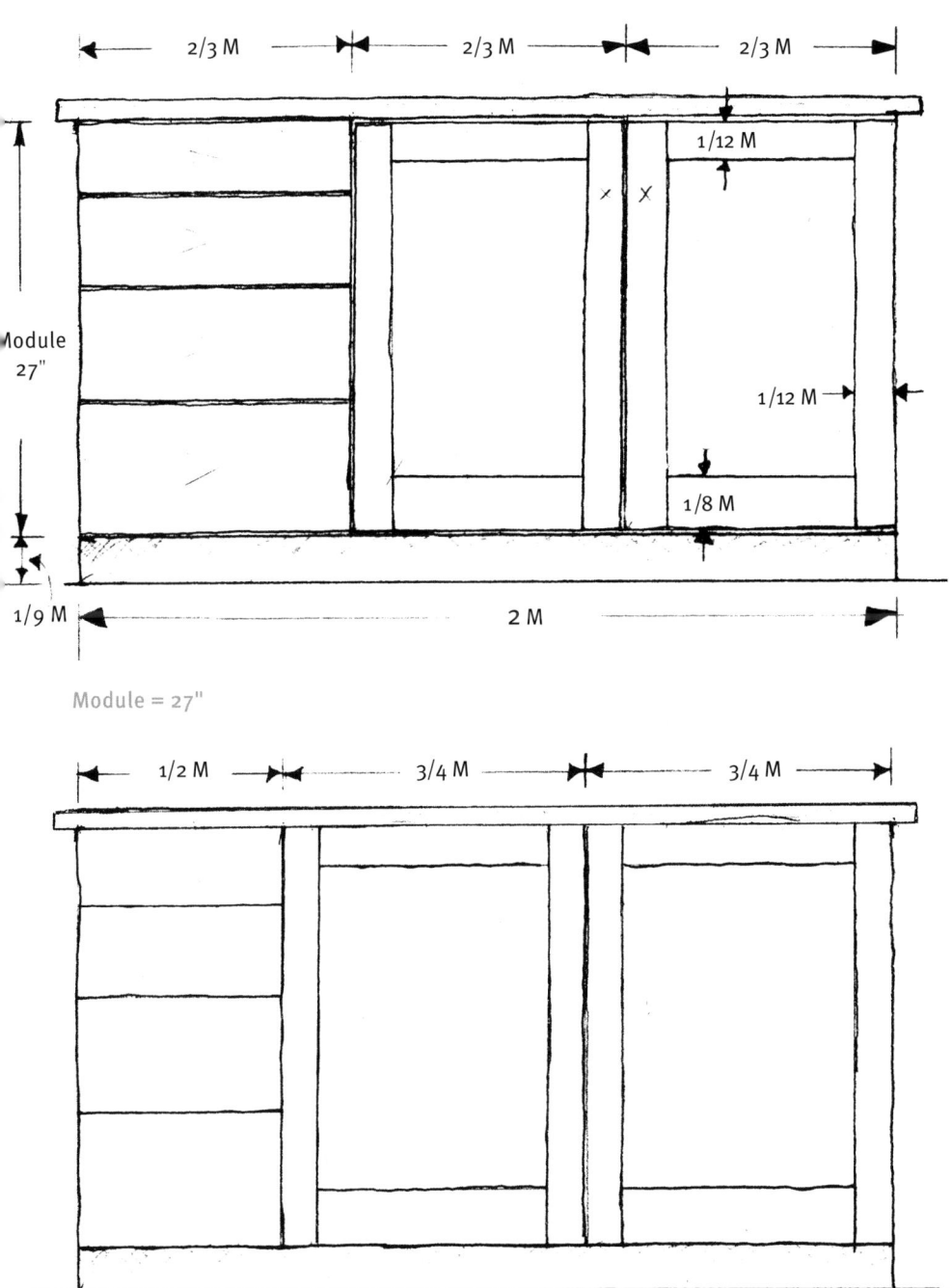

Module = 27"

ond version (at bottom on the previous page), I broke away from symmetry and reduced the drawer width from two-thirds to one-half a module. The doors share the remaining one-and-one-half a module at three-fourths of a module each. The result is a façade divided up with some contrast: Instead of 1:1:1 it's broken into a minor-and-major relationship of 2:3:3 (²⁄4, ³⁄4, ³⁄4).

• The door stiles looked to be appropriately proportioned when sized to ⅛ the door width on the two-thirds-module-wide doors and one-ninth the door width on the three-fourths-of-a-module-wide doors. What's interesting about this "looks right" strategy, is that it means both stile widths come out to be the same size: one-12th of the 27" long module or 2¼", which also happens to be the standard stile size of quality cabinetwork. See the detail in the drawing to learn how this bit of proportional magic works.

• I used the stile width for the width of the upper rail, but increased the width of the bottom rail to one-eighth of the module to account for visual parallax that would otherwise make the bottom rail appear narrower when viewed at an angle.

• Another detail in the drawing shows how to lay out the graduated drawers, starting with the top drawer face sized to one-sixth of the height of the cabinet face (i.e. the module).

Proportioning stiles:

1/8 of 2/3 M = 1/8 × 2/3 = 2/24 = 1/12 M
1/9 of 3/4 M = 1/9 × 3/4 = 3/36 = 1/12 M
1/12 of 1 M = 1/12 × 27" = 2 1/4"

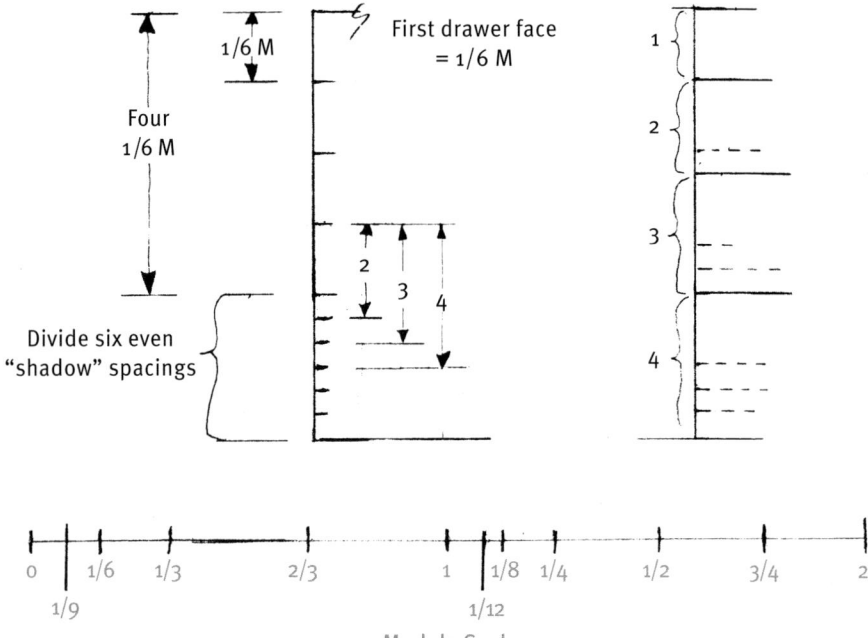

Module Scale

Acknowledgements

George and I wish to first acknowledge Christopher Schwarz and Lost Art Press for always fanning the embers of our craft into a warm inviting blaze – and Megan Fitzpatrick and Linda Watts whose skill at editing and layout made this a book a pleasure to read. Also, Nico Prins did an excellent job of converting our geometric layouts to clear animations.

Over the course of writing this book, I often consulted the following people to get informed feedback on a number of the ideas that George and I were exploring: Dan Packard, Greg Kossow, Tim Lawson, Abel Isaac Dances, Ole Kanestrom, Nat Natali, Rob Campbell, Catherine Stone and Stephen Cook.

Their responses helped me find clarity in my own understanding of how to best present my contributions to this project.

— Jim Tolpin

My heartfelt thanks goes out to Barb, my closest confidant and supporter, and to Jim Evans, who always took time to offer encouragement. Many steps led up to this book, and I'd like to thank the following:

Don McConnell, who offered feedback and questions, and his generous loan of valuable reference texts.

The Society of American Period Furniture Makers (SAPFM), many of whom offered photos of their work.

Mark Arnold, former editor of *American Period Furniture,* who got this rolling by nudging me to write several articles for the journal.

The enthusiastic men and women in the Ohio River Valley Chapter of SAPFM, who encouraged me to present much of this material and always rewarded me with thought-provoking questions.

My special thanks to Thomas Lie-Nielsen who got behind this early on.

Konrad Sauer, an awesome designer in his own right who, continues to offer kind words of encouragement. Finally, Walt and Dick Walker, two honest men who always encouraged me to dream.

— George R. Walker

Further Reading

Adam, Robert. *Classical Architecture.* Harry N. Abrams, 1990.

Alexander, Christopher. *Notes on the Synthesis of Form.* Harvard University Press, 1964.

Biddle, Owen. *Biddle's Young Carpenter's Assistant.* Dover, 2006.

Sutton, Andrew. *Ruler & Compass, Practical Geometric Constructions.* Walker, 2009.

Chippendale, Thomas, *The Gentleman & Cabinet-Maker's Director.* Dover, 1966.

Da Vinci, Leonardo. *Leonardo's Notebooks.* Ed. H. Anna Suh. Black Dog & Leventhal, 2005.

Denis, François. *Traite de Lutherie.* Aladfi, 2006.

Gloag, John. *Georgian Grace, A Social History of Design from 1660 to 1830.* Spring, 1967.

Hambidge, Jay. *The Elements of Dynamic Symmetry.* Dover, 1967.

Kimberly, Elam. *Geometry of Design: Studies in Proportion and Composition.* Princeton Architectural, 2001.

Langley, Batty. *The Builder's Director, or Bench-mate: Being a Pocket-treasury of the Grecian, Roman and Gothic Orders of Architecture.* Gale ECCO, Print Editions, 2010.

Lanteri, Eduoard. *Modelling, A Guide for Teachers and Students.* Chapman & Hall, 1902.

Mayborn, Mitch. *Seaplanes & Motors, Early Military Aircraft of the First World War.* Flying Enterprises, 1971.

Nicholson, Peter. *The New Practical Builder, and Workman's Companion.* BiblioBazaar, 2008.

Palladio, Andrea. *The Four Books of Architecture.* Dover, 1965.

Robertson, John. *A Treatise of Mathematical Instruments.* Ed. David Manthey, Invisible College, 2002.

Semes, Steven W. *The Architecture of the Classical Interior.* Norton, 2004.

Sheraton, Thomas. *The Cabinet-maker and Upholsterer's Drawing-book. In four parts, Second edition, with additional plates.* Gale ECCO, Print Editions, 2010.

Cliff, Stafford. *English Style and Decoration, A Sourcebook of Original Designs.* Thames and Hudson, 2008.

Vitruvius, Marcus. *On Architecture.* Penguin, 2009.

Wade, David. *Symmetry, The Ordering Principle.* Walker, 2006.

Walker, C. Howard. *Theory of Mouldings.* Norton, 2007.

Wittkower, Rudolf. *Architectural Principles in the Age of Humanism.* Norton, 1971.

Credits

Unless otherwise noted, all photos and drawings in sections I & II are by George R. Walker.

FIG. 1.1.2. Newport table by Allan Breed; photo by Lie-Nielsen Toolworks

FIG. 1.1.6. Detail from *Melencolia I*, an engraving by Albrecht Dürer

FIG. 1.1.7. Detail from *The School of Athens*, by Raphael

FIG. 1.1.8. Engraving from frontispiece of *Robinson's Proportional Architecture*

FIG. 1.1.12. Drawing by Jim Tolpin

FIG. 1.1.13. Engraving from Thomas Chippendale's *The Gentleman & Cabinet-Maker's Director*, 3rd ed

FIG. 1.1.14. Detail of swan's neck pediment by Brooke Smith; photo by Stephen Webster

FIG. 1.1.15. *Return of the Prodigal Son*, by Rembrandt

FIG. 1.1.17. Contemporary chest on frame by Brooke Smith; photo by Carolina Choroco

FIG. 1.1.19. Detail from *Anweisung zum Zeichnen der menschlichen Gestalt besonders für Dilettanten brauchbar, welche sich eine practische Kenntniß der Zeichenkunst zu verschaffen wünschen*, by Johann Heinrich Ramberg

FIG. 1.2.1. Photo by Dick Walker

FIG. 1.2.6. Engraving of double chest of drawers from George Hepplewhite's *The Cabinet-Maker and Upholsterer's Guide*, 3rd ed

FIG. 1.2.7. Drawing by Jim Tolpin

FIG. 1.2.13. Engraving from James Gibb's *Rules for Drawing the Several Parts of Architecture*

FIG. 1.3.2. Engraving of *The Monument to The Great Fire of London* by Sutton Nicholls, designed by Christopher Wren

FIG. 1.3.10. Drawing of a side table and mirror by John Linnell

FIG. 2.1.1. Photo from the Hubble Telescope, NASA

FIG. 2.1.5. Photo by Dick Walker

FIG. 2.1.6. Drawing by Josh Walker

FIG. 2.1.7 & FIG. 2.1.8. Drawings by Leonardo da Vinci

CREDITS

FIG. 2.1.9. *Spear-Bearer* sculpture by Polycleitus

FIG. 2.1.10. Engraving from Sebastiano Serlio's *Canon of the 5 Orders*

FIG. 2.1.14. Drawing from Edoard Lanteri's *Modelling, A Guide for Teachers and Students*

FIG. 2.2.3. Connecticut highboy by Larry Mauritz

FIG. 2.2.5. Federal game table by Robert G. Stevenson Jr.; photo by Craig Carlson

FIG. 2.2.8. Ladies' desk by Robert G. Stevenson Jr.; photo by Craig Carlson

FIG. 2.2.9. Engraving from Andrea Palladio's *Four Books of Architecture*

FIG. 2.2.10. Engraving from Batty Langley's *The City and Country Builder's and Workman's Treasury of Designs*

FIG. 2.2.16. Detail from side table by Allan Breed; photo by Lie-Nielsen Toolworks

FIG. 2.2.17. Inset photo of crown moulding by George R. Walker; photo by Lie-Nielsen Toolworks

FIG. 2.2.23. Drawing from HABS (Historic Architectural Buildings Survey) Library of Congress

FIG. 2.2.24. Engraving from Batty Langley's *The City and Country Builder's and Workman's Treasury of Designs*

FIG. 2.2.29. Detail from Newport table by Allan Breed; photo by Lie-Nielsen Toolworks

FIG. 2.3.1. Drawing from Ed. Lanteri's *Modelling, A Guide for Teachers and Students*

FIG. 2.3.6. Baltimore side chair by Peter Van Beckum; photo by the maker

FIG. 2.3.7. Edenton chair by Benjamin C. Hobbs

FIG.. 2.3.8. Hepplewhite card table by Sharon C. Mehrman; photo by the maker

FIG. 2.3.10. Engraving from Thomas Sheraton's *The Cabinet-Maker and Upholsterer's Drawing Book*

FIG. 2.3.20. Drawing from Edouard Lanteri's *Modelling, A Guide for Teachers and Students*

Unless otherwise noted, all photos in sections III & IV are by Craig Wester and all drawings are by Jim Tolpin.

FIG. 3.1.13. Photo of sector by Christopher Schwarz

FIG. 3.3.1. Photo of Philadelphia highboy courtesy of the U.S. State Department

FIG. 3.4.1. Three-drawer chest by Charles L. Phillips; photo by the maker

FIG. 3.4.6. Federal secretary by Robert G. Stevenson Jr.; photo by Craig Carlson

FIG. 3.4.7. Piece by Michael Colca (michaelcolca.com)

FIG. 3.4.9. Detail of Federal table by Steve Latta; photo by Lie-Nielsen Toolworks

FIG. 3.4.14. Klismos chair by Philip C. Lowe; drawing by George R. Walker

FIG. 3.4.15. Demi-lune table by Gerald Curry; photo by Lie-Nielsen Toolworks

FIG. 3.5.1. Photo by Lie-Nielsen Toolworks

Index

Italic page numbers indicate information is found in a figure.
Bold page numbers indicate information is found in a sidebar or inset.

3-D, 24

Adam, Robert, 43
apprentices, 7, 21, 33;
   classic orders, 11, 13, 52
arc, 82, **83**, 116, *136*, 137;
   drawing, *114*, 115, *115*;
   endpoints, 139;
   expansion from circle, *137*;
   generating with joined sticks, 138;
   Gothic, 139, 140;
   Lancet, 140, *140*;
   locating a focal point, 139;
   quarter-, *89, 149*;
   relative to chord, 138, *138*;
   from station points, 137–38
Ark of Covenant, 64
artisan age, 2, 5, 6–8, 17, 81;
   curvature, 80, *82*;
   designers, 66;
   drawings, 21, 22, 25;
   end of, 10;
   language of, 10, 11, 12

artisan geometry, 33;
   basic constructions, 122–27;
   basic curves and tapers, 136–45;
   developing moulding profiles, 146–49;
   generating shapes, 128–35;
   traditional tools, 96–121
automation, 10
axis lines, 60; symmetry, 61, *61*

battens, 98, **105**, 113, 115, *115*, 116, *116*, 117, 123, 137, 145
Beethoven, Ludwig van, 24;
   Symphony, No. 5, 14
benches: boot (project), 165–66;
   techniques, 25
Breed, Al, 3
Brumbaugh Woods, 62, *63*

cabinets:
   cup (project), 168–69;
   New England corner, 126;
   rustic-design, 107, *107*
CAD. *See* computer-aided design software
candy box (project), 158–59
Capitol, 61
Chippendale:, 80;
   Gothic, 22

chord, 22, **83**, 84, 148, 154, 164, *164*;
  arc, 115, 138, **138**, 140;
  guitar, 53;
  imaginary, 82;
  making adjustments with, 84;
  musical, 55, 85
circumference, 46, 60, 125, 135
circles, 27, *47*, 35, 36, *36*, 37, 44, 45, 46, *46*, 64, *65, 82*, 84, *84*, 89, *89*, 148, 149;
  curves, 79, 81;
  drawing, 102, 103, *103*;
  erecting an equilateral triangle, 134;
  erecting a perpendicular, 125;
  erecting a square, 129, 129, 130, *130*;
  expansion in quadrants, *133*;
  focal point, 139, *139*;
  hexagon generation, 135, *135*;
  human form, 48, 50;
  intersecting with lines, 98, 106, 113, 124;
  in nature, 47, *47*;
  octagon generation, 135, *135*;
  outer edges of a form, 60–61;
  oval from melded, 142–43, *143*;
  proportional expansion, 137–38;
  quarter, *149*;
  semi-, **83**;
  squaring, 97;
  violin, *44*;
  visual scale, **29–30**
classic orders, 11, 13, 44, 45, 50–54, 69, 70, 71, *86*, 87–90, 170;
  Greeks, **72**
clues:
  looking in all the right places, 20–22;
  looking in all the wrong places, 22–24
Colonial style, **75**
compass, 9, **12, 29–30**, 44, 54, 81–82, **83**, 88, *96*, 97, 102, **104, 105**, 112, 115, *122*, 123, 127, 134, 139, 141, 144;
  tuning, 102;
  using, 102–3
Composite order, 50, 89
computer-aided design software: 21, 24
contrast, 22, 56, 67, *67*, 68, *68*, 85;
curves, 81;
  introduction, 62–64;
  three, 67;
  using to define a form, 64–66
Corinthian order, 50, 70, *86*, 89
curves, 17, *35*, 46, 74, 90, 98;
  in craft tradition, 80;
  generating tapers and, 137–45;
  human form, 77;
  incorporating, 77–85;
  light and shadow, 78;
  nature, *76*;
  tactile, 78–79;
  tools, **104–5**, 113, 115, 116, 134;
  visualizing, 79–80

da Vinci, Leonardo, 48
designers/designs:
  classical, 74;
  interior of room, 66;
  make them sing, 26–27;
  modernist, **75**;
  origin of word, 7
desks:
  lap (project), 160–61;
  writing, *20*
dividers (tool), 2, 3, 4, *4*, 6, *7*, 8–9, 10, 24, 33, 34–35, **38–39**, 54, **56,**

65, 66, *88*, 89, *89*, 90, 98–99, 103;
  dividing a line into equal segments, 124;
  elliptical arch, 142;
  hexagons, 135;
  layout of taper on stock, *109*;
  layout tools, **105**;
  legs, *5*;
  parallel line with, *114*;
  points, **49**, *99*, 112;
  rectangles, 131;
  referral boards, *101*;
  resetting, 101;
  and sectors, 106–7, *107, 108*, 110, *110*, 111;
  styles, *98*;
  tool sets, **104**;
  trisecting an angle, 127;
  tuning up, 99, *99*;
  using, 99–100;
  walking out even spacings, *5, 100*
Doric order, 50, 54–55, 70, 71, *89*;
  drawing, *91–93*;
  Roman, 88–89
dovetails, 124, 157, 164;
  drawer, 6
drawings, 21, 23, 27, 111, 118, 154–55;
  arc, *114*, 115, *115*;
  bright side of the brain, 24–26;
  circle with compass, 103;
  classic orders, 13;
  curves, 81–82, **83**;
  Doric order, **91–93**;
  exercise, **28, 38, 49, 56, 65, 83**, 88–90, **91–93**;
  freehand, *25*, 81, 88, 149;
  full-scale, 123;
  full-scale layout square, *119*;
  industrial, 22, 25;
  locked ratios, 56;

measured, 20, 22;
minor and major sides, **65**;
physical act of, 24;
proportional, 25, **38, 49**, 71;
scale, 99, 117, 123, 142, 143–44;
smaller-scale, 141.
See also da Vinci, Leonardo; drawing tools
drawing tools, 104, 104
Dürer, Albrecht, 54

edges:
  checking and truing, 112, *112*
ellipse, 113, 141, 142, 144, 157;
  making an, 116, *116*, 117;
  semi-, *142*, 143;
  -stick, *117*, 118, *119*
Erie, Lake, 19

Federal, **80**;
  Virginia sideboard, 14
focal points, 102, 103, 113, 115, 138, 140, *141*, 143, 144;
  locating, 139, *139*, 142;
  volute generated from gridwork of, *144*
forms, 3, 54;
  arc, *136*;
  architectural, 50–53, *67*;
  bilateral symmetry, *62*;
  boundary, 88;
  circle as outer edge of, 60;
  constructing, **29, 31**;
  Doric order, 89;
  furniture, *84*;
  harmonious, 46;
  human, 11, 33, 44, *45*, 48–50, 54, **72**, 74, 77, 79;
  ornaments highlight, **75**;
  punctuation used to organize, 68–71;

shapes combined into, 33–39, 46, 47, 74, **83**, 130;
using contrast to define, 64–66;
variable reflectivity, 78;
violin, 44.
See also *individual forms*, e.g., circles
freehand drawing. *See* drawings, freehand
Freemasons, 122

geometry, 7, *7*, 9, 24, 32, 33–35, 60, 81, 88;
bisecting a line between two points, 123–24;
bisecting an angle, 127;
cutting, 83;
dividing a line into equal segments between two points, 124;
dividing a line into segments of a specific ratio, 124;
dropping a perpendicular from a point above a line, 126;
erecting a 45° angle from a point on a line, 126;
erecting a perpendicular from a point on a line, 125;
intuitive, 74;
and music, 63;
trisecting an angle, 127, *127*.
See also artisan geometry
Gibbs, James, 30;
"Rules for Drawing," 31;
"Rules for drawing the Several Parts of Architecture," 88
Goddard family, *3*
Goethe, Johan von, 153
Gothic:
arch, 139–40;
Chippendale, 22

handsaws, 10, 162, 163, *163*
hexagons, 129, 135, *135*, 144, 148
highboy, 128;
Philadelphia, 15
historicist, 13–17

Industrial Revolution, 10, 11, 22, 34
Ionic order, *13*, 50, 70, 89

Keller, Helen, 13, 79

Langley, Batty, 13, 54
language of artisans:
classic orders, 86–93;
incorporating curves, 76–85;
proportions made simple, 58–75;
understanding proportions, 43–57
Lewis, C. S., 59
Lincoln Memorial, 61

Magee Marsh, 19
Mahler, Gustav, 5
Mall (Washington, D.C.), *60*, 61
Maloof, Sam, 14
McConnell, Don, **83**
measuring tools. *See* rulers
Michelangelo, 81
mirror image, 48, 50, 56, 89;
symmetry and, 61–62, 68
mirrors:
period, *37*
modernist design, 13–17, 15, *60*
mouldings, 50, *52*, 54, 69, *71*, **72,** *75*, 77, 78, *78*, 81, **83**, 88, 89, *89, 92*;
crown, *84*;
devloping profiles, 147–49;
traditional, *69*
music, 4, 8, 9, *14*, 17, 25, 27, **31**, 44, *45*, 50, 55–56, 63, 84, 130;

creating visual, 85, 90

Newport, R.I., *3*
Newport table, 3, 6

octagon, 129, 135, *135*
Old Street Tool, *83*
originality, 59, 50–61
ornaments, *37*, 92;
    designing with, **75**

Palladio, *65, 73*
Plato, 97
Pleiades, *42*, 43
Polycleitus: "The Cannon," 49
polygons, 97, 129, *134*;
    constructing, 134, *134*;
    generic, 135;
    six-sided, 135
projects, 153–74;
    boot bench, 165–66;
    candy box, 158–59;
    coffee-for-two tray, 167;
    cup cabinet, 168–69;
    lap desk, 160–61;
    side table, 170–71;
    step stool, 156–57;
    tool tote, 162–64;
    vanity, 172–74
proportions, 3, 4, *4*, 5, 6, 9, 10, *10*, 11, **12**, 15, 17, 22, 24, *24*, 25, 34, *34*, 37, 39, *39*, 89, 90, 103, 154, 155;
    connecting with architecture, 50–53;
    connection with human form, 48–50;
    curves, 148;
    expansion of a circle, 137–38;
    linkages, 54–56;
    made simple, 58–75;
    maintaining divisions from one station to another, 108–9;
    relationships, 13, 33, **38**, 131, 132, 153;
    sequences, 82;
    sine curves, 148, *148*;
    understanding of, 43–57;
    using arcs, 89;
    where they come from, 46–47;
    whole-number, 123.
    See also classic orders; sectors
punctuation, 56, 157, 161, 169, 171;
    combining curves, 85;
    contrast and, *85*;
    to establish a border, 71–73;
    introduction, 68;
    used to organize a form, 68–71
Pythagoras, **12**, 55, **56**, 63, **65**, 130

Quakers, *3*
Queen Anne period, 80

ratios, 64, 111;
    divisions, 124, *125*;
    harmonic tones, 65, 130;
    lancet arc, 140;
    locked, **56**;
    mirror image, 56;
    origin, 49;
    oval from melded circles, 142;
    oval to a fixed width, 143;
    simple, 4, *4*, 49, 61, 156;
    sine curves, 148, *148*;
    square, **56**, 118;
    whole-number, 11, **12**, 106, 131.
    See also mirror image
rectangles, *32, 35, 36*, 37, 38, 54, *67*, 74, 129, 144;
    contrast to define a form, 64, 66, *66*;

generating from squares, **12, 29–31**, 132–33;
graduated, 131;
harmonic expansion of, 130–31;
harmony, 56;
locked ratios, **56**;
proportional linkages, **49, 65**;
visual scale, **83**
Rembrandt, *14*
restrained style, *3*
rulers, *10*, 11, **12, 54**, 123

Scruton, Roger, 75
sectors, 97, 98, 100, *106*, 131;
deriving proportions on, *106*;
dividing a dimension into equal parts, 107;
geometry of, *106*;
how it works, 106;
laying out hardware locations, 110;
maintaining proportional divisions from one station to another, 108–9;
secret of, 103, 106;
using, 106–7
Semes, Steven: "The Future of the Past," 13
shapes:
combine into forms, 33–39;
definition, *35*
Sheraton, Thomas: "The Cabinet-Maker's and Upholsterer's Drawing Book," 103
sideboards, *4*, 45, **80**;
Virginia, 14
squares (tool), 4, **12**, 64, **104**, 111, *116*, 117, *117*, 118–19, *122*, 141;
miter, 35;
using, 120–21
squares (shape), *26, 27, 29–30*, **29**,

35, 36, 47, 48, **56, 65**, 74, *74*, 97, 129;
alternative erection, 130, *130*;
-and-a-half, 130;
erecting from two points on a line, 129, *129*;
generate spiral from corners, 144, *144*;
generating a geometric expansion of a rectangle from, 132;
truncate corners to create octagon, 135, *135*
sticks, 6, 102, *102, 115, 116*;
and battens, 113, 123;
creating arcs with, 113, *114*, 115, 138;
ellipse-, 117, *117*, 118, *119*;
hinged, 103;
pegged, 141;
tick, 111, 155
stools: step, 45;
step (project), 156–57
tables, 80, *80*;
apron, *84*;
card, *62*;
carving on, **75**;
conference, 115, 138;
demilune, *145*;
Newport, 3, 6;
period, 37, 81;
shape, 66;
side (project),170–71;
standardized heights, 45
St. Paul's Cathedral, *34*, 56, 58, 59, 60–61, 64, 67, 81, 90, 124, 158, 166, 174;
and axis lines, 61;
straightedges, 9, **12, 30**, 33, **38**, 88, 97, 98, **104, 105**, 111, *111*, 112, *112*, 119, 141, 142, 149
Swan, Abraham, **75**

symmetry, 46–47, 48, *48*;
   bilateral, *62*;
   diffusion, 132;
   layers, *62*;
   and mirror image, 61–62, 68

Tolpin, Jim: "The New Traditional Woodworker," 111
tool sets, 6, **83**;
   drawing, **104**; layout, **105**
totes, 79;
   tool (project), 162–64
Townsend, *3*
traditional design, 5, 15, *15*, 37, 39, 46, 61, 68–69, **75, 83**, *84*;
   Lancet arc, 140;
   moulding, *69*
trays:
   coffee-for-two (project), 167
try square, 98, **105**
T-squares, 111, 118, 120
Tuscan order, 50, 89

vanities (project), 172–74
visual scale, 27, 66;
   creating, 28–31;
   curved notes on, 83
Vitruvius, 19, 20, 25, 48
volutes, 88, 143–44;
   generated from a gridwork of focal points, *144*

Weinberg, Steven, 46–47
White House, 61
Wren, Christopher, 34, *34*

ISBN 978-0-9850777-5-4 $34.00